Miss Eliza Bowen, Washington, Wilkes County.
Historian; Educator; Author.

Photograph presented to the Georgia Department of Archives
& History by Mrs. Barron Hill of Washington-Wilkes.

The Story Of

WILKES COUNTY GEORGIA

by

Eliza A. Bowen

Edited, Annotated and Indexed

with Introduction

by

Louise Frederick Hays
State Historian of Georgia

Authority of Ben W. Fortson, Jr.
Secretary of State

CLEARFIELD

Originally published
Marietta, Georgia, 1950

Reprinted for
Clearfield Company, Inc. by
Genealogical Publishing Co., Inc.
Baltimore, Maryland
1997, 2005

International Standard Book Number: 0-8063-4731-7

Made in the United States of America

INTRODUCTION

On June 1st, 1773, His Excellency Sir James Wright, Bart., Captain-General and Commander-in-Chief of the Royal Province of Georgia, made a treaty with the Cherokee and Creek Indians, whereby he secured a tract of land for Georgia, beginning "at the place where the lower Creek Path intersects Ogeechee River and along main branch of said river to the source of the southermost branch of said river and from thence along the ridge between the waters of Broad River and Oconee River up to the Buffaloe Lick, and from thence in a straight line to the tree marked by the Cherokees near the head of a branch falling into the Oconee River, and from thence along the said ridge twenty miles above the line already run by the Cherokees, and from thence across to Savannah River by a line run parallel with that formerly marked by them." This land was ceded by the Indians in payment of debts owed by them to the Traders. The new ceded land was composed of the present Counties of Wilkes, Lincoln, Elbert and parts of Madison, Oglethorpe, Greene, Taliaferro, Warren and McDuffie.

As soon as the treaty was effective, Governor Wright opened a post at the confluence of the Broad River and the Savannah and called it Fort James. This Fort became the gateway into Georgia for settlers from Virginia, North Carolina and South Carolina. The new settlers crossed the Savannah River at Fort James where they registered and secured their tracts of land. The Land Court Record is in the Georgia Department of Archives and History and it shows the names of those who entered Georgia, the number in their families, the number of slaves, if any, the tract of land they bought and how much they paid and promised to pay for it.

In 1777, the County of Wilkes was created, with Fort James about the center of its eastern boundary. At that time Wilkes County comprised most of this "new Purchase." From Wilkes County many of the settlers gradually moved west into new tracts of land as they were obtained from the Indians, and consequently many of the families of North Georgia trace their ancestry to Wilkes County.

Miss Eliza A. Bowen of Wilkes County wrote stories of Wilkes County people and published her articles in the *Washington* (Georgia) *Gazette and Chronicle* from 1886 to 1897 and later some of these articles were published in a small pamphlet, very few of which are still in existence.

My personal thanks are extended to the following librarians for their interest and loans of their copies: Miss Ella May Thornton, State Librarian; Miss Margaret Jemison, Librarian, Emory University; Miss Kathleen Colley, Librarian, Mary Willis

Library; Miss Lucille Simcoe, Reference Librarian, Duke University; Wimberly DeRenne of the University of Georgia Library; Miss Virginia Satterfield, Librarian, Georgia State College for Women; Mrs. Bessie Sims DeVaughn and her family and Miss Minnie Stonestreet of Washington, Wilkes. Dr. T. B. Rice of Greensboro was most helpful with his newspaper clippings from the *Gazette and Chronicle* and his comments used as footnotes.

Not one of these copies was complete. I have put these articles and pamphlets together so that it makes the most complete copy of Miss Bowen's *Story of Wilkes* to be found. There is a missing part in Chapter XXVI and unfortunately the story ends in the middle of a sentence. In spite of every effort made to secure these missing parts, they have not been found.

Miss Eliza Bowen was by profession a teacher of Latin and was also, a student of astronomy. She was the author of *Astronomy by Observation* (D. Appleton & Co.), a book pronounced by Dr. Stone, noted astronomer of the University of Virginia, as the best elementary astronomy in the English language. Often at night, she wandered through the streets of the quiet town of Washington utterly absorbed in her study of the stars, not seeing or speaking to friends whom she chanced to meet.

Her *Story of Wilkes County* shows that at other times she was keenly interested in her fellow townspeople, observing their characters, personalities and acquainting them with many facts as to their ancestors and property. Although she wrote her *Story of Wilkes* more as a pastime than as a serious history, it is now valued as important source material for students of early Georgia history. She had a remarkable memory and to it she added much information from older residents whom she interviewed. She also studied Wilkes County records with great care. Her informal style makes the stories of locations, schools, churches and families of Washington, a charming chronicle of the period.

Miss Bowen was born in Columbia County, Georgia, on April 22, 1828, and died May 10, 1898.

Louise Frederick Hays.

PUBLISHER'S FOREWORD

It was with great pleasure that we received from the Secretary of State of Georgia authority to publish the typewritten copy of "The Story of Wilkes County, Georgia" owned by The Georgia Department of Archives and History, and edited, annotated, and indexed, with Introduction by Mrs. J. E. Hays, State Historian.

This book is a faithful transcription of the typewritten copy except for the correction of obvious typographical errors attributed to the original newspaper publication in the nineteenth century.

Due, likewise, to typographical error there will be found instances in which proper names and surnames, obviously intended to be the same, are spelled differently on diverse occasions. Such we have not attempted to correct for fear of error on our own part.

Through the courtesy of Mrs. Frank Hill of Washington, Georgia, Mr. Robert Quin of Atlanta, and Mr. Hugh Quin, of Macon, Georgia a copy of Miss Bowen's original manuscript was located at the last moment before the book went to press and compared with the book as it now appears. The comparison revealed that the newly located copy could supply no additional material to the book, as it contained much less than the Georgia Department of Archives and History copy from which the book was composed.

We hope that our publication of this book will fill a long felt need in making generally available a work so important to Georgia's annals from standpoints both historical and genealogical.

Continental Book Company.

The above sketch of the home of Col. Micajah Williamson, in the town of Washington, Wilkes County, Georgia, was found in the Plat Book of Wilkes County. The wording, 'Col. Williamsons house', shows plainly, but the wording, 'Built in 1787' is very dim.

The commissioners appointed by the Georgia Legislature on July 31, 1783, to lay out a town to be called Washington, and to be located in the County of Wilkes, were Stephen Heard, Micajah Williamson, Robert Harper, Daniel Coleman, and Zachariah Lamar, Esquires.

(See Watkins Digest of the Laws of Georgia, p. 284)

CHAPTER I

DATE OF FIRST SETTLEMENT

THE CHEROKEE INDIANS were the chief original inhabitants of the territory afterwards formed into Wilkes County, but there were also Creeks found in it. There are oral traditions in Wilkes which place the first white settlement as early as 1769. Gen. B. W. Heard, who is a descendant of one of the first settlers, who is an intelligent man, with also a somewhat accurate memory of dates, thinks that these settlers came in 1769. There is also a printed statement from a newspaper reporter who talked with Gen. Robert Toombs in his later years, placing the first settlement in 1769. There is, however, no original written evidence to sustain this tradition of an event that took place more than a hundred years ago. It is true it is printed in the *Life of Rev. Jesse Mercer* that his father, Rev. Silas Mercer, removed from Virginia to North Carolina and resided in Currituck County until about 1769, when he emigrated to Georgia and settled in what is now *Wilkes County*. The Life of *Father Mercer* was written by Rev. Charles Mallary. While this is printed, it is not an original document, as Mr. Mallary lived long afterwards; nor does he give his authority for the date.

After a good deal of reading on the subject, I am disposed to think that the original settlement of Washington and Wilkes cannot be placed earlier than the latter days of 1773, and I will state the reasons which lead me to this conclusion.

There are two treaties with the Indians, which may still exist in the collection of state papers in England; but at any rate the terms have long been printed by persons who have had access to them; first by Capt. Hugh McCall in his *History of Georgia*, printed at Savannah in 1816. Afterwards, in 1859, Rev. Dr. Stevens an Episcopal clergyman living in Savannah then, but who was subsequently made Bishop of Pennsylvania began a *History of Georgia* printed in Philadelphia, and he printed the terms of the treaties from the original documents. Lastly, Mr. Charles C. Jones, who has published two vols. of a *History of Georgia*, also prints the substance of the same treaties. Mr. Jones is a nephew of Rev. Dr. John Jones well known in Washington.

The first of the two treaties was made at Augusta in 1763.

The colonial governors of Georgia, Virginia and of the two Carolinas were present, and seven hundred Indians, chiefs of the Cherokees, Creeks, Choctaws, Chicasaws and Caharobas. This treaty fixed the northern boundary of the white settlements in Georgia. The treaty states that the line runs up Savannah River to the mouth of Little River and then to the mouth of Williams Creek, situated in what is now Taliaferro and, I think, Warren County; then it met the *Creek trail* which went to the Ogeechee.(1)

This was thirty years after Gen. Oglethorpe came to Georgia. This treaty was in force until 1773. Sir James Wright was then the Governor of Georgia, appointed by King George II. He was a native of South Carolina and had been attorney general of that colony. The people of Georgia considered him a very good Governor and especially as he was a man who could be trusted to keep his word. It is true that when the Revolution came on, he took the side of the king and made the rather funny blunder of telling the people of Georgia that they would be entirely ruined if they separated from England. *Foresight* is not as good as *hind sight* and so we seem to be wiser than the old governor. In the school *History of Georgia* written by Lawton Evans of Augusta, Governor Wright's *rule of Georgia is said to have been wise, zealous, and popular.*

The Indians were thus confirmed in their titles to the lands which afterwards became Wilkes County. They, however, wanted to trade with the whites and it was provided by the treaty that the governor was to give licenses to traders whom he thus authorized. Governor Wright absolutely forbade the sale of rum and liquor, by the traders, and this is somewhat interesting as the first prohibition regulation in the counties which constituted original Wilkes. Also they were to give credit for only a small amount but this order was changed when the treaty and orders were sent to England for approval.

After a while, the Indians got deeply in debt to the traders; and having no other means of payment, a new treaty was made in 1773 at Augusta, between Gov. Wright and the Indians. This treaty opened up Wilkes County for settlement. The new northern boundary ran from the northern part of Wilkes, now Elbert, to Cherokee Corner, as it was called. This territory was ceded by the Indians in payment of debts which Col. Charles C. Jones says amounted to about sixty thousand pounds sterling, or $300.000 nearly. The governor was to sell the land to settlers and from the proceeds pay the traders.

Thus by the treaty of 1767, the territory was confirmed by the governor to the Indians. He agreed to prevent and punish

(1) These Treaties are in Candler's *Colonial Records*, XXXIX, 496-499; and in the Manuscript Treaty Book, 1773-1796, 1383-1392, in the Ga. Dept. of Archives and History.

infractions. By all accounts of him, he was a man who could keep his word and, in 1773, he made an address, at Augusta, to the assembled chiefs and said that he had kept it. Now under these circumstances, all of which are proved by important published documents, and are in no sense matters of mere tradition, I do not think that any small body of men insufficient for self-defense, would have ventured to make settlements in this territory. They would have been at the mercy of the Indians and could have counted on no protection from the white government of the colony, which indeed must have been on the side of the Indians. I know many white men do not regard treaties with Indians. Of this we have examples in our own day. Silas Mercer, certainly, was not that kind of man. We might suppose that small bodies of settlers made their own trade with the Indians, if the Indians held their lands in fee simple as the whites do. In that case, they could have come in and bought lands from private owners. But a cession of lands could only be gained from chiefs acting for their tribes. The Cherokees are said to have been the most intelligent of the Indian tribes found in Georgia, as indeed they are to this day noted for their superiority. They would have been very indignant with settlers violating the treaty and would probably have destroyed them.

Governor George Gilmer, who had the very best opportunity of knowing about the early settlers of Wilkes, especially those upon Broad River or near it, says that before the Revolution a certain Lord George Gordon came to Wilkes county with a body of Scotch settlers who were apprenticed to him for five years to pay for the cost of their passage to this country. Gov. Gilmer tells us of this in his book called *Georgians*. He says that when the Revolution came, Lord George Gordon, who was very much opposed to independence, returned to Britain. I think myself that it is more than probable from Gov. Gilmer's statement that this Lord George Gordon was a half crazy fanatic who created riots about *popery* in London in the reign of George III. The story of the riots is of a good deal of interest and is a good subject for some of our young people to look up in the Library. Gov. Gilmer says that Lord George Gordon is a character in Scott's novel the *Heart of Midlothian* and I remember myself, that Dickens' story of Barnaby Rudge is founded on these riots.

In upper Wilkes there are traditions to this day in regard to these settlers. On the plantation of Mr. Henry Hill, there is a field called the *Red House Field* to this day, and tradition says, that these Scotch settlers had built here a framed house painted red and from this house the field took its name. The land on which they settled is, to this day, called *Scotchtown*. Traditions in Wilkes county represent this body of settlers as having come in considerable numbers, sixty or seventy families, and these numbers might have sustained them against the Indians, if they had come, as tradition says, early in the sixties of the last century. But a reference to Gov. Gilmer's book dispels the idea that they could have come so early. Gov. Gilmer says on page 237 of *Georgians - when fighting for independence commenced, Lord George Gordon carried his people to South Carolina and sold them & etc.* If now the indenture of five years had not expired in 1776, this settlement could not have been long prior to 1773. Gov. Gilmer, besides knowing the early settlers, who lived on the lands relinquished by the Scotch colony, tells us that he went to school in South Carolina, somewhere near Vienna, to Dr. Moses Waddell, and that he boarded with an old Scotch couple called Sutherland who had belonged to the colony of Lord George Gordon and who had been sold to Gen. Perkins. Gov. Gilmer was born in 1790 and was about fourteen years old when he attended this school. I am quite sure Gov. Gilmer is accurate. When his book was published, he was accused of party prejudice in what he wrote and, it seems to me, justly in some cases, but his veracity could not be questioned.

Rev. S. G. Hillyer, well known in Washington, is a descendant of an early well known settler of Wilkes, John Freeman, who lived in or very near Scotchtown. In investigating this subject, I wrote to Dr. Hillyer. He tells me that judging by the remains left by the Scotch settlers, they could not have lived in Wilkes long. Some broken pottery was nearly all.

Thus I have come to the conclusion that the first settlers probably came in the latter part of 1773. But I tell the facts and leave others to judge for themselves. I am like other people who tell a story, I like to make it interesting and thus I would like to put the first settlement as early as possible. But as I take it, the value of what I say depends mainly on its truth. I shall, in what I say, remember the immortal aphorism of Artemus Ward, *that it is a great deal better not to know so many things than to know so many things that are true.* For an earlier settlement than 1773, it seems to me, that we have nothing but tradition and a tradition that conflicts with written and published documents.

In regard to Rev. Silas Mercer, perhaps it is well to add, that the *Life of Jesse Mercer* p. 16 shows that his grandfather moved to Burke county first and afterwards came to Wilkes and this date, 1767, refers, in all probability, only to his coming to Georgia, which was prior to his settlement in Wilkes.

The lands ceded by the Indians in 1773 were called the *New Purchase,* sometimes, merely the *Ceded Lands.* They extended between the Savannah and the Oconee[2] and were bounded south

(2) This should be Ogeechee River.

by Little River and Williams Creek. They included all of present Wilkes, Elbert, Lincoln, and Oglethorpe with parts of Green, Warren, Taliaferro and Madison (which was subsequently formed from Elbert). I hope I may some day find time and data to draw, for our Library, a map of original Wilkes, showing the successive boundaries.

Gov. Wright was to sell the lands and pay the traders. The lands were ceded by the Cherokees and Creeks, both having some claim. On June 11, 1774, he issued his proclamation, stating that he was about to have the lands surveyed and parcelled out in tracts from 100 to 1,000 acres, for the convenience of the settlers. He said that 100 acres would be sold to the head of the family, fifty more for each child and for his wife, 500 for each slave owned and 50 more for every able bodied white male servant whom he could bring, 25 for each woman servant from 15 to 40 years old. The lands were described as good for wheat, indigo, tobacco, hemp, flax etc. Not more than five (5) shillings an acre were to be charged and five dollars was to be paid as entrance money for 100 acres. A land court was opened where the Broad River joins the Savannah and a stockade fort was built enclosing an acre and called Fort James. There was a garrison of 50 rangers and there were barracks and officer's quarters. Each corner of the fort had two story block houses with swivel guns and openings for small arms. The fort was on a slight eminence in the fork equally distant from both rivers and also from the extreme point of land. Higher up, a town was laid out, called Dartmouth for the English earl who had induced the king to sign the treaty. This town, however, soon gave way to Petersburg.

The sale of the Wilkes county lands gave rise to a much talked of claim against the U. S. government, which was called the Galphin Claim, and 1 think it may interest people who live here now. When Gov. Wright sold Wilkes county lands the Revolution had begun; and of course, as he was appointed by King George, he was a Tory. So in selling the lands he favored Tory and discriminated against Whigs. Also, when the money was paid in, he again paid the Tories and refused to pay the Whigs. One of the Whig traders, George Galphin by name, was a gentleman of high character and much intelligence, living at a place still called Silver Bluff on the Carolina side of the Savannah river, just below Augusta. George Galphin had a handsome brick residence there which was still standing a few years ago, an antique old mansion. He traded with the Indians for furs and skins and was very much respected for honest dealings by the Creek Indians. He traded chiefly in Georgia, though his home and large warehouses were in Carolina at Silver Bluff. He was a strong Whig and had several times aided the state of Georgia, when its resources were very low, and he also exerted his influence with the Creeks to keep them from attacking the Wilkes settlers. His claim amounted to about $50,000 which was audited and accepted as correct by the Governor, though its payment was refused along with other Whig claims. When the Wilkes lands came into possession of Georgia the claims of these traders were recognized. The United States Government, however, took charge of all revolutionary obligations of the States and among others of the Galphin claim.

For some reason or other, this debt both of justice and honor, though often presented, was unpaid until Taylor became President. By that time, it had come by inheritance to Col. John Milledge, the only son of Governor Milledge,[3] and also George W. Crawford, as attorney, had come into possession of a part. Crawford was in General Taylor's cabinet and when it was paid there was a great clamor, because he was interested. When the money was granted by Congress, a court of arbitration was necessary to settle the shares of persons interested, and Judge Garnett Andrews of Wilkes was on the court. They gave Col. Milledge a snug fortune. He was the only child of Gov. Milledge and had been the richest young man in Georgia of his time. I knew him well, one of the most agreeable and amiable men in the world, but with a most unexampled talent for getting rid of money. He had spent all his father left him when this windfall came to him and he set to work at once in the most systematic manner to spend this. But he had great luck of receiving fortunes, for after this Galphin money was all gone, he received and also spent two other fortunes. At last, when his aunt, Miss Polly Milledge, the Governor's sister, died she left her comfortable little property to the wife and children of her nephew. Capt. John Milledge, now State Librarian, one of the most polished gentlemen in Georgia, is the son of this Colonel John Milledge.

(3) John Milledge was Governor of Georgia, 1802-1806.

CHAPTER II

SETTLEMENT OF
THE TOWN OF WASHINGTON

FROM ALL I can learn, I believe that the first settlement on the site of the town of Washington was made by a party of emigrants from Westmoreland County, Virginia, who reached the spot on the last day of the year 1773 and, on New Year's day 1774, began to cut down the first trees in the unbroken forest of magnificent oaks which stood on the site of Washington. They began with them, the building of a stockade fort. It was called Fort Heard. One of the party was Stephen Heard and with him came his brothers Barnard and Jesse and, it is said, also their father, John Heard, Benjamin Wilkinson and his wife, Ann were of the party. Gen. B. W. Heard whose property on the north side of the Court House Square is, partly at least, on the site of Fort Heard, is the descendant of Jesse Heard and Caroline Wilkinson, daughter of the same couple just mentioned. I have already given the date which Heard assigns to this emigration, viz 1769. The territory of the *New Purchase* as Wilkes Cy. was called, must have settled very rapidly during the revolution. It was called the *Hornets' Nest* by the Tories, as Gov. Gilmer tells us. It is probable that the traders had spread widely the knowledge of these desirable lands. Gov. Gilmer tells us that the North Carolina settlers, the Clarks, Dodys, Waltons, and Murrays came here before and during the Revolution and settled on Long's Creek southward from Savannah.

There is a curious old monument of the early settlers of Wilkes found in the southeastern part of the county on what is now the plantation of Mr. and Mrs. Fortson. I saw it, Sept. 27, 1889. It is a flat rock, of granite of gneiss, on which is cut in the stone a square; and joined on one side of the square, a smaller parallellogram. At the top, there are cut in large bold letters the words, *John Nelson*. At one side are the words *Land granted in 1775* and on the other side of the square is the date *1792*, which evidently is the year in which the cutting was made. Among the old records in the ordinary's office at Washington, there are minutes of the Superior Court from 1779 to 1790. In them, the name of John Nelson is found two or three times on the Grand and Petty Juries. But I have had a fuller account of him from Rev. F. T. Simpson, School Commissioner of Wilkes County, who is his great nephew. John Nelson was a

7

Marylander who came here and settled and the figure I have described cut on stone was a map or plot of his land. Mr. Simpson took me to see this curious old monument. It was completely hidden in tall weeds and when these were torn away, it was necessary to scrape on the dirt with which the stone was encrusted before anything could be seen. As this was done, the letters came out clear and distinct, though they had been exposed to wind and weather for 97 years.

Mr. Simpson's grandmother was Kitty Nelson, sister to this John Nelson, (and great grandmother of Miss Annie Lane who wrote this). Kitty Nelson married Archibald Simpson who enlisted as a Revolutionary soldier after John Nelson came to Wilkes County; and the brother went back to Maryland and persuaded his sister, for protection and security, to come to Georgia. She had two little boys, of whom the youngest, William Simpson, was not much more than a baby. And she came to Georgia on horseback, bringing that child before her on the horse. After the revolution was over, Archibald Simpson joined his wife and children. This shows the attraction Wilkes had for settlers. This monument is the oldest one on stone in all the up country of Georgia. The oldest gravestones in the county are those of the family of Gen. Elijah Clark, in the Jordan-Hill burying ground near Clarke's Station Church; but none of these date back to 1792. It would be a great misfortune to have this stone destroyed and I am in hopes that some of the Simpson family will have it moved to our Library grounds, if it can be done without breaking the inscribed portion of the rock.

The boy, William Simpson, whom his mother brought on horseback from Maryland grew up to be the first person in Wilkes county to take out a patent. The old yellow document still exists in the hands of Rev. F. T. Simpson. It was a patent for a machine for the transmission of power and it is dated 1818. There is a drawing of it attached and the letter bears the autograph of John Quincey Adams, who was then Secretary of State, and who afterwards became President of the United States. The autograph was a frank of the letter, making it go through the mail free.

Note on date of settlement. Mr. F. Colley, a descendant of one of the first settlers of Washington, called Staples, who came with the Heards, tells me of the tradition in his family placing the settlement of Wilkes prior to 1773. The strongest argument for an earlier settlement comes from the fact that 1779 Col. Elijah Clarke raised 300 men in Wilkes county.

By settlers, I mean, not traders domiciled for purposes of trading, of whom there were doubtless a good many, but settlers claiming and cultivating farms. If there were any of the latter, it is inexplicable that they were not mentioned in the Treaty or negotiations about it. If any documentary evidence can be furnished, I shall be glad to print it. I think it is useless to look for land deeds before 1773 but there may be letters or other documents. I will add, what I had not noticed before in *Mercer's Life*, that while giving 1767 as the date of Silas Mercer's emigration, Rev. Mr. Mallory says that Jesse Mercer was born in North Carolina in 1769. Mr. Colley's ancestor, Staples, was the man who is remembered as having 16 daughters and one son. Wives are hard to get in a new country and Mr. Staples seemed to have taken a large contract for supplying them.

CHAPTER III

WILKES COUNTY
IN THE REVOLUTION

WILKES COUNTY was laid out in 1777 by the convention which met at Savannah to form the first constitution of Georgia, that which organized the state. It was named for John Wilkes who was a member of the English Parliament and took the side of the colonies in their opposition to taxation. He was, however, a somewhat unscrupulous demagogue. North Carolina also named one of her counties for John Wilkes. Our Wilkes County, in the section laying it off, is described as *the lands north of the Ogeechee.*

The traders with the Indians had probably talked a good deal about the fine lands, for certainly Wilkes began to settle with astonishing rapidity. It is probable that it owed the strong Whig character which it had during the Revolution, to the fact that the settlers came mostly from states where the great questions of the Revolution had been much discussed. But the manner in which Gov. Wright granted the lands had brought many Tories here so Wilkes was in the unfortunate condition of a community divided in itself. From this; it was preserved in the late *War Between the States.* The effect was, the Tories made war upon women and children wherever they had a chance. Many stories were told of their cruelty. The impression these produced was so lasting that in the late war, there was a strong tendency among old country people to call Union men Tories.

Phillips Church, in the south western part of Wilkes County, takes its name from a revolutionary soldier who built a mill on Kettle Creek. The name was at first the *Church at Phillips Mill,* but the congregation long afterwards bought out Salem church from the Presbyterians and then called their body *Phillips Church.* When Mr. Phillips was away with the revolutionary army, his wife was much annoyed by Tories. On one occasion, it is said that she had been washing clothes and had hung them out to dry when a Tory came up and, seizing a shirt, started to run off with it. In the day when the work of women, spinning and weaving, furnished nearly all the clothing worn by both sexes, the shirt would have been a serious loss; so Mrs. Phillips, seeing the danger, ran out to protect her property. She seized one end of the shirt and the Tory held the other and both pulled. Mrs. Phillips, seeing that she was getting the worst of it, suddenly let go, and pointing her raised forefinger at the Tory, said scornfully, "Sir, were you born of a woman?" Her adversary was not wholly devoid of shame, for he left the shirt to Mrs. Phillips.

It was not until after the taking of Savannah and Augusta by the British in 1778-9 that there were bodies of troops in Wilkes. In reading the account of events subsequent to this time, I have been much surprised to find that so honorable a record of events is so little known by people living at the present day. The revolutionary history of this county is, in every respect, as honorable as that of any part of Upper South Carolina of which so much has been said and written. In fact, it was simply a part of the general contest in the up country, Gen. Pickins and the Carolinians coming to help upper Georgia; and also Gen. Elijah Clarke and the Georgians going over to help the Carolinians. When George Walton, signer of the Declaration of Independence, came in 1785 as chief Justice to hold court in Wilkes, he spoke in his charge to the jury, of the revolution as, 'a seven or eight years war in which you have greatly distinguished yourselves'. No one knew better than George Walton, the whole history of the contest and so it is high praise. But it is no higher than the circumstances warrant and I hope I may in some degree revive the knowledge of the history.

Colonel Campbell, the British officer, who was in command in Augusta at the beginning of the year 1779 sent a Lt. Col. Hamilton to Wilkes to disarm the opponents of the British, and drive off Whigs. Col. Campbell then thought that the whole of Georgia was conquered, and that he would meet with submission. But it is evident that many of the people of Wilkes had already shown their sympathy with the Revolution; for many fled to Carolina while those who could not remove went into the stockade forts which had been built as a protection against the Indians. Then Col. John Dooly, living in the part of Wilkes which is now Lincoln, issued an address to stir the people to resistance and he collected a body of troops to oppose Hamilton. Dooly was, however, forced to retreat across the Savannah river, when he was joined by Col. Andrew Pickens and the two recrossed the river to attack Hamilton. Hamilton had succeeded in taking Carr's Fort from a small body of old and infirm men who had defended it. The Americans were about to recapture Carr's Fort when they received, through Joseph Pickens, a brother of Andrew Pickens, a message telling them that Col. Boyd was coming from Ninety-Six in Carolina forwards to Georgia, with 800 British and Tories, who were plundering and burning as they marched.

Col. Boyd had been sent by Cornwallis to enter Georgia from the north and marching southward, enforcing submission, to go to Savannah, thus completing the full conquest of the state. A force of 600 men from Augusta under McGirth was to meet him on

Little River and the two were to co-operate in reducing the colony. In reading of this contemplated march through Georgia, from the up country to the sea, I was reminded of a later invader, Gen. Sherman, whose track I traced in Sept. 1865 by the chimneys of the houses he had burned.

As soon as Dooly and Pickens heard of Boyd's approach, they thought best to leave Hamilton at Carr's Fort and to go to prevent Boyd from crossing into Georgia. Some Georgians under Capt. James Little, who lived in the fork of Long Creek, had already gone over to help Capt. Anderson of Pickens regiment, who endeavored to annoy Boyd in crossing. Boyd tried to pass at the Cherokee Ford, a place which is, I presume, known now to people in Elbert which was then Wilkes. But there was a block house there with two swivel guns garrisoned by a lieutenant and eight men. They refused Boyd a quiet passage so he took his men five miles higher up and the horses swam across, the men crossing on rafts. Capt. Anderson had only a hundred men and the canes on the river impeded his operations but Boyd lost a hundred men in killed, wounded and missing. The Americans lost sixteen and some prisoners were taken. Soon after, Anderson joined Dooly and Pickens and they crossed the Savannah at Cedar Shoals, which I suppose is still known to the Elbert people.

The comprehension of Boyd's movements will be much aided, if my readers will look at a map of Georgia such as is contained in the children's geographies (or ought to be) and afterwards at Callaway's map of Wilkes County. Maps hang in the Library which are excellent for this purpose. It will be seen that Oglethorpe county lies just west of Wilkes and Broad river, running north of both counties, separates them from Elbert; while Long Creek and its branch, Dry Fork separates Wilkes and Oglethorpe.

All these counties were then Wilkes. Boyd, after crossing the Savannah, marched along the Broad River and his course was westward. He crossed at Webb's Ferry near the fork. The Americans, who had been joined by Colonel Elijah Clarke with a hundred men from Wilkes, crossed Broad River at what is called the Fish Dam Ford, known now to Wilkes county people. This was Feb. 13, 1779; nearly one hundred and ten years ago. The former position of the church now called *Clarke Station* was not far from the place on which Gen. Clarke encamped on the night of the 13th. The burying ground known now as that of Dr. Will Jordan and which was the burying ground of Gen. Clarke's family, is said to be nearly where they encamped. The names *Clarke's Station* and Clarke's Creek are of course derived from their connection with Gen. Elijah Clarke. Gen. Clarke afterwards owned large landed property on this creek and all the original deed and titles to land run back to him.

The next day, Feb. 14, 1779, Valentine's Day, the battle of

Kettle Creek took place. The *Gazette* ought never to mark St. Valentine's Day without reminding young people that it is the anniversary of the battle. There were a great many young fellows in the army of Pickens, Dooly and Clarke, but they were not making verses to women. They were trying to keep from them, a burning and plundering invader.

CHAPTER IV

THE BATTLE OF KETTLE CREEK

IF THE READER will again look at Callaway's map of Wilkes County, which hangs in the Mary Willis Library, he will see, in the southwestern part of the county, the battlefield of Kettle Creek. Then he will see how Boyd and also Clarke, marching southward after crossing Broad River must have passed near Centreville and Sardis Church. The Americans are said to have marched in line of battle, Pickens being in the middle, Dooly on the right and Clarke on the left. They had in all 500 men and Boyd had 700. This, he told himself, after he was wounded. The reader who sees how near Kettle Creek is to Little River where McGirth was awaiting Boyd with more than 600 men, can understand how timely the battle was. Boyd himself said, when wounded, that he had expected to join McGirth the same afternoon. In six hours more, Boyd would have had 1500 men and it would have been useless to oppose him.

I have myself seen the battle ground of Kettle Creek, which is on the plantation now belonging to Mr. Henry Slaton. There is a steep bluff on the south side of the creek, which is to this day called the *War Hill* by people living in the neighborhood. On the north side, there is a low meadow, then swampy near the creek. Part was then covered with a cane brake. The British were surprised by their enemy. Boyd's men had a long march and little to eat and they were busy killing bullocks and parching corn when they heard the firing of pickets. Col. Boyd at once tried to form his men and he was helped by a fence and fallen trees. But Pickens, turning a little to the right, attacked him from a higher position and the men of Dooly and Clarke forced their way through the cane. Col. Boyd showed great courage but he was forced to retreat and as he did so, he received three wounds, any one of which would have proved mortal. There used to stand a large tree, Walnut I think, which was said to mark the spot where Boyd fell, but I think it has been cut down. The British now ran through the swamps and crossed the creek, leaving behind horses, baggage and arms. The battle had lasted an hour.

Just then, Elijah Clark, with a sound judgment and prompt action which always distinguished him, was impressed with the idea that the enemy would try to gain the hill on the south side of the creek and rally there, so he prepared to cross the creek with his left wing. Just as he gave the order, his horse was killed under him. But he mounted another horse and led his men by a ford to the other side. There he found the enemy under Major Spurgeon, trying to do exactly what he had foreseen. Gen. Clarke had at first only a part of his men, as there had been a mistake about the order. But the firing attracted the attention of the others and soon the whole force of the Americans had crossed and were aiding Gen. Clarke. Then the battle lasted three quarters of an hour longer on the south side of the creek. The British struggled for the hill with obstinate bravery and it seemed doubtful who could win. But finally they were defeated and fled in every direction. They had seventy dead and about seventy-five wounded. The Americans lost nine killed and twenty-three wounded. The success of the battle was undoubtedly due to the foresight and promptness of Elijah Clarke though all the others did their duty.

When the fight was over, Col. Pickens went to Col. Boyd and offered him every relief in his power. Col. Boyd thanked him and asked about the result of the engagement. When told of his opponents entire success, he said that it would have been different had he not fallen. He gave his watch and other articles to be sent to his wife in England with an account of his death and burial. All this was carefully observed by Col. Pickens. At his request, Col. Pickens detailed two men to give him water during the night and to bury him. He died before morning.

His followers fled, some to the Indians, and some reached Augusta. McGirth, who had been awaiting Col. Boyd at Little River, also fled to Augusta. Some of the prisoners, who were South Carolinians, were taken to that state, tried for treason and executed.

In this battle and that of Carr's Fort, the Americans gained some 600 horses and a large quantity of arms, ammunition, and clothing. These were very much needed.

When we compare the numbers engaged in this battle with those, which, in the recollection of many of us, fought at Missionary Ridge, and Chickamauga, it seems an insignificant affair. But the prowess of soldiers is shown not so much by the number engaged, as by the relative proportions of the contending parties. The Americans had 500, the British 700 (by Boyd's own statement) that is, the British were two fifths stronger than the Americans. When we compare the number engaged in both periods with the then population of the state and county, the Revolutionary battle does not suffer much by comparison. The victory was complete for the enemy was scattered; the stake was great, the full possession of Georgia. It was fought by the men of Wilkes County, aided by Gen. Pickens and his Carolinians. The sound judgment and ready decision of a Wilkes county man, Elijah Clarke, stood between the enemy and their own firesides, to strike a blow for homes, for the old men, the women and the children. In wounds and personal bravery Gen. Elijah Clarke and doubtless others, were equal to the honored heroes of our day. He was one of the North Carolina settlers who came to Wilkes County just before the revolution. He was wounded in 1778 at Alligator Creek, where he was shot through the thigh and at Kettle Creek his horse was shot under him. In 1780, he was again wounded at Musgrove's Mill in South Carolina. Charles C. Jones, in his *History of Georgia*, says of Col. Clarke at this battle (Musgrove's Mill) "Col. Clarke, who fought with a desperation worthy of all praise, received two sabre cuts, one on the back of his neck and the other on his head. In fact, his life was saved by his stock buckle, which turned the edge of the weapon. At one time, he was actually surrounded by the enemy and in charge of two stout cavalrymen. Renowned for his strength and activity, and exerting himself to the utmost, he knocked one of them down, put the other to flight and thus liberated himself from his unpleasant situation. Colonel Clarke was every inch a hero." He was the most noted partisan leader in Georgia. In 1781, at the battle of Long Cane in South Carolina, he received a wound in the shoulder which was supposed to be mortal and he was carried off the field in great pain. When he came back to Georgia, he was attacked with small pox, a disease which gave Georgia people a great deal of trouble during the Revolution. There was no vaccination then. But he was no sooner up than he raised 100 men in Wilkes county whom he took to aid in the final siege of Augusta. He was at a number of the important battles in Upper South Carolina. He was thanked by the legislature of Georgia and at the close of the war, two European nations, one of which was France, offered him high command in their armies. Clarke County is named for our brave old general. One of his grand daughters married Eldred Simpkins, a lawyer in South Carolina and her daughter married Francis Pickens, the grandson of Col. Andrew Pickens who in our day was governor of South Carolina. Mrs. Dr. Dred Hunter, now living very near Washington, is a grand daughter of Governor Pickens. Consequently she and her sons are lineal descendants of two of the commanders who fought at the battle of Kettle Creek. Gen. Elijah Clarke is the great, great, great grandfather of Mrs. Hunter. On inquiry I find that Mrs. Hunter remembers a picture of General Clarke in the family, an antique old figure with a cue and ruffled shirt. I wish we could get the original, or a photograph of it, for our Library. Among other persons who fought at Kettle Creek, may be mentioned Gen.

Clarke's son John, who afterwards became Governor of Georgia.[1] He was not much more than a lad when he was at Kettle Creek. Stephen Heard, Micajah Williamson, and Capt. James Little are mentioned Wilkes county men who were there.

It is not generally known that there was a mulatto youth among the troops of Gen. Clarke at Kettle Creek. He was living with a man named Aycock and was supposed to be his slave. When he enlisted, this was made an objection to receiving him until Aycock said that he was free. He was an excellent soldier under Gen. Clarke throughout the Revolution. He was shot at Kettle Creek and left on the battlefield dangerously wounded. Governor Gilmer says that he was taken home and cared for by a man living near the battlefield named Harris; that he was very long sick and was so grateful that he remained with Harris and his family and worked for them. The Harris family moved to Madison county in 1811 and he went with them. He took the greatest interest in the son of his benefactor and helped him to go to Franklin College and afterwards to study law with Judge Upson. His name was Austin Dabney. Gov. Gilmer says that when young Harris was admitted to the bar, Austin Dabney stood outside the railing with tears of joy trickling down his mulatto face. He drew a pension from the U. S. Government on account of his thigh, broken at Kettle Creek. When Judge Upson was in the legislature, he used his influence to have Austin Dabney receive a land lot. One of the members of the legislature from Madison county voted for it and it is said that his constituents resented this favor to a Negro. Gov. Gilmer says that Austin Dabney was generally respected by his old Revolutionary associates. Dabney and his friend Harris moved finally to Zebulon in Pike County where he is buried there with the Harris family.

Rev. George White says that Col. Wylie Pope, the ancestor, I suppose, of the family now living in the county, used to tell the following story with much glee. Austin Dabney was his neighbor and on one occasion when the former went for his customary annual pension, he was in company with Col. Pope. They travelled together socially on horseback until they reached Savannah, when the Colonel observed to Austin, that he (Austin) was a man of sense and knew that it was not suitable for him, (Mr. Pope) to be seen riding side by side with a colored man through the streets of Savannah. Austin replied that he understood that well. So when they reached the principal streets, he checked his horse and rode behind: Col. Pope had passed the house of Gen. James Jackson,[2] then Governor of Georgia. On looking back, he said he saw the Governor run out from his house, seize the hand of Austin Dabney and give it a cordial

(1) John Clark was Governor of Georgia, 1819-1823.
(2) James Jackson was Governor of Georgia, 1798-1801.

shake and then draw him off the horse and lead him in the house where he was the Governor's guest while he was staying in Savannah.

But Dabney never pushed himself into any social notice. It is said that when Judge Dooly went to Madison county to hold court, Dabney would always go to the tavern in the evening, where the Judge put up and, seated on a low seat, listen and take part in talk about the Revolution.

For a long time, pieces of muskets, of bayonets, and also musket balls were picked up at the battlefield of Kettle Creek. During the year 1876, when we were celebrating the Centennial of our independence, an old silver coin was picked up on the battlefield and, when I last heard of it, was in the possession of Mr. Henry T. Slaton. I wish that he and any others who may have old relics of the battlefield would give them to the Mary Willis Library where they would be preserved, for the benefit of the county.

I saw the battlefield in the summer of 1865, not very long after Sherman's march through Georgia. Sherman did not come through Wilkes county, but he turned off the road leading through, so near us, that the people living on the Union Point and Washington Road drove their stock off to keep them from falling into the hands of his bummers. Some of these thought of the old battle ground which is an out of the way place off the main roads. So they drove a lot of stock there for security and when I saw the battlefield in 1865, there were charred remains of their camp fires on the top of *War Hill* and corn cobs and shucks where they had fed their cattle. Thus the two armed invasions of the up country of Georgia, eighty-five years apart, that by Boyd and that by Sherman, came into curious connection on the old battlefield. We shall come to another curious coincidence of the kind in recalling the story of Wilkes county.

I suppose that it is partly owing to the out of the way, remote situation of the battlefield of Kettle Creek, that so few persons have seen it. With the solitary exception of Mr. William Fluker, who was raised in the neighborhood, I think I am the only person in Washington who has been on the battleground. Mr. William Fluker's ancestor, was living in the neighborhood, when the battle was fought and this man's brother Owen Fluker, was one of the soldiers engaged. It would make a very pleasant summer day's excursion to go up to the battlefield and carry a lunch.

A few years ago an interesting article in regard to the battle field was published in the *Washington Chronicle*. I think it was probably written by Gen. Graves. In it a very entertaining revolutionary story is told, which I have heard from other sources. The scene was at Anderson's Mills on Fishing Creek in the eastern part of the county. It seems that six American soldiers went in to get meal for their comrades. I think While so engaged, some Tories came up and killed three. The other three saved themselves by jumping out of the window, one of them holding a bag of bullets, which was a very valuable possession. In the freshet of 1840 - the Harrison freshet - Fishing Creek rose and washed from their graves the bones of the three dead soldiers. A concourse of people from the surrounding country met together just after, and buried the dead with great reverence.

The story is both true and interesting but I do not think the Tories could have belonged to Boyd's men, as is stated in the account. The account of the battle which I have followed was originally published in *McCall's History* in 1816. McCall was himself a revolutionary soldier, a Carolinian by birth, and there was a Capt. McCall in Col. Pickens regiment who was either the historian or his brother, I think. In addition, this account was published while one at least of the men who fought the battle was living, Gov. John Clark, who might have been expected to read with much interest the account of the battle in which he took part when little more than a boy. Thus it seems that the account must be substantially true, or it would have been corrected. By this account Boyd followed by Dooly and Pickens, was on the northern side of Broad River until February 13th. After they crossed, they both marched southward, camping within four miles of each other that night. To this, all the traditions in regard to *Clarke's Station* agree. Thus I do not think the Americans could have camped near Anderson's Mill on Fishing Creek the night before the battle. But since the account which I have followed states that Gen. Clarke joined Pickens and Dooly after they crossed the Savannah and before crossing Broad River, Gen. Clarke and his men may have previously been in the vicinity of Fishing Creek. This however, would put the occurrence at Anderson's Mills at some days before the battle.

After the successful battle, those citizens of Wilkes county who had retreated into South Carolina when Hamilton was sent to the up-country, returned to their homes. But they had not long been in the country when an attack by Indians was threatened. Alex. McGillivray, a Creek half-breed, and a man named Tate were agents of the British and they stirred up the Creek Indians to attack the settlements. There were 800 Indians collected at Fulsom's Fort, a point I am unable to locate. Gen. Clarke guarded the frontier and the danger was so great that all male inhabitants over sixteen years were called out. Col. Pickens came to help. He prepared to surprise the Indians.

They were warned in time by some Tory, but Col. Pickens move had the effect of dispersing them in small parties. In pursuing, some of the Indians were killed and three Americans. But quiet was restored. This was in March 1779, after the Battle of

Kettle Creek. What the people of the settlements suffered from Indians appears from many anecdotes. On Boyd's Creek in Elbert, lived a Mr. Richard Tyner, a poor, respectable man. In his absence, the savages came one day and killed his wife, then they dashed out the brains of the baby against a tree. A little son called Noah hid in a hollow tree and escaped. The tree was called for many years *Noah's Ark*. There were two daughters, Mary and Tamar, and the Indians carried them off to Coweta. Many years after, an Indian trader called John Manack bought Mary and bringing her to Elbert married her. They would not sell Tamar. They had resolved, however, to burn her alive, because they supposed that she was trying to escape. She was warned by an Indian woman, by whose help she obtained a canoe and provisions with which she floated alone down the Chattahoochee, traveling by night. She reached Apalachicola, where she found a vessel which took her to Savannah, and there she found help to get back to Elbert. She married a man named Hunt and when Rev. George White passed through Elbert, some of her descendants were living there.

Another story is told of an Indian attack in Elbert in which they carried off a little girl twelve years old. A gun smith named William Sutton determined to rescue her, or die in the effort. He came up with the Indians in the night and shot one, who seemed to claim her. She ran in the direction from which the noise of the report came and was seized by the hand of Sutton and carried on a swift horse home.

Gov. Gilmer says that an old woman once told on oath in Elbert Superior Court, of a party of Indians who came to her house at about the close of the Revolution, and who seized her infant child and before her eyes, beat out its brains against a stump.

Gov. Gilmer tells also of an old man in Oglethorpe named Bridges, who went out to hunt, and taking his little grandchild as far as the garden, placed her in a mulberry tree near by. Indians came who shot Bridges and seized the child, and while the father of the child who had been startled by the shot, was running up, they held it up by its feet, and cutting out the lobes of its heart, threw them at him. This happened in 1791.

This is what an Indian invasion meant and it will show readers what women in Wilkes endured from fear when the 800 savages threatened in 1779. The bitterness people felt toward Tories who would bring these horrors upon them can be well understood.

In all these things, the history of Elbert, Lincoln, and Oglethorpe was the history of Wilkes county. The county remained as one until 1790. The people of these other counties ought to be interested in the common history. Elbert and Lincoln were settled very early, being near the Savannah River;

and were active participants in the revolutionary struggle. The scene of the battle of Kettle Creek chances to be in our present Wilkes, but the men who fought it came from all three counties. When Chief Justice George Walton spoke of a war "in which you have greatly distinguished yourselves" he was talking of what we now call Elbert, Lincoln and Wilkes but then called only Wilkes county.

CHAPTER V

THE FIRST COURTS IN WILKES

THE BAND OF Tories who fought at Kettle Creek had been collected first in North Carolina recruiting as it passed through South Carolina. These collections of Tories had given much trouble in North Carolina, being largely actuated by the wish for plunder. It is said that the defeat of Boyd acted as a check to them and they did not collect again in large bodies. Another effect of the battle was that Augusta fell into the hands of the Whigs again. The battle took place February 14 and before the end of the month, Col. Campbell evacuated Augusta in such haste as to leave behind a large quantity of horses and military stores.

On the 25th of August, 1779, that is in the summer after the battle of Kettle Creek and the advance of Tate and the Creek Indians, the first court was held in the up country of Georgia north of Augusta. The old yellow book containing the records of this court is the oldest record in the office of the Ordinary of Wilkes County in Washington. This book is, by thirteen years, an older record than John Nelson's inscription on the rock, before described, though of course the grant of John Nelson's land in 1775 was earlier.

This book, which in 1889 was 110 years old, has always excited great interest among visitors who have examined the records in Capt. Anthony's office and I, myself, have looked it it over several times with much curiosity. But it became much more interesting to me after knowing in detail the events in the county, which immediately preceded the session of this court. It is stated in the book that the court assembled under an order from the Executive Council of Georgia. It is called a Court of Oyer and Terminer and General Gaol Delivery. Thus I suppose it cannot be classed with our *Superior Courts* which became familiar afterwards. There were three Justices, Absolom Bedell, Benjamin Catchings and William Downs. Henry Manadue was appointed Clerk and Joseph Scot-Riden Sheriff. John Dooly was attorney for the State. This gentleman must have been the Col. Dooly who was at the battle of Kettle Creek. Judge Dooly, his son, was too young to have acted as attorney. Some little doubt as to whether there were not two John Doolys was excited in my mind, by finding in *White's Historical Collections,* in a list of officers and soldiers who applied for land under the Act of 1783 of Georgia Legislature, and a resolution of Congress Sept. 1776, the names of Captains John and Thomas Dooly, both Captains. Col. John Dooly who fought at Kettle Creek was dead in 1783 and so was his brother Thomas. But there is no trace whatever of two of the name. White gives another list of officers in the Georgia service and there were but the one John Dooly and one Thomas Dooly. I presume the application was made in 1783 for land, for the children of these men, and as the land was given for the services of the dead John and Thomas Dooly, it was entered as if in their name. Thus, it seems quite certain, that the States Attorney General in this Court was Col. John Dooly of Kettle Creek fame. The court met, not at Washington but at the house of Jacob McClendon. From the best information I can get, Jacob McClendon lived where Mrs. Toliver Jones lives now.

As the Grand Jury was the first appointed in the county and was up country, I will give their names as they appear: Stephen Heard, foreman; Barnard Heard, George Walton, Daniel Burnett, Thomas Carter, Richard Aycock, Robert Day, John Gorham, Dionysius Oliver Esquires. Holman Freeman, Sen. Daniel Coleman, Thomas Stroud, Micajah Williamson, James McLean, Jacob Ferington, William Bailey, John Glass, Charles Bedingfield, Gentlemen. William Harper was appointed Deputy Sheriff.

The proceedings of the court would now be called irregular. It was evidently appointed mainly to try Tories. These had been guilty of great outrages in Wilkes County and it was doubtless felt that a trial and punishment of some of them for treason might add security for the women and children and old men in Wilkes when younger men were away. The Grand Jury first found a true bill against Joshus Rials for high treason and 'acting in conjunction with Tate and the Injuns'. This was evidently a man who had sought to bring the horrors of an attack by a large party of Creeks on the people of Wilkes. They found another indictment against James Mobley for the curious combination of 'Treason, Horse Stealing, Hogg Stealing and other misdemeanors'. This man was tried and pronounced guilty. He was not discharged but remanded to jail for further evidence, and thus coming before the court adjourned, he was tried again and found guilty and condemned; five other persons were tried and found guilty but recommended by the jury to mercy. Nevertheless, on August 28th they were all sentenced to be hung, one on the 6th of September. Besides this, the Grand Jury presented as a grievance that 26 men whom they named were at large and recommended that they should be arrested and tried for 'assisting the British troops and the avowed enemies of the United States of America'.

These were severe proceedings and also irregular. When

I first read them, I knew little of the history of the country just preceeding. They did not appear nearly so violent and inexcusable after I had read about the invasion of Boyd and especially the arming of the Indians to attack the white settlements of Wilkes. The manner in which the British carried on their warfare in Georgia and Carolina brought about reprisals. In those days, they thought if you could call a man a *Rebel* you put him out of the pale of the law. We changed the meaning of that word.

One very odd thing appears on this record. The Grand Jury summoned before them a man called John Crutchfield and inquired into the conduct of Cols. Pickens and Dooly in sending him into the British camp as a spy, and in regard to this matter they report that "After the most Strictest Scrutiny, we are of the opinion, that they did it with an Intent of Serving their Country and their Conduct is highly approved by us". That is just as the clerk Henry Manadue wrote it, capitals, spelling and all. This is still more curious when we remember that Pickens and Dooly had, but six months before, fought a successful battle which protected the county when invaded by a cruel and unscrupulous foe. And also to make the matter still more strange, Col. Dooly was the prosecuting attorney of the very court for which this Grand Jury was summoned! It is odd, but I tell exactly what the record reports. Nearly a hundred years afterward, the South was engaged in another war and certain natives of Wilkes County were much disposed to criticise certain military necessities of the times. It is somewhat curious to find Wilkes County starting out on that line from the very beginning. It has occurred to me that the Grand Jury may have investigated this matter, not because they needed to be satisfied, but to satisfy and correct some outside opinion and to justify Pickens and Dooly.

Just after the war, when Francis Asbury, Methodist Bishop, used to come on annual tours preaching the gospel in Wilkes, there was a John Crutchfield noted among the early Methodists. It was doubtless this same revolutionary soldier, Holman Freeman, Sr. on this Jury, I suppose to be the father of two younger men, Holman and John Freeman. He is, I suppose, the ancestor of old Major Freeman who is now (1889) the oldest man in Wilkes County. Major Freeman is I think, descended from his son Holman. From his son John, a gallant revolutionary soldier, are descended Rev. S. G. Hillyer well known in Washington and his late brother Judge Junius Hillyer - together with other younger members of the Hillyer family. The descendants of the Waltons and Aycocks are, I suppose, still in the county. I presume Francis Triplett, one of the witnesses, was the ancestor of Mrs. Mary Turner Maddox. The descendants of Barnard Heard live in Wilkes I think. Stephen Heard, was a noted and honored actor in the revolution. His descendants live in Elbert, but Mrs. Marcus Pharr, Jr., the daughter of Mr. Robert Heard of Elberton, represents Stephen Heard now in Wilkes. She is his great grand daughter.

Augusta did not long remain in the possession of the Americans. The British took Charleston and the attempt of the Americans and French to take Savannah was unsuccessful. After this, the defeat of Gen. Ash on Brier Creek, and the treachery of Gen. Andrew Williamson who went over to the enemy, caused Augusta to be occupied, in April 1780 by the British under Brown and Grierson. In 1780 the city was considered in such danger that an order was issued for the Executive Council of Georgia to go for safety to Heard's Fort in Wilkes County Georgia. They moved here in February 1780. Stephen Heard of Wilkes County was a member of the council and when Governor Howley left Georgia to attend the session of Congress, Mr. Heard was elected President of the Council. This made him, in the absence of the Governor, the acting executive of the state. Stephen Heard was a man of fine sense and character and a devoted patriot from beginning to end. Georgia named Heard County for him. He did and suffered much in the revolution. During the contest, his first wife was turned out of her home by Tories and caught a cold which caused the loss of her life. One of his sons afterwards represented Elbert County in the legislature for nearly twenty years. He was the grand father of Mrs. Marcus Pharr the younger. Another son who died early used to be spoken of by the older lawyers of this county as a young lawyer of uncommon talents.

Since Heard's Fort occupied in part at least the site of what is now Gen. B. W. Heard's garden, that is the spot to which the Executive council was removed. It is a curious fact that eighty five years afterwards President Jefferson Davis, leaving Richmond, Virginia, after the surrender of Gen. Lee, passed through Washington, and was entertained in what is now Gen. Heard's residence and that the last Cabinet Council of the Confederate Government was held in one of the rooms of this house, then occupied by Dr. J. J. Robertson, Cashier of the Bank which was then kept in the building. Thus the lot fronting Court Street, once the bank property, has been the resort of two runaway governments but with how different fate. It is another curious coincidence in the history of Wilkes County.

In April 1780, a session of the Superior Court for Wilkes county was held in Washington. The records of this court are contained in the same old book which holds the minutes of the Court of Oyer and Terminer held in 1779. This was a regular session of the Superior Court, and the Chief Justice of the State, Wm. Stephens, was present and presiding. He was assisted by five Justices of the Inferior Court, viz; those who held the former court, Downs, Catchings, and Bedell, and added to them, Zachariah Lamar and John Gorham. The name Lamar, afterwards well known in Georgia, and perhaps somewhat characteristic of it, is found early in the records of Wilkes county. The names Basil, Zachariah, James and John were kept up. There was also a Samuel Lamar mentioned in the early records. All these appear during the revolution.

Some entries in the old book help to settle a question which I have heard much discussed viz; when the name Washington was applied to what had been called Fort Heard. In the records of the court of 1779, held in the country at the house of Jacob McClendon, the names of witnesses are given, and one of these is called *Sarah Wright of Heard's Fort.* Thus in August 1779, Washington, in a written document still existing is called *Heard's Fort.* To this, it must be added that the order of council for the removal designated *Heards Fort.* When this court of 1779 adjourned, the words of the old record are as follows: "Ordered that the court be adjourned till the court in course at the Court House in the county aforesaid." The word court house may, in common parlance, mean the building erected for the court, or it may mean the village, town or city, containing the building. The latter is a very common use. In Wilkes, I have often heard people in the country speak of going to *the Court House,* meaning to Washington. The expression is not so much used as formerly people say *going to town.* It is evident that in the old record, the words are used in the latter sense, and they indicate the anticipation that the site of the *Court House* was soon to be fixed.

In the book, the record of the Superior Court in 1780 is headed as follows, "The Superior Court begun and holden at Washington in the county of Wilkes in the state of Georgia on Tuesday April 4th 1780."

In addition to these documents, the digest of the laws of Georgia gives the act of January 23rd, 1780, which appointed a Court House for Wilkes county. "Wm. Downes, Barnard Heard, John Coleman, John Dooly and Zachariah Lamar or any three of them shall be a board of commissioners under this act respecting the town at the Court House in Wilkes county which shall be called Washington." Note the words *shall be.* I think all these facts prove beyond a doubt that this town of Washington in Wilkes county Georgia was first so called in 1780.

CHAPTER VI

DARK DAYS IN WILKES

AFTER THE Superior Court of April, 1780 adjourned, there were dark days until June 1781. And strangely they were ushered in by a literal dark day, a strange phenomenon of nature, which took place May 19, 1780. At nine or ten o'clock in the morning, a singular yellowish fog, or cloud, filled the air, and by noon, it had so obscured the sun that it was necessary to use artificial lights. It was again seen on the morning of the 20th but soon dispersed. It excited great alarm and is remembered as *The Dark Day*. It is supposed now that it may have been due to some volcanic eruption in some part of the world. A few years ago the unusual redness of the sky at dark was attributed to some substance in the air thrown out by the volcano Krakatoa. The account of the *Dark Day* has come to us from those who saw it at the North and in neighboring states, but no tradition of it descends from the persons then living in Wilkes.

When Brown and Grierson took Augusta in the spring of 1780 they did not send troops to attempt the permanent occupation of Wilkes county, but they frequently dispatched raiding parties of soldiers to the up country to force submission and drive away Whigs. One of these went to the part of Wilkes which is now Lincoln, and forcing their way into the house of Col. John Dooly at night murdered him in the midst of his family. On reading in our old record book the account of his prosecution of Tories in the court of 1779 when he acted as attorney for the State, I cannot help thinking that it inspired his murderers. It is impossible to read the account of things in Wilkes without pity for the unfortunate people. The warfare was carried on by British and Tories in the most barbarous manner. They robbed and plundered and killed, and I have no doubt that the seven Tories who were hung deserved their fate. The object was to prevent such conduct in future but it led to reprisals.

A part of this body of Tories afterwards went to the house of Nancy Hart on Broad River, then in Wilkes but now in Elbert County, and were captured by her, two of them shot and four hung by her husband and his friends. The story of their visit to Nancy Hart's cabin, and their order that she should cook their dinner, how she got possession of their guns and shot two of them, how her husband came and they hanged the others, has been told so often that I will not repeat it here. I am sure those who read will be glad to know that these were the Tories who had just come from murdering Col. Dooly.

It is said that on one occasion when news was wanted from the Carolina side, no one but Nancy would go to obtain it and that she crossed the Savannah on a raft made by tying logs together with a grape vine and returned with the information.

Again, she met a Tory on the road and diverted him by conversation, until she could seize his gun when she made him walk before her to an American fort to whose commander she delivered him as a prisoner.

On another occasion, when news was wanted from the British in Augusta, she dressed herself in the attire of a man and went into the camp at Augusta, where pretending to be crazy, she gained the information wanted and brought it to General Elijah Clarke.

Governor Gilmer tells us that she was a kind hearted though rough determined woman. He says that at the close of the war, she moved to Alabama but afterwards returned and finally she died in Edgefield County, South Carolina. When the Methodist preachers came through, she became converted and was a shouting Methodist.

Rev. George White shows that her husband's family was related to Hon. Mr. Benton whose name was Thomas Hart Benton. Virginia and perhaps some of the other older states have counties named for English princesses and queens, but I do not know of any other county named for a woman until Georgia named one for Nancy Hart.

In September 1780, Gen. Clarke and Col. McCall came from Carolina and made an attempt to retake Augusta from the British. They had a fair chance of success when there were reinforcements of troops from Ninety-Six in Carolina for Brown and they were forced to raise the seige. The discouragement was very great from the fall of Charleston and the unsuccessful attempt to take Savannah and Augusta. There is no farther record of the Superior Court in our Ordinary's office until 1782.

After the unsuccessful attempt upon Augusta, Col. Elijah Clarke and the Wilkes County volunteers, seeing they could make no advance in Georgia, determined to go over to Carolina and help in the active movement of Whigs there. When Gen. Clarke returned from the seige of Augusta in September, 1780, he appointed Dennis Mills on Little River as a rendezvous for his men, who assembled there to the number of 300. I wish somebody living now in this county or Lincoln could tell us where Dennis Mills was situated, for it was the scene of a very pathetic encounter. When Gen. Clarke and his soldiers got there he found, says *Jones' History of Georgia,* "four hundred women and children with their personal effects, craving permission to follow the army to a place of safety. For two years the operations agricultural - of this portion of Georgia had been so much disturbed that very many of the fields remained uncultivated. Poverty lay down at the door of not only a few, and the curses of the tyrant were heard everywhere. It was the part of humanity to harken to the prayers of this helpless population and to guide it into abodes of peace and plenty. For eleven days did Col. Clarke and his command escort this congregation of women and children through mountainous regions and unaccustomed paths to avoid interruption by the enemy. It was a journey replete with difficulties and privations, but there were no murmurings by the way and at last the patient travelers, footsore, weary, and pinched by hunger, found rest, homes, and entertainment, at the hands of the generous dwellers by the banks of the Watauga and and Nolachuckie rivers. In this beautiful region with its sweet waters, grand forests, and fertile valleys, unvexed by royal proclamations, unvisited by the despoiler, and rejoicing in the hospitality of a brave, honest, virtuous, and liberal people, did these refugees abide until the storm of war was overpast, until the gentle sounds of assured peace lured them back to their Georgia homes."

I found some trouble in fixing the exact situation of the place to which emigrated the Wilkes county refugees of the time of the revolution. But at last I settled the matter and found it to be in a community which has always excited great interest in the readers of our early history. It was the Watauga Valley. This is a beautiful valley lying on the western side of the Alleghany mountains which divided North Carolina from Tennessee. It was discovered not long before the revolution by James Robertson, who was one of the pioneers of Tennessee. It was first settled by another pioneer of Tennessee, John Sevier, who established there the first organized government west of the mountains. It was first called Watauga county of North Carolina and included all Tennessee. Soon after the Revolution, Tennessee became a state and John Sevier was the first governor.

Some time afterwards when Sevier was a member of Congress, he was appointed Commissioner, U. S. to settle the boundary between Georgia and the new state of Alabama. While thus engaged, he died. During the year 1789, the Tennessee people removed his remains to that state - his dust and ashes I suppose, for there could have been little more - and they had a great ceremony at the reinterment. The Watauga people were greatly in favor of independence and John Sevier came down to South Carolina and helped to fight at Musgrove's Mill, a battle in South Carolina where Elijah Clarke had been wounded. I imagine it was there and then, they had met and talked of the Watauga valley and its security from invaders, and probably this made Clarke think it a good place to carry the defenceless women and children who did not want to be left in Wilkes. Perhaps Sevier had invited this.

I think my readers will find this account of more interest and will remember it better, if they will take Cram's Atlas in the Library and find the spot to which the refugees were taken. The map of North Carolina contains a Watauga county in the northwestern corner and there the two rivers, Watauga and Nolachuckie take their rise. But you must turn to the map of Tennessee to find the actual valley, which is in Carter and Washington counties of Tennessee. Those who have travelled northward by the E. T. & Va. R. R. have, at Jonesboro, been in or near the Watauga Valley to which the Wilkes county refugees went a little more than a hundred years ago.

There is an account of both Sevier and Robertson in the Encyclopedia of American Biography at the Library. It tells how the wife of Robertson, who was a famous early heroine of Tennessee, saved her husband's life. The story would be out of place here.

But it would be in place to tell a little of the battle of King's Mountain, for some of the Gen. Clarke's men from Wilkes helped to fight it. Cornwallis had despatched an officer called Ferguson to the western upper portions of the Carolinas, to recruit Tories for his army and carry out his brutally severe orders against the lovers of liberty; and Ferguson collected a large band of Tories on King's Mountain which lies between North and South Carolina. John Sevier and another noted pioneer, Isaac Shelby, from what is now Kentucky, and who was afterwards the first governor of Kentucky when it became a state, planned an expedition to go down and attack the Tories on Kings Mountain. Ferguson had learned that Gen. Clarke was going up the Watauga Valley and he determined to intercept him. Gen. Clarke could not leave the Wilkes refugees until he conducted them to a place of safety, but he sent some of his men under Major Chandler who joined Sevier and Shelby. They fought the battle of King's Mountain in which Ferguson was killed, and a stop put to the operation of recruiting by Cornwallis in the mountains. King's Mountain can be found in Cram's Atlas in the Library. Some years ago, I had a beautiful view of this mountain from an elevated rock in *Jones Gap,* a narrow pass in the Saluda Mountains in South Carolina. The gap is walled in on both sides by mountains whose successive peaks seen, one behind the other, looked bluer and bluer as my eye ranged down the narrow defile. Between the two most distant of these, I could see a glimpse of the sunny plain beyond the entrance to the Gap and standing alone, bathed in light, far away on the plain, historic King's Mountain made the beautiful landscape more impressive by its suggestion of a memorable conflict and victory for human rights. But how much more it would have impressed me, if I had known then that soldiers from our own Wilkes county in Georgia fought in that battle!

It is not my part to say anything of the war in Carolina further than concerns the soldiers from Wilkes, who had gone to help the common cause. For this account I am indebted chiefly to Jones' *History of Georgia*. They were at Blackstone's where the only man killed "was a Georgian from Wilkes county named Rogers" and where it is said that the skill of the Wilkes county Riflemen excited general admiration. They were at the battle of Long Cane, where Col. Clarke was desperately wounded and then under Major John Cunningham at Cowpens, where they were in the front line of battle, also in skirmishes at Haw River and at Beattie's Mill.

In 1781 Gen. Nathaniel Green was appointed commander of the Southern Division of the U. S. army and there was a prospect of doing good in Georgia, so Col. Clarke gained permission to return to the state from South Carolina with his men. They dispersed themselves over the county in small parties to visit their homes. In Jones' *History of Georgia,* he quotes the following from McCall's book: "When these small parties entered the settlements where they had formerly resided, general devastation was presented to their view; their aged fathers and brothers had been hanged and murdered, their decrepit grandfathers were incarcerated in prisons where most of them had been suffered to perish in filth, famine or disease, and their wives, mothers, sisters, daughters and young children had been robbed, insulted and abused and were found by them in temporary huts more resembling a savage camp than a civilized habitation". McCall adds, "There is damning proof of the truth of this unvarnished tale and the reader may imagine the feeling of the Georgians of that day and the measure of his resentment. Mercy to a loyalist who had been active in outrage became inadmissable and retaliative carnage ensued".

Brown and Grierson, entrenched in Augusta had sent out parties to do this work and Cornwallis was also responsible as a circular letter can be read, sent out by him directing that the people of the Provinces shall be treated "with the utmost rigor". I find that the descendants of people then living in Wilkes remember to have heard the old people speak of this man Grierson. In several instances, prisoners were turned over to the Indians by him and killed barbarously by them.

It was soon after his return from Carolina that Col. Clarke took small pox. Therefore when the soldiers assembled in April 1781 at Dennis Mills, they were under the command of Lieut. Col. Micajah Williamson, whose name appears so often in the old court records of Wilkes county from 1779-1790. He took the troops to Augusta and began to erect works for attacking the town. As soon as Gen. Clarke was able to get up, that is in May, he joined Col. Williamson with 100 men from Wilkes county. They had hardly begun the seige, when they had to send back to Wilkes and drive away Indians and Tories.

I do not design to relate the story of the second siege of Augusta further than to tell the part taken in it by the soldiers from Wilkes County. Col. Lee,[1] the father of our great Robert E. Lee and Gen. Andrew Pickens came to conduct the siege. Among the Whigs was Capt. Samuel Alexander, who was, I presume from the part of Wilkes county which afterwards became Warren. I find his name several times on the list of jurymen in Wilkes before 1787. The old father of Capt. Alexander had been captured by one of the raiding parties sent out from Augusta and he was placed by Col. Brown with other prisoners in the bastion of the fort which was most exposed to fire. Capt. Alexander commanded one of the companies attacking Fort Cornwallis, in which they were placed. Augusta was taken in July 1781. It is told in White's *Statistics of Georgia* under the head of Heard County, that Stephen Heard found his old father in Augusta where he had been carried by Grierson. Jones says in his *History of Georgia*, that the father of Capt. James and Samuel Alexander had been arrested by Grierson in his eightieth year, "chained and dragged by the tail of a cart for two days. When attempting to obtain some rest for his feeble limbs by leaning against the vehicle he was ignominiously scourged by the driver". These old men had been held as hostages for the neutrality of the up country. Grierson was shot through a window after the surrender. The perpetrator could not be found, but it was believed to be one of the sons of old Mr. Alexander.

In November 1781, there was an invasion of Cherokees in Wilkes county with the usual accompaniment of robbery and murder. Gen. Pickens with his Carolinians and some Georgians went into the Cherokee territory and burned every village south and east of the mountains. After this, the Cherokees and some Creeks began another invasion but were met and driven by Col. Clarke beyond the Oconee.

In October 1781, Cornwallis surrendered at Yorktown. Gen. Twiggs had already been advancing on Savannah and it was soon after invested by Col. Wayne. On July 11, 1782, the British evacuated Savannah. In November of that year, Independence was acknowledged and Peace was proclaimed. It must have been a grateful sound in Wilkes; but there has no word come down to us about their joy. In that year, 1782, begun the regular records of our Superior Courts.

The exertions of the men and the sufferings of the women in Wilkes equalled those of the up country in the Carolinas, of which so much has been written.

(1) Col. Lee was Richard Henry Lee called 'Light Horse Harry Lee.' See Hays, 'Hero of Hornets' Nest', pp. 123, 127, 131, 132, 134, 135, 136, 137, 139, 182, 322, 339.

In White's *Historical Collections of Georgia,* there is an account of Mrs. Hannah Clarke, the widow of Gen. Elijah Clarke, who survived him twenty years, dying at the age of 90 in 1829. The burning of her house and its contents by a party of British and Tories is recorded and the turning out of herself and children. When her husband was so desperately wounded at Long Cane in Carolina, she started on horseback to see him and was robbed of the horse she was riding. It is stated that she accompanied him on one campaign and that she was moving from place of danger when her horse, on which she was riding with her two children, was shot under her. She was at the siege of Augusta.

The hatred of Tories which was felt so long is not remarkable. The following anecdote illustrating it has, I think, never been printed. I have before spoken of Mr. Phillips, from whom Phillips Church was named, in the southwestern part of the county near Kettle Creek and I related a story of the troubles of Mrs. Phillips. When Phillips and the other soldiers came back, of course the women told of their sufferings. When the church was first built, they could not at once get it floored, and so the congregation used it for public worship, sitting on the logs which were the sleepers of the building. One Sunday they were seated there before their worship commenced, when Phillips looking round spied a Tory. Jumping up dressed in what used to be called a *smock frock,* he walked on the logs to the place where the Tory was seated and, seizing him by the collar, marched him to the door, giving the Tory a parting kick as he pushed him out. This was perhaps not a very Christian like performance but it was natural. Nature will sometimes get the better of grace, as those of us know who lived through Sherman's invasion. I imagine, however, that this occurrence took place before good brother Silas Mercer had got to the church on that Sunday morning.

In our county records, prior to 1788, I find two Phillips, Joel and Zachariah. One of these I presume was Phillips of Phillips Mill. It is curious that I find these names as signatures in another place. Early in the Revolution, Georgia was somewhat divided about joining in the effort to gain independence. There was a public meeting in Savannah, at Tondee's Tavern, in which there was an expression of sympathy with those who wished to declare the colonies independent. The people in the country above Savannah were not ready and there were meetings in both Burke and Columbia to protest against the meeting at Tondee's Tavern, as expressing the feeling of the colony. Columbia, it must be remembered, was then in Richmond. To the papers of protest in what is now Columbia, I find appended the names of Joel and Zachariah Phillips, evidently brothers and also Absolom Bedell. Absolom Bedell was one of the judges who sat in the court of 1779, which hung seven Tories, although the jury recommended mercy for five of them. The two Phillips, who were evidently brothers and Absolom Bedell were, it is clear, emigrants from Columbia. Sometimes there are two of a name, father and son, but since there is no senior or junior to either Bedell, it is probable there was but one man. The strong feeling evidently felt by both men later, is an example of the way in which popular sentiment spreads and grows. When Georgia finally took position there was no wavering at all in Burke and Columbia or elsewhere. Never in the darkest day, and I have shown that there were very dark ones, did Georgia or any part hesitate or think of making separate terms with the enemy. I hope I shall interest in this account of the Revolution in Wilkes those who live in the county and inherit its memories. Nothing will so inspire us with patriotism as an account of what our fathers did. I myself am a native of Appling, Columbia County, but I have lived so long in Wilkes, that I feel as if I am a part of it and also my grandfather, John Andrews, a Revolutionary soldier who was at Yorktown when Cornwallis soon afterwards came to Georgia and settled in the part of Wilkes which afterwards became Oglethorpe. My paternal grandfather was a revolutionary soldier also, not in Georgia, but a kinsman of mine, Commodore Oliver Bowen, took an honorable part in the revolutionary history of the state. He is buried in St. Pauls churchyard, Augusta.

In writing this account, I have had no access to any original documents, except those in our Court House, which are of much interest.

I am indebted to Jones *History of Georgia,* to Gov. Gilmer's *Georgians,* and to the two books of Rev. George White, *Statistics* and *Historical Collections.* So that what I have said is in a large measure mere compilation, and therefore, a very humble performance. But I hope I have so put the facts together that those who live in Wilkes county can know something of its honorable history.

CHAPTER VII

IN THE LAST CENTURY

THE TREATY OF peace was signed November 1782, but for Wilkes county the fruits of independence began as soon as Augusta returned into American possession in July 1781. There are no records of the sessions of the Superior Court in the year 1781, and a knowledge of the state of things in Wilkes and all over Georgia renders it pretty certain that the gap is occasioned, not by the destruction of records but by the fact that no court was held. A session of court was held in October 1782 and thereafter regularly, twice a year, up to the late session held by Judge Lumpkin November 1889, one hundred and seven years afterwards. The Chief Justice, George Walton, was not present until 1784, when he delivered the charge from which I have made a previous quotation. This charge has some sentences which bear very strongly on a question discussed in my first article, viz.: the date of the first settlement in Wilkes, so I will quote it at greater length.

Chief Justice Walton said, "Gentlemen of the Grand Jury Fourteen or fifteen years ago I several times rode over this country when it was a wilderness, and nothing to be seen but the Savage and his Game of the Woods. The Indian line being soon moved further out, it began to settle, and altho it has been interrupted by a seven or eight year war in which the first settlers greatly distinguished themselves, it has increased in number strength and cultivation to an astonishing degree, this rapidity of settlement is an incontrovertible proof of the goodness of the soil, the climate, &c."

I took the liberty of putting commas in his Honor's charge, but spelling and capitals are his. It is evident he gave a written copy to the clerk, and I presume the clerk copied it exactly. Even the best educated of our Revolutionary heroes did not spell correctly as we call it, from George Washington down. I rather enjoy their license, for I think English spelling is a tyrannical imposition, though I am obliged to follow and teach it so long as the rest of the world does not rebel.

Judge Walton's charge brings out three points with various degrees of clearness. First, that there were no settlers when he was here in 1769. "Fourteen or fifteen years" before 1784 would take us to 1769 or 70. George Walton says he traveled through this country several times, and I imagine he was a trader or trader's agent, for Walton was a poor youth, a carpenter who had worked his way up though his descendants in my time were aristocrats.

He says in effect that there were only savages and wild animals here in 1768 or 1770, and I think this point must be regarded as settled almost to demonstration, for he was an eye witness and in character one of the first men in the Georgia of his day. It is true we have merely the written report of his testimony, but it comes down to us with the highest possible authenticity of a written document. It is found yellow with age, in the carefully preserved official records of the county.

Another point brought out by Judge Walton's charge is the extreme improbability that settlers came before 1773. The friends who have reported to me traditions that settlers came in 1769, also report that these found many others already here. Now from the point already made out unmistakably from Judge Walton's charge, it is clear that both these statements cannot be true. If they found white inhabitants here, they must have come after 1769. But more than this, Judge Walton expressly says "The Indian line being soon after moved further out, it began to settle." Thus he makes the beginning of the settlement follow the moving of the line, which as we know took place in 1773 when the treaty was made. The treaty again is preserved in a carefully kept document, and there can be no doubt as to its date. In telling of the actual settlement, Judge Walton's statement does not come so near furnishing demonstration, because here he was not an eye witness. Nevertheless, he makes it extremely improbable that the settlers came before 1773. He lived contemporary with these events, and he is likely to have been interested in hearing of matters in a part of the country over which he had traveled. But in addition to this, there were several persons on the jury which he addressed who were here from the first, and who must have known of their own personal knowledge, when the first settlement took place. John Freeman and Dury Cade were Jurymen. Barnard Heard must almost certainly have heard Judge Walton's charge for he was a witness in one of the cases which was brought up for trial. If there were any incorrectness in the judge's statement he would have been better informed. I do not of course think that he would have altered the copy of his charge given to the clerk to be recorded, so as to make it report what he did not say but he would have stricken out an incorrect statement from the record copy. Thus Judge Walton's charge gives an extremely high degree of probability to the view that the first settlement of Wilkes followed the treaty of 1773.

But there is still another point. At first I was disposed to think that the number of soldiers raised by General Clarke in Wilkes an argument for earlier settlement, because on any other theory, there must have been an extreme rapidity of settlement which without positive evidence seemed improbable. Judge Walton furnishes just that positive evidence. He says that the county did fill up with astonishing rapidity notwithstanding the war.

Now I wish so to state the facts that all readers can form their own opinion in regard to this matter; but in my own judgment these facts show clearly that settlement began in 1773. I am far from thinking tradition valueless, but no recollection so easily becomes indistinct and altered as that of dates, and this tradition is confronted by very powerful positive testimony.

In Dr. George Howe's *History of the Presbyterian Church in Carolina*, it is said that Pendleton county, (a tract of about forty miles square on the eastern side of the Savannah, not far from the part of original Wilkes which is now Elbert,) contained in five years after its early settlement, nine thousand inhabitants, as shown by the United States census. This rush of emigrants reminds one a little of Oklahoma in our day.

Wilkes county was settled in 1773. In 1790, the U.S. census reported for it 31,500 inhabitants. This was of course the original county, including Wilkes, Elbert, Lincolnton, Oglethorpe, and parts of Taliaferro, Warren, Green, Hart and Madison. The whole state of Georgia had by the same census of 1790, 82,548 inhabitants. Thus Wilkes county in seventeen years, had gained more than a third as many settlers as the whole of Georgia had in nearly sixty years. These figures astonished me, and I cannot account for the rapid emigration in this direction only by supposing that this Piedmont region in Georgia and South Carolina was the one direction in which settlers could reach larger tracts of fresh land without putting the great barrier of the Alleghany mountains between themselves and other white settlements.

There was a Virginia regiment in Georgia during the latter part of the revolution. It came with General Wayne under a Colonel Posey and was at the siege of Savannah. They seem to have marched through the up country and they learned a good deal about the desirable lands in Wilkes. General George Matthews, afterwards governor of Georgia, came during the revolution and bought the Goose Pond settlements in a part of Wilkes which is now Oglethorpe county. He went back to Virginia, as we are told by Gov. Gilmer, and induced a large number of friends to come and settle. They formed the Broad River settlements. The grandfather of Judge Thomas Merriwether now living in the county east of Washington, Gen. David Meriwether was among the Virginia soldiers who were at the last siege of Savannah. He was taken prisoner and paroled, and while on parole came to Wilkes county and married Frances Wingfield, coming here to settle when the fighting was over. Gen. Merriwether was a great Indian fighter afterwards, and was appointed by the President, Commissioner with Duncan Campbell to make that treaty with the Indians which gained the territory between the Flint and Ocomulgee Rivers. Merriwether county was named after Gen. Merriwether.

Among the noted revolutionary soldiers who settled in what was then Wilkes, but now Lincoln, was Col. John Graves. He had been a distinguished officer, was at the battles of Brandywine, Germantown, Monmouth and at the siege of Yorktown. When General Green crossed the Yadkin coming south in 1781, Col. Graves with 200 men was ordered to protect the passage of the troops from Cornwallis. He acted with great gallantry and was entirely successful in a desperate encounter.

He settled near Grave's mountain to which he gave name but afterwards moved just beyond what are called the *French Mills,* where he died. His grave can be found on the place where Mr. Enoch Johns now lives, who occupied the house his son built. Col. Graves was the grandfather of the children of Mrs. John T. Wingfield and Mrs. F. T. Simpson. John Temple Graves, editor of the *Rome Tribune,* a Wilkes county boy whom we all remember, and in whose success we take pride and pleasure, is the great grandson of Col. John Graves of the Revolution.

I am making a somewhat rambling paper, but I have just room to tell the curious fact that in Columbia county, and in Wilkes each, there was a revolutionary soldier who had also been at Braddock's defeat in the old French war, in 1755, and both lived to be 102 years old, and also each married, in extreme old age, a much younger woman. The story of the two men is so similar that a reader might fancy there was but one, who had been multiplied into two by imagination and imperfect memory. But this is not so, there were really two men. Of one of them, in Wilkes county, Mr. John Wright, I personally know something, as his first wife was my grandmother's sister, Sarah Goode by name, and I have heard my cousin, Mrs. Stephens, his grand daughter say he never was married until he was sixty years old. That was rather an old bachelor for aunt Sarah Goode to tackle and civilize. But he lived to marry again and at an extreme old age and by his last wife, was the father of Mr. James Wright who lived near Mallorysville.

His Columbia double was named David Hodge. The marriage of this one was announced as follows in the *Augusta Chronicle;* "The Spirit of seventy-six. Another hero of the Revolution has fallen--before the shrine of Hymen--but even in his fall he triumphed. Thus runs the proud memorial of his glory. On the 25th ult. was united in the holy bands of matrimony by John McGhee Esq. Mr. David Hodge, aged one hundred and two years and two months to Miss Elizabeth Bailey aged forty years, both of

Columbia county, Georgia. Mr. Hodge was at Braddock's defeat; and served through the whole period of the Revolutionary War." How long after this David lived with his Elizabeth does not appear. John Wright died at 102 years, but I have heard his daughters, whom the young wife very soon caused to leave, say that he would have lived longer but for the lack of attention from the young woman. Mrs. Esther Gresham and Miss Polly Wright were his daughters, two excellent and sensible women. The two brothers H. T. and F. P. Slaton of this county, are his grandsons. He has a son living in extreme old age at Woodstock, "uncle Jack Wright."

I wonder if any of our Confederate Vets will rival these old fellows in age and love making?

*(Note:---*In the last number, Col. John Temple Graves soldier of the Revolution, was, by inadvertence, said to be the grandfather, instead of ancestor as should have been written of the children of Mrs. J. T. Wingfield and Mrs. F. T. Simpson. He was the ancestor also of John Temple Graves of 1889.)

CHAPTER VIII

WASHINGTON LAID OUT

THERE WERE two acts of the Legislature relating to the laying out of Washington. One of these was dated January 23, 1780, and I have already quoted it in regard to the name of Washington. This was during the Revolution, just at the beginning of the *dark days*. The other act was passed in 1783, just at the close of the Revolution.

The Act of 1780 appointed William Downs, Barnard Heard, John Coleman, John Dooly, and Zachariah Lamar commissioners to lay out the town. There was some defect in the work done, probably owing to the disturbed state of the county. John Dooly was murdered that very summer. So when the Legislature met in July 1783 they said, "Whereas a town was ordered and actually laid out in the county of Wilkes at a place called Washington, under such instructions as were then laid down, but the same were not complied with, and the said lots are reverted," then the act goes on to appoint another set of commissioners, Stephen Heard, Micajah Williamson, Robert Harper, Daniel Colman, Zachariah Lamar, to carry out the intentions of the legislature, and make another "admeasurement." It is not altogether clear what the defect was---except that they had not taken measures regarding a church and academy---of which I shall speak further on. But this time, the work stood, and we say that Washington was laid out in 1773, one hundred and six years ago.

In the office of E. M. Anthony now Ordinary of Wilkes county, there is recorded a plan of the town made in 1805. That is the year in which the town was incorporated by the Legislature and it's pretty certain that this plan was drawn for the purpose of showing the territory subject to the act of incorporation. The plan is certified by the town commissioners of 1805, viz. N. Long, President, John Griffin, Wm. Prince, Joel Abbott, R. Worsham, Felix H. Gilbert, G. Hay, Commissioners. David Terrell the clerk of the county states that he recorded this plan at request of the commissioners. I will state in passing that a plan of the town, found in 1888 among old papers of Mrs. Martha Andrews by Mr. Floyd was a copy of this recorded plan. Richard Worsham was the grandfather of Mr. Samuel Barnett and Dr. F. T. Willis. This is merely the old original plan of Washington as made in 1783, and afterwards modified, as I shall show in 1793, and it is merely put on paper, not made in 1805. It, however represents the town as it was in 1805, when incorporated. On this plan, the town is a square, and within that square, which is drawn in black ink, there is another portion, a rectangle enclosed in a line of colored ink, and David Terrell writes a note on the margin in which he says that this colored line marks the limits of the *Old Town*, but the surrounding portion was originally laid out in residence lots. This as I will show was done in 1793.

Now I want to make the reader understand what part of our Washington, known to us in 1889, belonged to the *Old Town* of 1783 and what part was the Common of 1783. It will be very easy to make this understood to anybody acquainted with the town,--- easier than if you had that plan of 1805 before you, for on it the lots are known by numbers, and the names of some streets are not those which we now know.

The western boundary of the *Old Town* is a line running through the middle of what we now call Pope Street passing between the residence lots of Dr. Robert Simpson and of Mrs. Dr. Lane. This street is closed up on the north by Mr. Hogue's fence but it formerly extended further along the east of what is now the residence lot of Mr. Theodoric Green, formerly Judge Andrew's orchard. The street was closed up by Rev. Dr. Tupper by permission of the town council, but I remember well when it was open. But in saying that the middle line of this street was the boundary of the *Old Town* on the west the reader must not suppose that the street was laid out in 1783, or existed in 1805. It is not down on the map as a street, but there is merely a line marking the western boundary of the *Old Town*.

The eastern boundary of the *Old Town* was the street called by us Alexander Avenue, the street passing by the Female Seminary and running on the north to the Danburg and Elberton roads, on the south to the Double Wells road. This street was laid out in 1783, and exists on the map. It is there called, however, 'East Street.'

The south Boundary of the *Old Town* can be understood as follows. Let the reader imagine himself standing in Jefferson street on the pavement, and just half way between the Library corner and the corner of Mr. Wm. Johnson, or in other words half way between Liberty Street and Water Street. Having fixed this point, let the reader imagine a line extending east and west through the point on which he stands. That line would show the southern boundary of the *Old Town*. The line would cut exactly in half all the squares on the south side of Liberty Street.

The northern boundary of the *Old Town* can be found as follows. Let the reader imagine himself standing on Alexander Avenue about 60 yards north from its intersection with Court Street (that is, north of the street in front of Mr. John

Cozarts house.) Then let him imagine a line running east and west through the point on which he stands. It would be the northern limit of the *Old Town*. This line would run just back of Mr. Cozart's lot and the Bank lot. It would leave in the *Old Town* a row of half squares on the northern side of Court Street. Court Street is now closed up on the West by Mrs. Kemme's fence, that is west of its intersection with Allison street, but it is open all the way on this map. It was closed up by Dr. Tupper with consent of the town commissioners, and I have heard that they gave him a lease of 99 years on the two streets that he closed. Dr. Tupper was so much and so justly loved and honored in Washington, that his requests were granted. I remember well when Court Street was open to the line of Judge Andrew's fence,---through what is now Mrs. Kemme's garden, and my cousin now Mrs. Troup Butler, then Cora Andrews, used to get over the fence and go up Court Street on her way to school then at the Seminary.

Thus I have stated the four boundaries of the *Old Town*. Before going further, I must state that on the old map or plan, the open space which we call the Court House Square does not exist. It was not opened until the building of the present Court House in 1817. Previous to that time, it formed one square with the still built up square or parallelogram east of it. It used to have stores on it. My Uncle, Judge Garnett Andrews told me that at the time he thus spoke, there could be still seen somewhere near the Court House steps, part of the brick foundation of what used, at an earlier day, to be Thomas Terrell's store. I presume that this can still be seen.

Within the boundary of the *Old Town* which I have described there were eight whole or complete squares, four between Main and Liberty Sts., four between Main and Court Sts. Then there were also four half squares on the south side of Liberty Street which were within the boundaries of the *Old Town*, and also four other half squares on the north side of Court Street. Thus there were eight whole squares and half squares within the limits of the *Old Town*. Now every square was divided into 4 equal lots. Thus 8 squares contained 32 lots and the 8 half squares 16 lots. Together, they made 48 lots within the boundaries of the *Old Town*. The reader who has followed me sees that it would amount to that number within the *Old Town* as I have described it in nature, and there are 48 numbered lots on the map, without the colored line which represents the boundary of the *Old Town*.

And now I want to show the reader what was the outside boundary of the Common. Its interior boundary was the line around the *Old Town*, and its outside boundary ought to enclose 100 acres. I will show this. First let me describe the position of the boundary. The north boundary would be a line running along the north side of North Street, that is the street crossing Alexander Avenue by the place of Mrs. Isabella Colley. This street is on the Common of the *Old Town*. Of course it was not a street in 1783, but was made one in 1793, and is down on the map of 1805. Mrs. Isabella Colley's property is just where she could have escaped paying town tax in 1805. The north side of North Street ends on the west at the great white oak in the front yard of what was once Judge Andrew's residence at Haywood. He told me that this oak was at the northeast corner of the original town boundary. In calculating the limits of the town including the Common, from the old map, I find that it corresponds exactly with what I have said. I think that the old surveyors in laying off the rectangle of 100 acres begun at this White Oak, now a hundred years older. Thus this old white oak is a historic landmark. The north outside boundary of the Common extended from the white oak up to Mrs. Isabella Colley's corner and then across Alexander Avenue, and then extended 66 yards further over into what is now Capt. Alexander's lawn where we have the northeast corner of the old Common, and of the incorporated area of 1805.

The southern boundary of the Common and the corporation of 1805 was the south side of what we call South Street that is the street running between the residence lots of Mrs. George Dyson and Mr. William Toombs. This line did not end with Mr. Toombs fence corner, but crossed Alexander Avenue and extended 66 yards beyond its eastern side over what is in 1889 the property of Mr. Charles Smith, on which stood 66 yards east of his front fence, the southeastern corner of the old Common and of the earliest incorporation. A line drawn north from this corner would it is evident meet the northeast corner of the common on Mr. Charles Alexander's lawn. It would take in on the Common, the residence lots of Judge Reese, Mrs. Stephen Palmer, Mr. E. G. Binns, Mr. Lowe, Dr. Lyndon, Mr. Charles Smith (now occupied by Mr. E. M. Anthony, County Ordinary.) All of these persons would have been subject to town tax in 1805. The old plan which shows the town as it was after the Common was laid off in building lots in 1793, and as it was when incorporated in 1805, does not show any street laid off along the eastern line of the Common. The short street which lies between Judge Reese's property and the Presbyterian church is of much later origin. It was made when the Presbyterian church was built about fifty years later. I do not know that Judge Reese's eastern fence marks the Common limit, though I suspect that it does, and that his property on Main Street and Alexander Avenue comprehends exactly one of the lots of the old plan.

South Street on the old plan, crossed Main Street and extended into what is now Dr. Simpson's property and then it crossed our present Pope Street to the South of Mrs. Mary Lane's property. There is nothing by which I can mark its northern terminus. All the people south of it, Mr. Walter Shelverton, Mr. Chapman, Dr. Andrews, Mr. Walter Binns, Mr. Toombs DuBose, Mr. William Toombs would in 1805 have been living in the country and they would have had no town tax to pay. Mrs. George Dyson, the Methodist Parsonage, Mrs. Julia Ficklen's lately purchased home, Merriwether Hill, Mrs. Neeson, Boyce Ficklen, Mr. Fluker, Marcus Pharr, Jr., Mr. Wm. Johnson, Mr. Kendrick and Mr. J. R. Smith, all live on what was the Common. Had they lived in 1805 and where they do now, they would have been subject to town tax. But the people on Main Street east of Judge Reese and Mrs. Palmer would have been out of town in 1805, and would not have paid town tax. The northern boundary of the old Common and of the early incorporation was a line extending directly southward from the great white oak on Mr. Theodoric Green's property at Haywood. It would have run down the western side of Judge Andrews old Avenue across Main street and somewhere between Mr. B. S. Irvin and Mr. Hines, somewhere back of Mrs. Mary Lanes house where it would have met the south boundary of the Common. I cannot point out the southwest corner of the Common and the old corporation with definiteness as there are no landmarks to help me. If starting at Mrs. Lane's corner, that is at the corner of Pope and Liberty Streets, one walked directly south 204 yards, and then he turned exactly at right angles and walked 66 yards westward he would come to the southwest corner of the old Common and corporation of 1805. Mrs. Lane, Mr. Hines and the new residence of Mr. Theodoric Green are all on the old Common. In 1805 they would have been subject to town tax but our present Mayor, Mr. B. S. Irvin would have been free from this impost. Perhaps he might have been Mayor notwithstanding, if he had lived then, for it is a little curious that, of the town Commissioners who got up that plan in 1805 and had the town incorporated, several lived out of their corporation. Mr. Felix Gilbert, who lived where Mr. Charles Alexander now lives; Dr. Abbott, who lived in what will always be known as Gen. Toombs place: Mr. Nicholas Long, who lived in the house burned a few years ago near the big gully, and Dr. Hay, who lived in Judge Andrews old house at Haywood, were beyond the corporate limits. Mr. Gilbert, who was a merchant, was a pretty large taxpayer, however, and perhaps the rest were also.

There is one point more. The old plan makes a street called "West Street" run along the western boundary of the Common, parallel with our Pope Street. I think the street would have run east of Judge Andrews avenue, between Mr. Hines and Mayor B. S. Irvin and back of Mrs. Lane.

There is a little more to say about the old plan but I shall be too long unless I put it off.

There is a little more to say in regard to the original plan of Washington. First: I must show that the area of the town (Old Town plus Common) contained the 100 acres called for in the Acts of 1780-1783. The *Old Town*, as I have said, contained 48 lots. On the plan of 1805 found in Capt. Anthony's office, the whole of what had been Common in 1783 is divided off into lots.

There are 62 lots on what had been Common and these with the 48 of the *Old Town* make 110 lots in all on the paper containing the old Plan. David Terrell, clerk of Wilkes county in 1805, made a note in which he tells us that the original lots, i. e. the lots of the *Old Town*, were just 3 chains in length and breadth, each, including the street, that is to say, extending to the middle of the street. This would make each lot contain 9 square chains, and the 110 would contain 990 square chains. There are 1000 square chains in 100 acres, and 990 square chains are, in round numbers 100 acres. If lots are to be made of the same size and measured with surveyor's chains, this is about as near as we could make of them a rectangle equal to 100 acres. Thus the original lots of our town to the middle of the street contain nine-tenths of an acre; and since 10 square chains make an acre, our squares to the middle of the street contain each three and three-fifth acres.

It is sometimes said that the centre of the town, as at first laid off, was a point at the middle of Main and Spring Streets where they intersect. This is the centre of the *Old Town*, that is to say this point is at the middle of its length and breadth. But it is not true of the whole rectangle of the hundred acres, for the *Old Town* is not in the middle of the rectangle, as one can easily see on looking at the space enclosed in a colored line on the old plan of 1805. I have said that the area of the 100 acres is a square; this is not exactly accurate; it is a rectangle measuring 33 chains from east to west and 30 chains from north to south. In other words, there are 11 lots from north to south; 10 lots from east to west. Anybody can calculate this who remembers that the squares are two lots wide, and that there are as the plan shows, three lots between the intersections of Alexander Avenue with Court and North Streets. Also, that the property of Judge Reese and that of Mr. Hines are about a lot's width from east to west.

On the map, there are lots and streets in the southwestern part of the town, Jefferson and Water Streets extending across Main Street, and Allison Street crossing them. Also, the space between North Street and Court Street is regularly laid off in lots. But I doubt if ever all these divisions existed off paper,---and I doubt whether the "West Street" laid down on the map was over a real thoroughfare in nature. I fancy that the incorporators of Washington had some of the same enterprise about laying off on paper with which we are familiar in our day. They planned streets and were ready to carry it all out--but it did not *materialize* at last.

And now in regard to the act of 1793 which led to the sale of the Common. The act of 1780 gave directions to the commissioners under it to reserve acre lots which were to be used in establishing an Academy or Seminary of learning which was to be free. Minute and specific directions are given, and the commissioners are to have power to contract with builders for erecting the Academy, and afterwards with professors and teachers for ruling the school. A section of the bill of 1783 provided that on application to the Governor, he shall give them a warrant for laying off a thousand acres of land in the county for the use of the said school. Large powers are given to the commissioners to sell the land and to use the money or invest it. It is stated that the overplus from building is, after erecting a church, to be reserved and applied as a fund for the said school. It is provided that they shall make an annual report to the governor. They are even provided with the services of a paid clerk.

In the act of the Legislature: provision is made for building a church "with the overplus." There was perhaps no overplus, for after diligent inquiry and research, I can find no tradition or trace of a church building in Washington until nearly fifty years afterwards. There was preaching in Washington, but it was done in the Academy or Courthouse.

But the Academy was built, and we can point out its site. It was on the spot where the Catholic orphanage now stands upon Mercer Hill. It was a brick house and Mr. Samuel Barnett tells me that in due course of time his mother went to school there. Probably the building was upon a part of the 1,000 acres of land, though there is no evidence that they lay there. But this land produced no income unless rented, and nobody wanted to rent land when it was so abundant, and so easily gained in absolute possession. But the commissioners had to begin at once their contracting with builders and professors. The legislature was urgent upon them and when Chief Justice George Walton came to hold court he began talking to them about this academy. In 1784 in that charge which I have already quoted several times, he said, "It gives me uncommon satisfaction to see the forward improvements of this town, which promises to be of considerable importance in a short time, and it gratifies me beyond expectation to learn that an Academy is erecting. Nothing is so desirable, so necessary to a free and virtuous people as education. This pleasant and Healthy Situation will invite scholars. Go on with the Business with order, and the patrons of it will deserve well of their fellow citizens, of Mankind, and posterity." This was said Nov. 1st. 1784, but when Judge Walton came again in November 1785 he saw reason to

be a little urgent, and he said, "It were to be wished that your
academy were in such forward state" (as other enterprises) "the
brilliant Improvement which in a few months the students of
Augusta have made should warn the Trustees at Washington not to
delay theirs too long. Most of the counties begin to see the
consequences of a further procrastination, and are taking
measures to expedite their constitutional principles. Augusta
has already the start, and if the same right in the other counties is not speedily pursued by a Laudable Emulation and per-
severance she will draw in her school all the bright Youths of
the State."

I must remark that the same act of 1783 which provided for
the erection of an Academy in Washington also provided in the
previous sections of the Act, for an Academy at Augusta. This
is I presume the institution now called Richmond Academy at
Augusta, now a famous and rich corporation which celebrated its
centennial a few years ago. There were also other Acts about
the same time, providing for Academies in other counties. There
is a later Act providing an Academy for Louisville, and I have
seen it stated lately in some of the papers that Louisville
boasts of her old Academy dating back into the last century.
It is not exactly pleasant now to think of Augusta and Louisville glorying in their ancient Academies while we in Washington have not so far as I know, a single thing to show for our
1,000 acres, and the acre lots besides, with which we were provided. It is true that the legislature was somewhat partial
and gave Louisville 2,000 acres. And also Richmond Academy
received a productive piece of property, the Sand Bar Ferry as
it is called, across the Savannah River below Augusta, which
is, I think, still in its possession. Waynesboro and other
county towns also received gifts of land for academies, and
also, so did Wrightsboro, but I think like Wilkes and the
prodigal son, they spent their living.

After a while the free Academy began to encumber its trustees with burdensome pecuniary obligations in paying teachers,
for it had no income except what was derived from the sale of
land, and that speedily came to an end when used for running
expenses. So the commissioners applied for relief to the Legislature which in 1793 passed an "Act to dispose of the Common of
the town of Washington." This Act says, "whereas the commissioners did in pursuance of said Act, (that of 1783) dispose
of certain lots and did take certain steps towards building an
academy, and did employ professors and teachers for the in-
struction of youth in said Academy, whereby considerable sums
are by the commissioners due to individuals which they in justice and good faith wish to pay; and whereas a certain quantity
of lots were by the Commissioners reserved as a Common to the
said town of Washington, the timber whereof is already consumed,

nor is the said Common of any use to the lot holders in said town. Be it enacted they may sell". &c.

So the Common was sold in lots, and the professors and the teachers, who were doubtless as impecunious in that day as this, got their money; and having been a teacher myself, I rejoice to know it. Rev. F. T. Simpson has sent me a copy of an old book long since out of print in which this academy is mentioned. The book is *Morse's American Geography* published in 1796, the first school Geography ever issued in this country. Of course, it came from the progressive town of Boston, and Jediath Morse wrote it. He tells us that Washington has an academy which possesses a fund of 800 pounds sterling (which is nearly $4,000) and he adds that this school has sixty or seventy pupils. At the same time he informs us that Washington contains 34 houses.

I shall speak further of one of the teachers, most of whom were ministers. In 1804, when Mr. Barnett's mother was going to school there, a storm came which blew the academy down. But it was repaired, for it was used again, probably up to the time when Washington's present academy lot on Main, Liberty and Jefferson Streets was bought and a house built. The old brick academy on Mercer Hill had as we know a bell, for according to the testimony of those who remember it was the bell which was afterwards used on a market house which used to stand, in the memory of many persons living, on the southwest corner at the intersection of Liberty and Jefferson Streets; this is, on the lot where Mr. Wm. Edmundson now lives, opposite the Library. Mr. Stummer, since the War, pulled down the market house and built a dwelling house on that lot, and it is a great pity that the old bell had not been preserved as a relic of early Washington. Very likely it is now in existence, and I am sure that anybody who would recover and put it in the library would do the town a service.

I have seen several letters written in 1812 to a young girl thirteen years old who was a pupil at the old brick Academy in that year. She was then Miss Nancy Anderson, and became in after years the wife of Col. James D. Willis and the mother of Mrs. Lucy Simpson of 1889. She boarded in Washington at the house of Mr. Osborne Stone, the father of our Mrs. Samuel Barnett, then married to his first wife. Her father Mr. Thomas Anderson, writes that he is coming to the examination "next Wednesday" and hopes "you may be one among the best." Her aunt, Miss Mary Anthony, writes a little later and says, "I was informed that you have got the praise of the whole school." Her grandfather, Mr. James Anthony, who has several descendants around Washington now, says, "Remember, a virtuous young lady is like a piece of clean white paper; if it once gets blotted, it cannot be got out without injuring the paper." There is a letter written in

September after Miss Nancy Anderson left school, by one of her school mates, Miss Nancy Booker, who was I presume a great aunt of Mr. S. Booker. It was evidently written in the school room, for she complains of the boys shaking the desk. School was *out*, and I suppose the boys were preparing to go home. From her letter, I find that Mr. Ezra Fiske was the teacher. The writer says, that Mr. Fiske is going away, and adds, "I am so sorry." Thus at the lapse of nearly eighty years Miss Nancy Booker shows us she was a good girl---for good girls always love their teachers. A letter written by one of the pupils of a school is a pretty good test of its merits. Judging by this test, the old brick Academy was a very good school in 1813. Miss Nancy Booker's letter, in spelling, penmanship and composition, would not discredit a school girl of 1889.

    Mr. Barnett tells me that Rev. Ezra Fiske married his mother to the father of Dr. T. F. Willis, her first husband. That is a union to which the town of Washington owes a good deal. Mr. Fiske did not remain long in Georgia, and was a man of some eminence afterward in the State of New York. He was elected professor in the Western Theological Seminary, but died before he could serve. I should have said that he was a Presbyterian minister.

NOTE.---In a previous number I stated that the name Washington was given to this town in 1780. It has been believed that it was the first town which was ever named for George Washington, but our knowledge about this has been vague and uncertain. I have since been investigating the dates of which other towns were named for the Father of his country, and in this I have been aided by Mr. Edwin M. Anthony, ordinary of Wilkes now, who wrote to the ordinary of Washington, Beaufort County, North Carolina. The result is the statement, that the records of county and state both show that Washington, N. C., was named in 1782. Our correspondent grants our priority. Through Dr. Willis I learned that we are in advance of Washington, Rappahannock county, Virginia. I think I have settled it as a fact that Washington, Wilkes county, Georgia, is the first town of the U. S. so named. There is a Washington county in Virginia which was named in 1776.

    There is still another matter. A friend suggests to me that I have made a mistake---what is called an anachronism---in speaking of the *Wilkes Riflemen* during the Revolution. The words were copied exact from Charles C. Jones' *History of Georgia*. It is not an error in Mr. Jones, for the word is used by a good many authors who write of the Revolution. For example, one of the latest and most accomplished, John Fiske, in the December *Atlantic Monthly*, in an article on *Border Warfare* in the *Revolution*, p. 821, speaks of the *Maryland Riflemen*. The Magazine is in the Library. Mr. Barnett, who looked the matter up, tells me that the large Encyclopedias state that rifles were invented before the year 1600. I suppose rifles as now used are a recent invention.

    I am very glad to receive fair criticism. Very likely I shall make blunders, and shall be glad to correct them. I take a good deal of time getting up facts, but I have not the time to give literary finish to what I wrote. It was printed from my first draft, with the exception of an occasional page which is rewritten. It is the only condition on which I can write these articles at all, so everybody must excuse imperfections, as I am putting all these facts down, only to preserve the history of Wilkes County. I have nothing. In fact, I may lose in credit, for if the facts about the country carry my memory a little further, I may go down as a slip shod writer.

CHAPTER IX

THE SETTLERS

WHEN GEORGE WALTON[1] signer of the Declaration of Independence, came again in 1785 to hold court in Wilkes he was struck with the increase in immigration since peace, as he had been previously with the "astonishing rapidity of settlement." He uses even stronger language than ever before. He speaks of "this county in which there is such a prodigious influx of inhabitants," and "of the rage which has taken place in the northern and neighboring states of removing into this."

The old records in the office of Ordinary give us the names of grandjurors, petty jurors and in many cases witnesses. These bear out George Walton's words and show also the very fine class of immigrants which the county was receiving. Among the persons whose names we find prior to 1778 are George Lumpkin, John Rutherford, John Hill, Thos. Ansley, Nathaniel Howell, Thomas Wooten, Burwell Pope, John Lindsey, Frederic Sims, William Pollard, Wm. Morgan, Cornelius Cohron, Thomas Branham, John Nall, Henry Mounger, John Wingfield, Benjamin Taliaferro, Nathaniel Christmas, Job Callaway, Jacob Early, Wm. Glenn, Walker Richardson, Benjamin Joyner, Reuben Saffold, Jas. Findley, Curtace Welborne, Samuel Cresswell, James Anthony, Wm. Terrell, George Mathews, John Talbot, Daniel Grant, Thos. Grant, Wm. Boren, John Armstrong, Sanders Walker, Nicholas Long, David Merriwether, Thomas Welborn, Micajiah Megahee, Thos. Carter, Spencer Crane, --- Pharr, James Jack, Garland Wingfield, --- Cuthbert, Thos. Napier, Wm. Moss, Capt. Lipham, Horatio Marbury, John Barksdale, Henry Pope, Chas. Tate, James Marks, Henry Gibson, Francis Meriwether, John Pope, David Lowry, Thos. Wingfield, Wm. Stokes, Henry Gibson, Wm. Gilbert, Daniel Mills, Edward Butler, David Hillhouse, Micaijah Anthony, John Pope, Jno. Chandler, John Cain, Elizabeth

---

(1) GEORGE WALTON b. 1741 or 1749; died Feb. 2, 1804.
Signer, Declaration of Independence, July 4, 1776.
Governor, 1779-1780; Jan.-Nov. 1789.
Chief Justice of Georgia, 1783-1786.
United States Senator, 1795-1796.
Judge, Western Circuit, 1789-1796.
Judge, Middle Circuit, 1799-Feb. 2, 1804. (Died while serving as Judge of Middle Circuit.)

Darden, Gabriel Toombs, William Toombs, John Shepherd, Williamson Bird, George Willis, Humphrey Burdett, Chiltson Hitson, (or Eidson) Joel Hurt, Pressly Rucker, Wm. and James Sansom, Wm. Heard, Alexander Cummins, John Callier, Joseph Wilson, Sampson Harris, Anthony Poullain, John Colley, Phillip Combs. Of course the names that get into records show but a small part of those who came. But this list, to the older people who have known his and the neighboring counties, tells us much of the number and character of early immigration. I will a little further on say a few words in elucidation of it to others. The rapid influx makes us understand why, about the first business that came before the courts when they were held in 1782 was the licensing of Thomas Carter's Ferry. Ferries were especially needed, for the ancestors of more than half of our present Georgia, Alabama and Mississippi were coming across the Savannah river on the roads leading from the northeast through old Wilkes county. The people living in Carolina and Georgia at the junction of Broad River with Savannah got such grand ideas in their heads that they named the town Venna; the Elbert county town in the fork St. Petersburg; the Lincoln county town, Lisbon. These were magnificent names, and when one crosses the river at the point now, there are a few old houses, and in Carolina, the duelling ground with its melancholy associations. In the last century, the ferries and the roads were thronged. Soon after Carters Ferry, Barksdales Ferry comes up in the old records. It was the building of the Georgia and other Rail Roads in the present century which I well remember, that diverted from this route the travel from the northern States, Virginia and the Carolinas. At the close of the Civil War in 1865, when the railroads were cut at Augusta, the returning Confederate soldiers poured into Georgia by this route, across the Savannah traveling on precisely the roads which brought their immigrating ancestors to Wilkes to settle Alabama and Mississippi and other States. President Jefferson Davis (dying it is feared while I write this) came by the very route which brought his grandparents to live and find their graves in Wilkes county.

Among the names on the foregoing list, may be found that of John Talbot. He probably came in 1783 or '84. The house which he built for himself not far from the Augusta road is I think the oldest house in Wilkes county, and that makes it the oldest in Georgia north of Little River, and the oldest north of Augusta, unless my native county, Columbia can show an older. The oldest house in Washington is the old Allison house, which stood on the site of the present Episcopal church and was removed a little to the northeast of the church, where it still stands. But I think the Talbot house to be older. John Talbot's house is not at all like the Allison house, any

typical middle Georgia house. I saw it a few years ago, through
the kindness of Mr. F. T. Simpson who took me there. It is on
the place of Mrs. Thomas Merriwether, who was Mrs. Florence. It
is now used for a negro house. It struck me as soon as I saw
it, how like it was to some of the houses which I saw before the
war in Virginia, in Mansemond and Isle of Wight counties. It
was not a large house, having at first two rooms below stairs,
and two above, with a stair case cut off in a dark passage. It
was afterwards enlarged by the addition of two more rooms. The
upper story is not weatherboarded, but shingled on the side
walls, very much as are many of the Queen Anne houses now so
fashionable. To people of our day it would look somewhat cramp-
ed and uncomfortable,---as indeed some of the new Queen Anne
houses do. But all the work upon it is of the very best character. One of the rooms is panelled up to the ceiling in a way
that at once reminds the visitor of the panelling in the hall of
Mr. Burwell Green's beautiful new house in Washington. The old
piazza in front has a brick floor. The bricks are square and
almost as smooth as our best pressed brick, and many are still
firm though they were burned more than a hundred years ago. The
ceiling of the piazza was plastered, and the manner in which
portions of the plaster still remain shows the thoroughness of
the old workmen. There are two benches in the old piazza which
might have been bought in 1789 from some fashionable warehouse
of antique furniture for piazzas. The old house is an exceed-
ingly interesting relic of antiquity, very characteristic of the
old Virginians who conquered Wilkes county from the wilderness
and the Indians. If a settler from the north had owned that
place and wanted to build, he would have carefully restored
every part of the Talbot house exactly as it was at first then
he would have painted it in terra cotta color (it was probably
colored in the beginning) and he would have built an addition in
the Queen Anne's style, and the whole old and new, would have
harmonized perfectly. He would never let a visitor go without
showing the older part of the house, and telling of its association. If I had a new house in Washington, I should make a
strong effort to become possessed of those two old piazza
benches.

John Talbot died in 1798, and lies buried at old Smyrna
church which I stopped to see when I took my trip with Mr. Simpson. The church is a late erection, and has no special interest.
Our object was to visit the graveyard. There is no monument over
John Talbot's grave, but its position is manifest, as he was almost certainly the first person interred in the Talbot lot in
the graveyard at Smyrna. John Talbot was one of the most substantial and richest of the early settlers. Matthew Talbot, who
in 1889 was a young man in business in Washington, is a descendant of John Talbot, and now the only representative of a very

honorable name. Mrs. Mary Turner Maddox is a descendant of John Talbot through a daughter of his who married Francis Triplett. The descendants of the late Mr. Geo. Lamar of Augusta are also descended from John Talbot; John Talbot built good houses for his sons and daughters who settled here. Mr. Burdett lives now in one of them. But they are not like the old Virginia house that he built for himself. He was connected in some way with George Walton, signer of the Declaration of Independence. His son Matthew Talbot was representative of Wilkes in the Georgia senate of 1817 and when Governor Rabun died, like Governor Stephens, in the office of Governor, Matthew Talbot became Governor of the State. Like Governor Boynton of our day, he was not chosen again when the election came. He was much honored however, all over Georgia. Many of the older persons now living remember the patriarchal figure, white head and pleasant face of his brother Thomas Talbot, who was one of the elders of the Presbyterian church in Washington.

In the list of names of settlers taken from the records of early courts in the office of the ordinary, George Lumpkin is found. He was probably the ancestor of the Chief Justice Joseph Henry Lumpkin and his descendants among whom are Prof. Lumpkin of Atlanta, and the children of Capt. Harry Jackson and Mr. Hoke Smith. He was also ancestor of Governor Wilson Lumpkin for whom Lumpkin county is named. John Rutherford was the ancestor of Prof. William Rutherford of the University of Georgia, of Miss Milly Rutherford, now principal of Lucy Cobb and of many other Rutherfords. John Hill was probably one of several brothers from whom descend the Athens Hills, Hon. Joshua and Judge Edward Y. Hill, of LaGrange, and the large family of Hills now scattered through Wilkes county. Garland and John Wingfield are the father and uncle of the Garland Wingfield whom many of us remember. John is ancestor of Dr. Robert Simpson, Mr. F. T.' Simpson, Mrs. John Stephens of Atlanta, Mrs. Lane, Dr. Wm. S. Armstrong of Atlanta. Thomas Wingfield was the ancestor of Mr. Samuel Barnett and Dr. F. T. Willis, of Dr. Barnett, of Eufaula of all the children of Dr. Joseph A. Eve so long an eminent and beloved physician of Augusta, of all the descendants of Mr. James Nisbet formerly a prominent lawyer of Macon, including the children of Geo. Hazlehurst also two or three of the wives of Bishop Andrew, of Mrs. Wm. Reese and her sister Mrs. Cozart of Washington. The descendants of this old man are found among persons of high character in nearly every town in Georgia. Thomas or Curtace Welborne was the ancestor of the eminent occulist Dr. Abner Welborn Calhoun of Atlanta, also of Hon. Edward Hill of our town and his brother Wellborn Hill of Atlanta, of the late Mrs. Martha Andrews and her nieces. Thomas Napier was the maternal ancestor of a former well known lady of this place, Mrs. Maria Randolph and her cousins, Mrs. Leroy Napier of Macon, Mrs. George W. Price of Atlanta. Thos. Ansley was ancestor of the Augusta Ansleys. Daniel Grant was ancestor of Mr. John T. Grant and his son, Wm. Grant, two well known men of wealth in Atlanta, who live in elegance. Job Callaway was one of several brothers, ancestors of the Callaways whom we have known in Wilkes, of Professor Morgan Callaway and of his son of the same name who has lately distinguished himself at John Hopkins University. The descendants of Francis and David Meriwether and Micajah Megahee are wealthy and leading men of Alabama and Mississippi. James Anthony, besides his descendants in this county, was the father of Dr. Milton Anthony the distinguished physician who founded the Medical College of Georgia at Augusta. Gabriel and William Toombs were the brothers of the older Robt. Toombs who came with them and whose son in our day distinguished his county state and the whole south. Jacob Early was the father of Peter Early Governor of Georgia, for whom Early county was named. Wm. Pollard was ancestor or kinsman of the Pollards, a family of high repute in Alabama. David Hillhouse and Felix Gilbert, brother of Wm. Gilbert on the above list and who came with him to Georgia, are the ancestors of all the branches of the Alexander family who have filled Augusta and Savannah and Atlanta with citizens who are an honor and advantage to any state. Benjamin Taliaferro for whom Taliaferro county was named, became United States Senator from Georgia. He had been a distinguished revolutionary officer, and became a man of much eminence in Georgia. Gen. Heard says that Dr. Taliaferro of Atlanta was the descendant, not of Judge Taliaferro, as I had previously stated, but of his brother, one of the Broad River settlers who married a sister of Gov. Gilmer. Anthony Poullian was ancestor of the well known family of that name in Augusta and Madison. Reuben Safford was ancestor of a well known and much respected family who lived a long time in Madison.

This enumeration becomes tedious but it is a very small part of what could be given if the list of early immigrants to Wilkes were even partly complete. I simply selected a few as a sample, who chanced to be on the records of the court. The descendants of these people show what, in quality, was the *prodigious influx* which so struck George Walton. We know from Governor Gilmer's account that there were Gilmers and Bibbs who came from Virginia with some persons on this list. These two families furnished a Governor and a Senator in Congress to Georgia, Gov. Gilmer [2] and Dr. Wm. Bibb,[3] and Georgia named a county for each. Several of both families settled in and around Montgomery, Alabama, where they became honored and wealthy citizens; and two Bibbs became Governors of Alabama.

(2) George R. Gilmer was Governor of Georgia, 1837-1839.

(3) Dr. William W. Bibb was in Congress, 1807-1813.

Rev. F. T. Simpson showed me lately the deed of his plantation on Upton creek southeast from Washington. It was acquired by Mr. Simpson's father from the heirs of Gen. Nathaniel Greene who owned once, much land in this county; but the deed states that the tract was surveyed in 1785 for John Jack and William Barnett; William Barnett was the paternal grandfather of Mr. Samuel Barnett now among us. He came from Mecklenburgh county, North Carolina, and married Jean Jack the sister of John and James Jack from the same county. William Barnett and his wife Jean Jack lie buried at old Smyrna church where I saw their graves in the family burying plot, a few days ago. Mecklenburgh county, N. C., in which Charlotte is situated, is famous for the story of its Declaration of Independence, with which James Jack of my list of immigrants is closely connected. A year before the Declaration of July 1776 was passed, the Scottish Irish settlers of Mecklenburgh met and passed, with much ceremony and deliberation, a Declaration of their own. It was read over to the large body of people there assembled, and adopted. When the chairman of the meeting asked, "Who will carry the resolutions to the Congress?" then assembled at Philadelphia, James Jack replied "I will." They were carried by James Jack on horseback and delivered to some of the members of the Congress. The delegates were not then prepared to take such a declaration and took no notice of it. Gov. Gilmer says, "The fact that such a declaration had been made was unnoticed in history unknown to the public, and denied when asserted, until placed beyond dispute by the production of two copies which had continued in the possession of persons present when it was made, and by the finding of a copy which was sent to his government by some British officer in the Southern colonies, and deposited in the colonial office in London. James Jack and William Barnett came to Georgia about 1783. There was another family of Barnett's who came from Virginia and settled with the other Broad River settlers in what is now Elbert. Both families were descendants of Barnetts who had settled first in Newark, New Jersey, but who had separated. The Alabama Barnetts, descended from the Elbert stock.

One of the most entertaining persons on my list of settlers before 1788, is George Matthews who became Governor of Georgia 1793.[4] He was a revolutionary soldier of some distinction, for whom Virginia named a county. He is the governor who has excited so much amusement by his bad spelling. He spelled coffee kaughphy and other words with equal incorrectness. He seemed to think, the more letters he put in a word the better he spelled. Gov. Gilmer describes him as follows:

"General Matthews was a short thick man with stout legs, on which he stood very straight. He carried his head rather thrown

(4) George Mathews was twice Governor of Georgia, 1787-1788 and 1793-1796.

back. His features were full and bluff, his hair light red; and his complexion fair and florid. His looks spoke out that he would not fear the Devil should he meet him face to face. He admitted no superior but General Washington. He spoke of his services to the country as unsurpassed but by those of his great chief. He loved to talk of himself and spoke as freely and encomiastically as enthusiastic youths do of Alexander or Caesar. His dress was in unison with his looks and conversation. He wore a three cornered cocked hat, fair top boots, a shirt ruffled at the bosom and wrists, and occasionally a long sword at his side. To listen to his talk about himself, his children and his affairs, one might have thought him a puff of wind; trade with him, he was found to be one of the shrewdest of men. When he read, it was always aloud, and with the confidence which accompanies the consciousness of doing a thing well. He pronounced fully the l in 'should and would' &c; and ed at the termination of compound words with a long drawling accent. He wrote 'congress' with a K. When governor, he dictated his messages to a secretary and then sent them to an Irish schoolmaster to be turned into good grammar."

My readers can imagine his odd figure walking down our Court Street. But this he doubtless did in March, 1786, since he was foreman of the Grand Jury at that session of court, and what was then the new court house on the north side of Court Street had just been finished. Gen. Matthews became Governor of Georgia in 1793 and became very unpopular in 1796 from his signing the Yazoo Bill, which parted with twenty three million acres of land at two cents an acre. Some of the legislators were supposed to be corrupted. Gov. Matthews had been opposed to the sale, and Gov. Gilmer says that his secretary tried to prevent his signature by privately dipping his pen in oil so that it would not make a mark. This startled him, but he called for a pen and signed the bill. It created so much indignation that he left Georgia, and never after lived much in it. As he was going to Virginia on one occasion, he was taken sick and died in Augusta, where he was buried in St. Paul's churchyard---between 1784 and 1800. The Broad River settlers, of whom Gov. Gilmer gives a very full account, came in 1784-5. He says the Harvies were the most numerous. The children of Mrs. Eliza Pope Hull, and Mrs. Clifford Alexander Hull of our day, are descended from the Harvies through the marriage of their grandfather Mr. Asbury Hull of Athens with Lucie Harvie. Col. Benjamin Taliaferro married a granddaughter of Daniel Harvie, who was the first of the family to settle in Georgia. Daniel Harvie was one of a family all noted for great size and strength. He weighed four hundred pounds. Gov. Gilmer tells us it was said that he had righted the corner of a mill house which had been put out of place by a freshet; probably the great freshet of 1796. Also that he raised heavy hogsheads of tobacco over the ground sill through the door of the tobacco house, and that he could hold up for some time two men of ordinary size, one on each hand, with his arms extended their full length from his body. Daniel Harvie's name is found in our early records, but he took cold and died soon after he came to Georgia from hauling a drag for fish in Long Creek.

John Marks who is placed on my list of persons of the court records, before 1788, is one of two brothers, John and James Marks, whom Gov. Gilmer reports among the Broad River settlers. John Marks married as he says, a widow who brought with her to Georgia, Merriwether Lewis, her son by a former marriage. This is the Lewis who afterwards undertook what is called Lewis and Clarke's expedition, which explored the Northwest Territory and the sources of the Missouri. Lewis and Clarke counties in the new state of Montana, commemorate them. John Marks who had been a distinguished officer of the revolution, died and his widow and her son returned to Virginia where in 1794, he went into the Army. But it is remembered of his stay in Georgia, that at some time between 1790-1794, during an alarm from the Cherokees, the Broad River settlers sought safety in the woods. One night a gun was heard to fire, which occasioned a great panic, which was quelled by the presence of mind of the boy, Merriwether Lewis who suddenly threw water, extinguishing the light of the fire.

The MSS. documents entrusted to me enable me now to give a very interesting account (as it seems to me) of the old Academy on Mercer Hill and the early teachers. On Aug. 27, 1784, just after the laying out and sale of town lots, the commissioners met and it was stated that £800 ($4000) was the lowest bid for the building. Col. Micaijah Williamson urged them to postpone for a lower. Accordingly, when they met a week later, they awarded the job to Capt. Joseph Cook at 781 pounds ($3,905). It seems the sale of lots in the town was to be used in payment, and Col. Micaijah Williamson was empowered to collect and pay out monies for the building, which is called an Academy and Church. This Col. Micaijah Williamson's name is on the oldest jury list, that of 1779, so that he must have been a very early settler. He must have come from Virginia or the Carolinas. In 1784, he bought the property owned by Gen. B. W. Heard on the north side of Court Street. It is called a reserved lot. I think this may mean that he had before acquired it in 1780, when the lots were first laid out but the legislature ordered them laid out again. One of his daughters, the youngest, afterwards married Duncan G. Campbell. She was a sister of Mrs. Judge Griffin, not daughter as I once supposed. It is probable that she lived with her sister and was not married until after her father's death. Judge Andrews said that Col. Williamson's son, William Williamson was the first child born in Washington of white parents. There is a William Williamson in the first graduating class at Athens in 1804, but it hardly seems he would have been old enough to be this first white child. He may have been the grandson of the old Col. W., who evidently had older sons, probably born before he came to Wilkes. Col. Micaijah Williamson kept a tavern on the site of the old State Bank, as far back as could be remembered when Judge Andrews spoke of it. The records in the ordinary's office show that he applied for a license to keep tavern in 1786. He must already have sold the lot on which our first court house was built, viz.: where Gen. Heard's garden now stands, for this was finished in 1785, as the records of the county in the ordinary's office show. Judge Andrews said that this tavern consisted of two log cabins with a broad open space between the rooms, in which was the dining hall. Very likely if business was brisk, other detached log houses were built to accommodate the guests. People in a new country often enlarge house room in that way, and from Gov. Gilmer we learn that the early settlers of Wilkes did so. In this house, court was held before the first court house was built. Before the old tavern was planted a tall swinging sign; and on it there was a picture of General Washington.

Judge Andrews said that Col. Williamson had several daughters who were the leading belles in the early history of Washington. One of them married Judge Griffin and another Thompson Bird. The oldest married Gen. John Clarke who became Governor of Ga., another Mr. Thweatt of Milledgeville, who was the father of Mrs. Homer Howard and Mrs. Thacker Howard of Columbia and Mr. Peterson Thweatt. The youngest was married to Duncan G. Campbell some years after her father's death. The records of the marriage licenses of Sarah and Susan Williamson to John Griffin and Thompson Bird, are in the ordinary's office now. Judge Andrews said they were all very fine women, unsurpassed by any in Georgia. This was then a new country and it may seem to young ladies of this present luxurious day, that it was a rough time these young ladies had in their log home. But the most important thing in the society of young ladies, is to have an abundance of beaux of high character, talents and elegant manners. I do not mean that young ladies are all the time husband hunting---by beaux, I mean visitors. Girls who have male visitors of this character need not sigh for the glories of the pink teas and the blue balls of the plutocrats described in the *Atlanta Constitution*. A new country opening with fine resources throngs with men of enterprise, character and ability. There never was a finer county than early Wilkes and there is every evidence that there was a *prodigious influx* of fine young men. No doubt there was a constant procession of them up Court Street to see the beautiful Misses Williamson.

Col. Micaijah Williamson was a gallant old Revolutionary

soldier who fought at Kettle Creek, at the siege of Augusta, &c., and I am sorry I shall have to record the financial trouble he got into from handling the Academy funds. I do not mean that he was dishonest. Running away to Canada with trust funds is a later invention.

The commissioners of the Academy met again in June 1785. They were Stephen Heard, Zachariah Lamar and Micaijah Williamson, and Hon. George Matthews appeared with an appointment from the Governor as Commissioner. From what I have told of Governor Matthews, my readers can imagine the imposing dignity of his entrance, frills, cocked hat, (probably sword) and all. He was appointed, in the place of Daniel Colman, commissioner, who had died. The name of Zachariah Lamar, which has been so often on juries and important committees appears for the last time. This name appears afterwards in acts of legislature as a Trustee for the Louisville Academy and I suppose that he finally removed there.

When the Commissioners met in June 1785, they begun to discuss the best place for building an Academy. There had been six lots reserved on the Common for this purpose, when the town was laid out in 1784, and I think it will astonish my readers when I tell them where they were. Spring street runs directly through the rectangle formed by six lots which lie three on each side of it. They begin at the bridge where South street crosses Spring and run 198 yards north from the bridge. The lot extending 66 yards east and west from Spring street. The Academy lot would have closed up Spring street on the south, but I suppose that a street would have been laid out all around it.

The Commissioners in 1785 thought it best to build the Academy beyond the limit of the town altogether, but not feeling authorized to change the location they determined to wait until the Legislature met and get authority. It seems that a Mr. Chisolm who was also the contractor (undertaker they call it) of the court house had already got our stocks for timber for the church and the academy, so they agreed to pay the workmen 50 pounds (or about $250. about) for what they had done.

I will tell my readers that my evidence is all beyond doubt for these facts. Also, there was afterwards a brick yard on these reserved lots or some part of them, between 1785 and 1801. This is undoubted and it is my impression the brick for the Academy were burned there, but for this I have no evidence.

Next, on June 7, 1785, they proceeded to elect a teacher for the Academy and they elected Mr. Samuel Blackburn, to begin January, 1786. This Mr. Samuel Blackburn was the first teacher who ever taught in Washington, so far as evidence goes, and I doubt whether there has ever been a single one since of whom such a description could be given as Governor Gilmer gives of this man. The Governor says, "His fine voice, expressive features, noble person, perfect self possession keen wit, and forcible language directed by a well cultivated and powerful intellect, made him one of the most eloquent men of his time." This was one of the young men who doubtless visited the beautiful Misses Williamson on the corner where the Bank stands. It is good company---not luxurious grandeur which makes good society, though of course refinements and what are called manners are of value when they are accessories and not all in all.

Mr. Blackburn however married Miss Anne Matthews. He taught school in Washington for three years, studying law in the interval, and after he married Miss Anne Matthews he settled what had by that time become Elbert county. Elbert county was laid off in 1790. He was advancing in his profession and in political influence as Governor Gilmer tells us and was elected in 1795 to the Legislature.

Gov. Matthews was then Governor, and signed the Yazoo Act. Gen. Blackburn as he was called voted against it, but he was suspected of favoring it and accused of talking for it. His vote was unnecessary to carry it, and people said he so voted to prevent suspicion of his father-in-law the governor. Governor Gilmer says, "The allegations against the integrity of Gen. Blackburn were founded on the most trivial circumstances." Whether he was corrupt or not, a great storm arose, the like of which has hardly ever since been seen in Georgia, and every body who had the smell of fire on their garments, and some who did not, were ruined politically. So Gen. Blackburn went to Virginia and settled in Staunton. He several times went to the Virginia Legislature. Gov. Gilmer says he was a Federalist and "his strong abusive denunciations of the Republicans when he was in the Virginia Legislature made him remembered by the parties in that state." Gov. Gilmer tells of a visit which he himself made to Virginia, when he saw Gen. Blackburn, and he tells us that when the latter was full of liquor, which men of that day were occasionally, he abused the Broad River people of Georgia in the bitterest manner for their suspicions of him. He got into a fight with Gov. Gilmer's brother for abusing Col. Benjamin Taliaferro. But Gov. Gilmer says he was very agreeable when he became sober. The Governor tells us of the lasting impressions produced on himself by hearing Gen. Blackburn make a very powerful speech in behalf of a criminal at Rockingham Court. Gov. Gilmer says he was an Irishman (Scotch Irish) or the son of one. Such was the first, and I suspect, the greatest of our teachers in Washington.

The Commissioners agreed to give him for his services 150 pounds ($750 nearly) a year, and he was to have a Tutor, or assistant, whom they were to pay 40 pounds ($200 nearly.) They were to furnish Mr. Blackburn a room. They also fixed the price of tuition. The scholars were to pay $2. per quarter for spelling, reading and writing; $3. per quarter for English Grammar and Arithmetic; $6. per quarter for the Latin Grammar and forwards." For the first quarter one half was to be paid in advance, and the other half at the end of the first quarter. The pay for the other quarters was to be made at the expiration of the quarters, and in default the student was to be excluded. The commissioners agreed to make good any deficiency of salaries to the Rector, as they called him, or to the tutor. There were to be two vacations of from two to four weeks at the option of the teacher.

In the MS. which I follow, there is a statement that in April, Col. Williamson was requested by the other commissioners to get plank to loft and floor Col. Clarke's house, and be allowed the expense. From this, I infer that the school was held in a house belonging to Col. Clarke. Mr. Blackburn taught for three years, 1786, 87, 88. The next year a house was rented from Col. Micaijah Williamson, for 50 pounds (about $200) per annum. When the year 1788 came, Col. Francis Willis was a member of the board of commissioners, and he offers a house at the Chalybeate Spring, for 40 pounds. This house was built for the purpose, and that was its cost. The school went to it, and for the first time we know where the school was kept. The Chalybeate Spring is in the grove known as the Effie Pope Park, where the Sunday School meeting was held last summer. Col. Francis Willis who now comes before us, was the grandfather of our Dr. F. T. Willis, whom we always hold in grateful memory, and I know that will interest people in him. He was a Virginian from Williamsburg, the old colonial capital of Virginia. There are a great many gravestones of the Willis family in the graveyard at Williamsburg. They show that the family was one of consequence, entitled to a coat of arms, which shows that they belonged in England to the gentry. A large number of the early settlers of Wilkes were what is called Scotch Irish, that is from the north of Ireland. Dr. Willis is, I think, of pure English extraction. Willis and Wingfield are certainly English, and I think the names Terrell and Worsham indicate English blood. Col. Francis Willis had two sons that we hear of, Thomas Willis, the father of our Dr. F. T. Willis, whose name occurs several times in our early county records as a juryman, and Nathaniel Willis, whose names occurs once or twice on subscription lists in the MS. from which I am writing. I was told by Judge Andrews that Dr. Willis' grandfather (he said father but it was grandfather) built the first hotel on the site of the one now occupied by Mr. Foreman. In the MS. from which I draw my facts, there is under date of 1802, a Mr. Crocker, for whose board the commissioners bound themselves and on an account in the MS. there is the item of $20 due Francis Willis for Mr. Crocker's board. The house built by Francis Willis came into possession of Mr. Sneed, the father of Mrs. George Dyson of 1889, and about 1824 or 5 it was burned. Mr. Sneed built the present house soon after. The parents of Dr. Willis, Thomas Willis and Elizabeth Wingfield Worsham, were married about 1812, and soon after Col. Francis Willis and his sons moved to the vicinity of Columbia, Tennessee, where Mrs. Willis' daughter Mary Willis, who afterwards became Mrs. Lane, aunt to our Mary Willis, was born. But Thomas Willis and his wife returned to Washington, and so our Dr. Francis Willis was born here.

I have wandered a little from my subject, but I know my readers will be interested in the ancestors of Dr. F. T. Willis.

Gov. Matthews was friend to education even if he lacked it himself, for my manuscript shows that in April 1786 he bought "forty Latten books and eight copperplates" for the use of the pupils, at his own expense. They cost $24. "Latten" is the spelling of the MS. and not of General Matthews, who would have used a great many more letters. The Commissioners ordered him reimbursed. I do not know what "copperplates" are.

When 1787 came, they gave Mr. Blackburn 190 pounds (about $950) and the tutor, who seems to have been a Mr. Allen, 50 pounds (or about $250.) In April Mr. Blackburn came up and stated that he expected to be paid in gold or its equivalent. This was agreed to. Mr. Andrew Burns who had become one of the Commissioners, was directed to have proper benches and writing tables made for the use of the Academy.

The reader will wonder what has become of the public building, Academy and Church. I suppose it was put off because the lots sold were not paid for. As time went on the Commissioners got in debt to Mr. Samuel Blackburn, whose excellent senses made him awake to his business interests. He seems to have spent a moderate portion of his pay, and so he quietly let the rest run on, knowing that the Commissioners were responsible. Towards the end of 1788, they begun to see that they were getting pretty deeply in his debt, and so they offered him, for 1788, the profits of the school and 60 pounds. There were complaints about deficiency in payment of tuition bills, and prices of lots. There seems to have been no difficulty between the parties, but Mr. Blackburn did not teach again. They had an examination of accounts and found they owed him about $2,145.

In addition to this, Col. Micaijah Williamson was getting behind in money borrowed. They seem to have treated the old Revolutionary Veteran with a good deal of consideration, and so, for a good many reasons, they had to call a halt in the business of becoming responsible for teachers' salaries. I see no account of any appointment of a teacher to succeed Mr. Blackburn. In 1793, in ciphering out responsibility, it appeared that the interest on that 429 pounds due to Mr. Blackburn had brought the whole indebtedness up to 567 pounds (about $2,835). I presume, quietly as Mr. Blackburn took it, he began to want the interest on his money. Probably about that time he had married Miss Anne Matthews. Her brother, John Matthews, a young lawyer had been appointed clerk to the commissioners. I think, in addition to the rest, they began to see that they would have to sue Col. Micaijah Williamson. John Griffin who married one of the Williamson girls, had now been brought into the board of commissioners. As this gentleman either was, or was to be, Col. Williamson's son-in-law, I suppose he did not want to see the veteran pushed. The old fellow had made a tender of paper money, but they would not receive it. So they then determined to petition the legislature for power to sell the Common. This was granted as I have before recorded. Col. Francis Willis, Micaijah Williamson, John B. Ruston and John Griffin were appointed to superintend the sale and David Terrell surveyed and laid the lots off. The sale was made Oct. 18, 1794. The MSS. contains the names of the buyers of every lot and the price paid. I will a little further on state these but it would interrupt my story too much to tell it now. Suffice it to say that the whole sum received was 413 pounds, 18 shillings. This was about $2069.50. Mr. Samuel Blackburn himself spent 47 pounds in lots.

And now being out of debt, I suppose the commissioners began to wake up to the project of keeping up a school and building the Academy-Church, as I will call it for short. In 1794, they elected Stephen Burroughs Rector. They seem to have merely offered him the profits he could make, not wanting to get in debt again, I suppose. It does not appear whether he accepted and taught.

They determined to raise a subscription for building the Academy, and they proceeded to sue Col. Williamson. But the matter seems to have languished somewhat. Through 1795 and part of 1796 my MS. gives me no information as to their proceedings. But in August 1796 they seem to have turned over a new leaf. We find Rev. John Springer, Rev. Hope Hull, Hon. David Merriwether, John Griffin and John Wingfield constitute the board and when they met Aug. 11, the first thing they did was to elect Rev. John Springer their President.

The Rev. John Springer is the Presbyterian clergyman who, just one hundred years ago, come next July 20, was ordained under Mr. Charles Alexander's great poplar. I shall have more to say of him further on, and of Hope Hull also, who was a famous early Methodist preacher, the great grand father of Alex. Pope Hull, esq., of Atlanta, and Harvie Hull, whom we wrote of in 1889. Suffice it to say, for the present, that Mr. Springer was a famous teacher and scholar. Hope Hull was a teacher, a man of great energy and influence. I have heard it said that these two taught in Washington at one time. The MS. in my possession satisfies me that this is a mistake. It is probably their connection with the building of the Academy which gave arise to the report. John Wingfield is probably the father of Miss Anne Wingfield, Mrs. Garland Wingfield, and their brother Dr. Wingfield of Madison. He was Mrs. Lucy Reese's uncle. He was an elder in the Presbyterian church, who was present at that ordination one hundred years ago.

I do not know how much the zeal of the two teachers and preachers had to do with it, but the Commissioners now went to work and actually built the Academy. They determined to raise a subscription among the citizens for $3,000 and themselves to supply $1,000 of funds. The subscribers appointed a committee of managers as they called them to unite with the Commissioners. These were Gen. John Clarke (Gov. C.) Ebenezer Starke and Benjamin Branham. The latter is I presume the ancestor of Miss Mary Branham and the widow (still living) of Mr. Simeon Hester; Edward Butler was one of the Commissioners. He was ancestor of Mrs. F. T. Willis and of our Mary Willis. Robert McRae was the President of the united body of Commissioners and managers. He, Ebenezer Starke, and Hope Hull got up the plan. John Matthews was secretary and treasurer.

The subscription list still remains---or part of it in my MS. The largest amount subscribed came from the liberal ancestor of Mrs. Dr. Fred Hunter, Benajah Smith.(5) (He married the daughter of Gen. Elijah Clarke and his granddaughter married Gov. Pickens.) It was $232. I imagine that this was partly the land given, for Benajah Smith owned the lands around Mercer Hill, as my manuscript shows. The commissioners had long before proposed "a hill outside the western end of the town, as a site for the Academy church." On August, 1796, They went to see it, and agreed to it, "provided that titles could be obtained to ten acres from Benajah Smith." On Jan. 5, 1797, they finally ordered that it shall be the place, but they call it by a name that puzzles me no little. I can make it out as nothing else than "the head of the Razapeth or Prazepeth." This is a name which I never heard, but it is clearly one of those two words.

The subscription list, or a very large part of it, is contained in my MSS. John Clarke (Gov. C.) William Cox and John Griffin follow B. Smith with a hundred each, and then come many fifties, twenties, etc. The thousand dollars which the commissioners were to furnish from the fund, they endeavored to get partly by suing Micaijah Williamson, though they evidently

(5) Benajah Smith was Tax Collector for Wilkes County, 1790-1791, and J.P., Wilkes County 1796. He married Elizabeth Clark, daughter of Gen. Elijah Clark. Her grave was found by engineers working on Clark's Hill Dam in 1946, ten miles north of Lincolnton, Ga. She was born March 14, 1770 and died Dec. 24, 1813.

tried to be as lenient as their duty would permit to the old revolutionary soldier. And also they seem to have obtained some money from the confiscated lands. I do not see exactly how it is for they bought and sold the land. But so it was. Dr. Graves, the father of Gen. James Graves of 1889, bought from them in 1789, lands which had been the property of "one Graham who was on the bill of confiscation." I suppose they must be the lands now owned by Mr. Enoch Johns and they led to the removal of old Col. Graves of Graves Mountain, to Wilkes. By 1796, Wilkes was reduced nearly to its present proportions in size. Elbert was cut off in 1790, Warren and Oglethorpe in 1793 when the Common of Washington was being cut into lots, and finally Lincoln in 1796.

The house which they built for Church and Academy is fully described in my MSS. It was a brick house as large if not larger than Gen. Heard's house on N.E. corner of Spring and Court streets, built by the Bank of the State of Georgia. It was 40 by 60 ft. in area, with two stories, the lower 12 ft. in height, the upper ten. It had a foundation two feet in height from the ground, and a wall three bricks thick; the first story was two brick thick; the second a brick and a half thick. In the lower story there were sixteen windows with panel shutters containing 24 lights 10 by 12 each. Upstairs there were 30 windows with 18 lights each, but no shutters. There were to be 3 arched folding doors pannelled, 5 by 8 feet, and four other doors, 5½ by 7½ feet.

The house was divided into two equal parts, each 40 by 30 feet in area, and separated by a wall running from ground to roof and having no doors in it. One half was to be the church or chapel, the other half the school house, and the latter was divided upstairs and down by partitions, making a large school room 20 by 30, both up and down stairs, and two smaller rooms upstairs and down each, with a passage. The 60 foot side of the house was the front.

In the original plan, the floor of the 2nd story was to run over one half of the 2nd story only, but in an order in 1807, it appears that there was a 2nd story put in over the chapel for it is "resolved that the upper floor may be removed, and if necessary, a gallery put in." This order shows that it was then used for divine worship.

There were two chimneys with five fireplaces in each, and shortly after the house was begun the contractor was ordered to put in another fireplace. The builder or contractor, "undertaker" he is called in the MS., was David Gaddy. I think his workmen were Darby Henley, Phillip Henley and Timothy Warhurst, for on the list I find a subscription opposite these names to be paid in work. The proposals, published in the *Gazette of the State*, tell us the commissioners will advance $600, and we learn

that they called for bids. We learn that Jan. 5, 1796, they
accepted David Gaddy's bid, but we do not know what it was.
Rev. Hope Hull was appointed to superintend the work, a strong
security of its excellence.

In reading the description of this building I was impressed
with its size and appearance. It must have been very much such
a house as the Bank (Gen. Heard's house in 1889,) and I began to
wonder why it was ever torn down. I began to wish that I could
talk with someone who had seen it. Very fortunately, I found
that Mr. Gabriel Toombs went to school in this Academy when he
was ten years old,---that is 66 years ago. He says it was torn
down not long after 1823 when he was at school there. He says
it undoubtedly was a large, nice, well built house, and he
thinks it was a most unfortunate mistake to destroy it. There
was, he says, a large fine grove standing around it. There were
many fine trees. There was as I have heard from others, originally no avenue. Mrs. Mercer afterwards had trees cut down to
make one, which every body regretted. Subsequently, when the
property was owned by Mr. Nicholas Wylie, he began to cut down
trees after the war. Some well meaning persons began to remon-
strate, and Mr. Wylie, who was a strong headed man when his
opposition was roused, was rather incited to cut more. There
were still some rather handsome trees to the north of the house,
and I learn they were destroyed unintentionally by injudicious
trimming. The present owners, who certainly are disposed to
improve the property, will in time have the loss of trees
replaced.

The commissioners who moved the site of the Academy sometimes in the twenties of this century, probably thought they
were bringing it nearer the centre. But now in 1889 business is
moving up in the direction of the R. R. depot, and of course
nearer Mercer Hill. When one thinks what a property it would
have been with that hill covered with the fine grove, which
would not have been cut down--when one thinks of the building---
a large fine brick house of imposing appearance, which the detailed plan and our knowledge of the thoroughness of the old
workmen show to have been a well made building, which would undoubtedly have been the oldest brick house in upper Georgia
venerable with the associations of the past century and the
early settlers; when one thinks of this and reflects what we
have in place of this, that abominable, unsightly, insecure,
wooden building that we now call the "Male Academy," well I will
speak for no one but myself, I am lost in astonishment at the
mistake made by our forerunners.

If there were public schools in Washington, the very first
thing necessary would be to put up a brick house at the public
expense. Here would have been the very house to suit. I have
been a teacher, and know the requirements of such a house. I

have seen a large number of the best and most modern school buildings of Georgia, Tennessee and Alabama, and this house, I pronounce might have needed some repairs and some changes, but the plan was nearly as good as could be made.

Well, there is no use in lamentations over what was irrevocably settled nearly sixty-six years ago, so I will proceed with my chronicles. The new house was hardly more than well begun, for the building was let in January, 1797, when death carried away two persons intimately connected with the Academy. Rev. J. Springer died in 1798. I shall have occasion to speak of him in another connection, so I will say no more now. Also early in 1798, we find that our commissioners had to deal, not with the old revolutionary soldier Col. Micaijah Williamson, but with his estate and his son of the same name. Gen. Elijah Clarke, the companion in arms of Col. Micaijah Williamson, died the next year, 1799. They had obtained an execution on nine hundred and fifty acres of land owned by Col. Williamson in Jackson county. They seem to have acted with kindly forbearance and the old soldier's son honestly, for they agreed to give nine months for payment to the younger Micaijah Williamson, when they would reconvey to him titles for the land, and I judge that the terms were carried out in the end.

It appears that soon after the building was begun, they applied, through Gen. David Merriwether to the Senatus Acadimus of the University of Georgia assembled at Louisville in July 1797 to locate the University in Washington. They offer the funds and the building, but certain subscribers must be reimbursed it seems. The offer it seems was not accepted.

CHAPTER X

THE WASHINGTON LOTTERY

WHETHER THE Mr. Borroughs who was elected as a teacher ever filled the place cannot now be known; but in 1798, after the death of Rev. Mr. Springer, Rev. Hope Hull, who was elected President of the Board of Trustees, was empowered to employ teachers, and the tuition was fixed at $18, $12 and $8, per annum, or $5, $3.50 and $2.50 per quarter. As it appears, the Board made no special offer of salary. Dr. Moses Waddell, or they spell it "Waddle," who afterwards became President of the University of Georgia was appointed Rector and elected by the Board, but Dr. Waddell did not come. Probably they found it not so easy to get teachers for tuition alone, so in 1800, they determined to get the names to an annual subscription for a period of ten years, payments to be made quarterly. My MS. gives a list of persons who agreed to pay $10 per year and smaller sums. About $350 was promised in that way. Richard Worsham and Thomas Wingfield of this list have descendants here in 1889. Felix Gilbert on it is the ancestor of Mr. Charles Alexander of 1889. Perhaps John Lindsay is the ancestor of one of our young men. Benajah Smith has descendants. I presume Mrs. Sarah Hester's children descend from Benjamin Branham, but the list, though names are familiar, shows the change which the population of Washington has undergone in ninety years. Francis and Nathaniel Willis are on the list. I find James Corbett on the list. He built the house in which Dr. H. F. Andrews now lives. L. Prudhomme, of whom I shall speak hereafter is on the list.

Immediately after the list was made, they order the secretary to write Dr. Wm. Wright of Greene county to meet the board on Saturday to discuss his undertaking the Rectorship.---Also, they appoint formally, Mr. Wm. Crocker as teacher of English and Arithmetic for the ensuing year, and announce that the Academy will open Monday, January 5th, 1801. A few days after, James H. Ray was made assistant and under Dr. Wright. By an advertisement, the prices for the two higher classes were increased to $24 and $15 per annum. It is stated also that board can be obtained in the neighborhood for $15 per quarter, the boarder finding his own lodging.

On April 27, 1799, it is said that the Board of Commissioners met "at the new building intended for an Academy," but I judge that the Academy only was completed, for Mr. David Gaddy was ordered in March 1800, to finish up a room 30 by 40. This is the chapel.

In April, it appears Dr. Wright wished to leave.

In May, 1801, the Commissioners met to take into consideration the "present situation of the Academy." The MS. says they "concluded to repair as soon as possible the Academy part of the building." The workmen are "directed to take any part of the walls now standing." We are told also that the Commissioners "will meet on Saturday to make further arrangements to repair the residue of the building." Rev. Hope Hull and Gen. Meriwether are ordered "to employ workmen and superintend repair."

All this indicates some serious trouble to so new a building---greater repairs than could be made necessary by school boy depredations, though these can do an astonishing amount of mischief when uncontrolled by teachers. Traditions come from a good many sources of a great cyclone or hurricane which at some time, did great damage to trees and buildings on the grounds of the Academy. Mr. Gabriel Toombs tells me he has heard that all the trees were blown down on the property. Mr. Barnett says that the house was blown down, but he placed the storm at 1804. I think the facts of the MSS. fit perfectly into the supposition that this storm was in 1801, and forbid any other.

The school was ordered dismissed until August. About this time, the Commissioners had some negotiations with a Mr. "Gilbert," Gilbert probably, who was to teach French. But we hear no more of Mr. Gilbert. In July 1801, the commissioners appointed for the last of the year, Wm. Prince Esq. Rector, with Mr. Ebenezer H. Cummins, Assistant Tutor. There were two Wm. Princes, Sr. and Jr. It is probable this was the younger. They also made Wm. Crocker assistant at a salary of $300 and board. This Mr. Cummins was I presume a son of the old Presbyterian divine, Rev. Francis Cummins. At the end of the year, Mr. Cummins would not stay, so they elected a Rev. Isaac Jones. Mr. Jones did not come, so they elected Wm. Prince Jr. Rector for five years beginning with 1803. They told him he "must teach or cause to be taught Latin and Greek." Also he "must submit his pupils to quarterly examinations by the Commissioners or someone appointed by them." He remained only two and a half years, and in 1805 gave up, the Board making him a vote of thanks for his "exemplary conduct." During this time, Mr. Crocker was his assistant and at one time proposed to keep a boarding house at the Academy, but this does not appear to have been done. There is evidence that they had exhibitions at the Academy, for which they charged fifty cents entrance fee and used the money in some sort of repairs. Mr. Prince had the well "cleaned out and built." In 1805 they employed Rev. James

Wilson teacher of languages, providing that the tuition money should be his compensation. Rev. James Wilson suceeded Mr. Prince as Rector. The record shows that Mr. Crocker sued the Commissioners for his salary.

For the year 1807, they selected Mr. Ichabod Ebenezer Fisk, but he remained only a year. The MS. does not tell where Mr. Fisk came from, but if Ichabod Ebenezer Fisk did not come from the land of the Puritans then there certainly is nothing in a name. He remained but a year and at the end of that time he had to take the note of the Commissioners for $158, as part of his pay. For the year 1808, they advertised to obtain a teacher. Among the respondents, they selected Mr. McCoy who is, I suppose, the gentleman that became Prof. McCoy of the University of Georgia. But Prof. McCoy did not come. I suppose the prospect did not look encouraging. So they elected Mr. James Armour for 1808, and this is the last teacher of whom my MS. gives me any information.

I have gone on to give the whole list of teachers chronicled in my MSS. but I must return, to relate what is to me the most entertaining part of the story of the old Academy.

Whether the Academy was unfinished or injured by the storm as to require a good deal of money for putting it into order, I am unable to determine, but certainly they felt the need of more money. Once they asked the Legislature to lend them $1,000. In 1805, that body passed an Act to help them, not by a loan, but by a Lottery. It is called the Washington Academy Lottery, and the MSS. contains a copy of the act certified by Horatio Marbury. It passed in 1805. Rev. John Springer was dead, and in 1804 that good Methodist Rev. Hope Hull, moved to Athens, accompanied by that good Methodist, Gen. David Meriwether. What the two preachers would have said, I cannot tell, but David Meriwether often represented Wilkes County and may have been instrumental in getting the Act passed. At first the Act was limited to a year, but the time was extended, and the drawing took place in 1807. From 1805 to 1807, I think that Lottery was the talk of Washington and all interested to get the money were urging everybody else to subscribe. The Commissioners say that "the laudable object of the Lottery induces them to hope that there will be a rapid sale of tickets." Nothing more strongly shows a change, or in fact an advance of public sentiment than that Lottery; for in this year 1889, the Georgia Legislature has forbidden the newspapers to advertise the Louisiana Lottery even. In 1805-7, some of the best men in Wilkes County engaged in promoting one. I must give their names: Nicholas Long, President; Wm. Prince, Jr., Secy.; John Griffing, Joel Abbott, Gilbert Hay, F. H. Gilbert, Richard Worsham. Dr. Joel Abbott gave the ground on which the Presbyterian church now stands. I do not know how many were church members, but I believe many were Presbyterians in sentiment.

The scheme was as follows: They were to sell 4,000 tickets at $4. each; of these 2646 were blanks and 1354 prizes. There was one $1,000 prize, 3 of $500, ten of $100, 40 of $50, 100 of $20, 500 of $10, 700 of $5. Attention was called to the alluring fact that there were less than two blanks to a prize. Thus one in three was your choice of getting your money back. The profit to the Academy was gained by a deduction of 15 per cent from prizes paid. The tickets all made this statement. The account of this lottery is still more entertaining from showing that just as soon as that lottery scheme was put fairly afoot and tickets were ready for sale, the Commissioners commenced the charming and happy plan of paying running debts with lottery tickets. They paid David Gaddy interest on their note of $430 by 32 lottery tickets.

But there are still more amusing cases. There were two ladies, one was Mrs. Anne Springer, to whom David Gaddy was indebted, for board I suspect, and this bill presented to the commissioners was paid in lottery tickets at $4. Tradition tells us that when Dr. Springer died Mrs. Springer came to live in Washington, where in fact she became a somewhat noted personage. The other lady was also a widow trying to take care of herself, Mrs. Sarah Hillhouse, Mr. Charles Alexander's great grandmother, whose husband was the owner of a newspaper early in this century. He had died in 1805, and Mrs. Hillhouse had gone energetically to work to support herself and her children. She printed the tickets and other matter connected with the lottery and the commissioners paid her too in lottery tickets at $4 each.

Of course this was done with the full consent of Mr. Gaddy and the two widow ladies, but to my mind, that only makes the matter more amusing, for I doubt not these ladies were two as rigid old fashioned Presbyterians as ever made a child learn the Shorter Catechism and keep Sunday.

The drawing took place at some time in 1807, and the last record in the old MSS. contains an order for burning the tickets after registry. I presume the Lottery was successful in raising the needed money, but there is no record of it. One would like to know that the two deserving widows got some prizes. I should like to know that one of them drew the great $1,000 prize; and the other two of the $500 prizes. But the MSS. is silent. It was all over eighty years ago, and the night of oblivion envelops the successful winners.

CHAPTER XI

BUYERS AND PRICES ON LOTS

THE MSS. which I have followed will probably go out of the county and is in my hands but a very short time. I have worked hard to get the facts for preservation, and will give the buyers and prices of lots, so far as I can ascertain them.

The first permanent sale of lots in the old Town was in 1784. There is a full record of those only which were sold again because the first buyers had not paid. The reader must remember that these lots contain a fourth of an acre. As I shall draw plans with numbered lots for the copies of this work to be preserved in our library, they will be thus identified by future readers. For present readers, I designate them by the names of the present owners.

Mr. T. C. Hogue, Mr. Hogue's residence property contains three lots of the old Town, viz: 17 on Main street, 19 south of 17 and 1 south of 16. Lot 17 sold for £16 11s about $83; lot 16 for £8 3s, or about $42; both to Daniel Gaines in 1794, being resale. Lot 1 which was on the north side of Court street, before that street was closed sold in 1784 to Gen. Elijah Clarke, price unknown. But in Feb. 1794, Gen. Clarke had titles to lot 1 made to his granddaughter Susanna, the daughter of Benajah Smith, who is the ancestor of Mrs. Fred Hunter. Mr. Hogue's cottages on the south side of Liberty Street are on lot 46. Lot 46 sold in 1784, to Samuel Creswell for £12 1s, about $60. In 1794 he sold it for £8 1s or $40 nearly, to Richard Worsham the grandfather of Mr. Samuel Barnett. Mrs. Hogue's garden opposite his residence is lot 32. It was originally bought by Gen. Elijah Clarke in 1784, and in 1791 he sold it to Anthony Powell (price unknown.)

Mr. Hugh Quinn lives on lot 35, which sold in 1784 to Spencer Branham, for £20 8s, nearly $103. In 1786 it was sold for an unknown price to Absalom Jackson----Stummer Estate.

Lot 43 on which Mr. Edmondson lives, and lot 44 on which Postmaster Anderson lives, both sold in 1784 to Col. Micaijah Williamson. They cost, each £10, or about $50. In 1785, Col. W. sold them to Leonard Marbury.

Mary Willis Library is on lot 42, sold in 1784 to Micaijah Williamson and he sold in 1792 to Powel Stamper.

John Cozart's residence is on lot 8, and was bought in 1784 by Daniel Colman, and in 1792 titles were made to Daniel Teroudet. Price not known. Mr. Cozart's lot west of the former on Court and Jefferson Streets, is lot 7 which sold in 1784 to W. Davenport for ₤25 or about $150.

Mrs. Kemme's house is on lot 18, and was sold in 1784 to Leonard Marbury and in 1786 to Henry B. Gibson. Prices unknown. The lot south of 18 is 14. It sold in 1784 to Daniel Appling for ₤15 or about $75, and in 1794, Daniel Gaines bought it for about $55.

Mr. Ed. Hill's house is on lot 34, sold in 1784 to John Appling, price unknown. The lot just north of 34 is 31, bought in 1784 by John Nelson, the man who made the inscription on stone in 1792, described in the first part of these chronicles. As it is called a reserve lot, I think he may have bought it in 1780. Mr. Hill's house, is lot 33, and in 1784 Gen. Elijah Clarke bought it for ₤10 2s, about $50. In Feb. 1794, Gen. Clarke had titles to it made out for his granddaughter, Harriett, daughter of Benajah Smith.

Estate Wm. Simpson. Lot 58 on which Rev. Mr. Brown lives sold in 1784 for ₤13 15s, or about $66 to Micaijah Williamson. It was resold in 1784 for ₤5 11s, or about $27, to David Hillhouse, ancestor of Mr. Charles Alexander. The lot west of 88 is 37, on which is the cottage rented by Mr. Foreman. It sold in 1794 for ₤7 1s, or about $35, to David Hillhouse. Franklin's is on lot 28 and this was conveyed in 1791 to Col. James Williams. Price unknown. Dr. Simpson's residence is on lot 48 and this was bought in 1784 at an unknown price by Sampson Harris, the ancestor of Mr. S. H. Hardeman, who is named for him. Mr. Harris sold the lot in 1786 to Thomas P. Carnes, afterwards Judge of the Superior court, and for whom the town of Carnesville is named. Dr. Simpson's garden is lot 47 east of his house and on Liberty street, sold in 1784 for ₤10, or about $50, to John Appling.

Mrs. Ellington lives on lot 4, which was the first bought by a woman, Mrs. Milly Mann, but in 1786, by her order a deed was made to James Williams.

—— William Sims' home is on lot 25, which in 1792 became the property of James Williams.

Bigby's store, lot No. 26 also became in 1792, the property of James Williams.

Express Office. This is on lot 22. In 1784 it sold to Daniel Young for ₤9 2s, or about $45. In 1786 Absalom Jackson bought it.

Floyd's store is on lot 27 which was sold in 1784 to Frederick Lipham for ₤8 5s, or about $41.

Wm. Ellington's house corner Main street and Alexander avenue was sold in 1784 for ₤15, or about $75 to Col. Micaijah Williamson. In 1793 it was conveyed by sale or gift to John

Griffin who married Col. Williamson's daughter Sally. In 1814, John Griffin was buried on that lot. In course of time, I cannot say when or how, he acquired the whole square, and on it built the first house at least as early as 1797, just where Mr. Burwell Green's new house now stands. The old shop which many persons remember at the corner of Main and Jefferson streets, was built by Judge Griffin for a law office. The house which Mr. Burwell Green pulled down was John Griffin's house, altered, added to and turned round.

Charles Smith, on the square. Mr. Smith's house is on lot 13, as also is Patat house. It was bought in 1784 by Zachariah Lamar, deeded by him in 1791 to John Handley.

Burwell Green's warehouse is on lot 30, bought in 1784 by John Appling.

Little River parsonage is on lot 41, bought in 1784 by a Mr. Smith.

Gen. Heard's property on N. side of Court Street contains two lots, 5 and 6 which were bought in 1784 by Col. Micaijah Williamson.

Jail, this is on lot 3 and in 1784 was bought by Micaijah Williamson.

Masonic Hall, Lot No. 11. Deeds made out in 1786 for Joseph Cook. In 1792, titles were made for Mrs. Grace Little and David Creswell, and a little later, the more southern portion became the property of "Mrs. Ann Powell late Wilkinson."

When the Common was sold in 1794, I think it was bought mainly by speculators. Mr. T. M. Green owns now, lots 108, 107, 106, 105, 104, 103, 102 of the Common. Lot 108 contains his new residence. It was sold to Benajah Smith, the direct ancestor of Mrs. Fred Hunter, for £13 5s (about $60.) Lots 107, 106, 105, 104 extended in a straight line north from 108. These were bought by Samuel Blackburn for £4 10s, £3 5s, £3 5s. Lots 103 and 102, the two lots lying east of Judge Andrews old garden at Haywood, were bought for £4 7s, and £4 by Col. Micaijah Williamson but I suppose owing to his financial troubles, he could not keep them, and they eventually came into the possession of Mr. Samuel Blackburn. In 1805, Dr. Gilbert Hay, then living in Judge Andrew's old house at Haywood, came up to the Board of Commissioners and presented an order from Mr. Samuel Blackburn (who had moved to Virginia) for titles to lots 107, 106, 105, 104, 103, 102. They were thus in 1805 added to Dr. Hay's other property at Haywood. Lot 108, however, did not belong to Mr. Samuel Blackburn having been bought in 1804 by Mr. Benajah Smith.

As a Masonic Hall was first built on that lot, Dr. Hay did not acquire the lot 108, on which Mr. Green's house now stands, until about 1810.

Mr. Hynes front lot 109, and his back lot 110 were bought in

1794 by Benajah Smith, for £13 2s and £8 1s, or about $60 and $40.

Mrs. Dr. Lane's lot, 49, was bought in 1794 by Benajah Smith, for £6 or about $30. He also bought the lots lying south of Mrs. Lane, lot 50, for £7 5s; 69 for £3 10s and 70 for £2 15s.

Dr. Robert Simpson's house and garden on Liberty St. are 8 and 7. South of Dr. S.'s residence, three lots 51, 68, 71 sold respectively for £7 12s, £5 12s, £2 10s. South of his garden, three lots 52, 67, 72 sold respectively for £10, £3 1s, £3 2s. These six lots: were all bought by the teacher named Samuel Blackburn.

Mr. Hogue's cottages on the south side of Liberty St., are on lot 6 of the old town. South of this, on the Common lies lot 53, bought in 1794 by Mr. Samuel Barnett's grandfather Richard Worsham for £3 6s. In line with 53, but south of it, lie 63, 73 bought by John Hendley in 1794, for £1 15s, £2. Marcus Pharr Jr. and Wm. Fluker now live on the part of the Common reserved in 1794 to build an Academy. These lots are 55 Pharr; 64 Fluker; 75 south of 64, and 54, 56, 74 on the west side of Spring Street, built up in negro houses. These were not sold in 1794 but deeded to John Mathews a son of Gov. M. who had served on the board as clerk and attorney, and these were given in payment; but valuation not given. In 1805, when Dr. Hay acquired part of Mr. T. M. Green's property, James Corbet had titles made to him for 64, 54, 55, 74. Mr. Corbet built the house in which Dr. Andrews lives now, and his widow lived there a long time.

Mrs. Neeson's house is on lot 63, which sold to Richard Worsham for £4 10s or about $22.50 in 1794. South of Mrs. Neeson lies lot 76, which sold in 1794 to John Matthews for £4 11s. W. T. Johnson's lot opposite Mrs. Neeson is 56 and sold in 1794 to Thompson Bird for £3 10s, about $19. W. T. Johnson's new house is on lot 57, which sold in 1794 to Powell Stamper for £8 3s, about $40.

Mr. Merriwether Hill's front lot is 62, the back lot 77. They sold in 1794 to Thompson Bird for £3 16s, or about $20.

Mr. Gil Cade's lot occupied by Mr. Kendrick is 58 and sold to Thompson Bird for £4 1s, about $20.

The Methodist Parsonage, lot 61, to Thompson Bird for £4 7s. Mr. Charles Smith on Alexander Avenue lot 79 to Thompson Bird for £4 3s, about $20. Mrs. George Dyson's lot 78 to Thompson Bird for £4 11s, about $22. Dr. Lyndon, lot 60 to Thompson Bird for £4 11s.

Mr. Lowe, lot 59 to Daniel Terondet for £5 1s about $30. Mr. E. G. Binns, lot 80, to Daniel Terondet for £7 1s, about $35. Judge Reese's lot on Liberty Street is 81, and sold to Daniel Terondet for £6 3s, about $30. Judge Reese's lot on Main Street is 85 and sold to Judge Griffin for £10 or about $50. Mrs. Palmer's lot on Main Street is 83 and sold to Judge Griffin for

£20, or $100. Mrs. Palmer owns lots 84 behind her residence, which sold for £31 or about $152, to James Huling, and 85 north of 84 which sold to John Hunton for £13 11s, or about $68. The high price of 84 was probably due to fact that an old tobacco warehouse stood upon it. I shall speak of this warehouse again. Mrs. Palmer's whole property sold for £73 11s, about $320.

Mr. Charles Alexander now owns two lots 86, 87 and part of another 85 which were on the Common. They are on his lawn, extending along Alexander Avenue from North Street at Mrs. Isabella Colley's corner. They extend 66 feet east from the street. In 1794, John Mathews, son of Gov. Mathews, bought 86 and 87, paying £3 1s and £2 1s. John Mathews appears to have sold them to Samuel Blackburn for in 1805, Mr. Felix Gilbert, Mr. Charles Alexander's grandfather, appeared before the Commissioners with an order from Samuel Blackburn for lots 86, 88, and half of 85 (which Mr. B. must also have bought.) Thus two and a half acres in the western part of Mr. Alexander's lawn were acquired by his ancestors in 1805. This was three years before the building of the brick house in which Mr. Charles Alexander now lives.

Mr. John Cozart owns two lots north of his residence lot. These are 89, 88. He also owns two on Jefferson St. 61, 80. These are north of his field lying at corner of Jefferson and Court Streets. These four lots were bought by Francis Gordon and Bernard Kelly, partners. They paid for the whole £24 2s or about $120. They contain three and three-fifth acres. Francis Gordon was ancestor of the children of Mrs. Octavia Wingfield now living here.

Gen. Heard's property on Court Street has 4 lots lying north of it, viz: 93, 92, 94, 95, and they were bought in 1792, by Nathaniel Durkee for £48 11s, or about $220. Lots 93 and 94 the two on Jefferson Street sold higher than any other lots on the Common, except Mrs. Palmer's two lots. Lot 92 brought £16 10s, about $82, and 93 north of it brought £15 2s, or about $78.

Jail Square. I do not know who owns the property behind the jail. But the two lots 99, 98, sold in 1794 to Micaijah Williamson as also did 97, 96 lying north of Mrs. Ellington. Lot 89 brought £4 11s, 98 £6 11s, 97 £6; 95 8 pounds 5s. Micaijah Williamson also bought the lots now in Mrs. Kemme's meadow; 101 for £2 11s and 100 north of it, for the same.

Perhaps readers will say that this is a fatiguing summary. It has certainly wearied me to write it down. I did it, only because it is a very important record of the town history, in danger of going forever beyond our reach. But I have now put nearly all the information in print.

CHAPTER XII

THE FIRST COURT HOUSE

UNTIL THE FIRST Court House was built in Wilkes County, court was held Governor Gilmer tells us, in some log dwelling house near at hand. Judge Anderson told me that it was held in the log house belonging to Col. Micaijah Williamson, which stood on the site of Gen. Heard's present residence built by the Bank of the State for a branch. In the early days, when there was no room for the jury to occupy in their deliberations, they used to go into the woods and sit on fallen trees. The story was told here, and put by Governor Gilmer into his book, that on one occasion while they were seated on a fallen tree, a Tory passed by, and one of the jurymen spied him and exclaimed, "Oh yonder goes a d--d tory." This was in the early days when the bitterness engendered by the Revolution was still deeply felt, and the whole twelve jurymen left their duties and jumping up pursued the Tory. Judge Andrews said that the fallen tree on which the jury were seated was on the site of Mrs. Ellington's present property (N.W. corner of Court and Spring Streets, and that the Tory pursued by the jury ran down Court street which was open to the Common. But it is said that the Tory ran so fast that the minds of the jury reverted to duty before they caught him.

The first Court House stood on the north side of Court Street, opposite the public square in what is now Gen. Heard's flower garden. At the spring session of the Superior court 1785, it was completed and examined by the court. If there was ever any account in our county records of the builder, it cannot be found now. But in the old MSS. from which I have written, it appears that the undertaker or contractor, was a man named Chisolm, for on Jan. 7, 1785, he came to a meeting of the Commissioners of town and Academy, and stated that it had been no part of his contract to paint the Court House, nevertheless if the Commissioners would furnish paint, he would agree to have the work done. So they agreed and gave their treasurer an order to buy paint.

When the house was inspected and received by court, Hon. William Stith was Chief Justice, as they called it. He was evidently a man of great ideas of dignity, for one of the first things he did when he opened court, was to promulgate some rules to govern the court, and one of these was that all barristers practicing in the court should wear gowns when they argued a case. Also he ordered that the sheriff should wear in court a gown and badges of office. The latter, I presume meant that the sheriff should precede the judge into court holding up a drawn sword. This was the old English custom and prevailed in Carolina up to the Civil War. In the year before the Secession of Carolina, I was in Abbeville, S. C., when court met, and my cousin Garnett Andrews, Jr., who was with me, called me to the Hotel window to see the Judge going to the Court House preceded by the sheriff with his drawn sword. The fact that Georgia gave up Judge Stith's rule so long ago, marks a very characteristic difference between the two states so closely allied by situation.

It is a curious thing that when the new court house was just completed, the court put on record that it was not in a convenient place on the lot. It says that the jury room which is in front ought to be brought forty feet from the south line of the lot, that is from Court Street. The Court recommended that a change be made but not at the undertaker's expense. Also, they say that the tribunal should be enlarged. Among the County Records, I find no account of the contract for this Court House, of its cost and plan. But it remained standing a long time after the present court house was built in 1817, and within the past few days I have talked with an old citizen of Washington, James Roddy Sneed, Esq., the elder brother of Mrs. Geo. Dyson, who tells me he remembers it well. It was a wooden house, and was rented as offices for doctors for a long time after the county ceased to use it. Dr. Reese who married the daughter of an early citizen, Henry B. Gibson, afterwards had offices in it. It is said that it was finally sold for the lumber in it, and that this lumber was used in building an addition to the house in which Dr. Simpson lives in 1890, on the southeast corner of Pope and Liberty streets. It was the first addition made to the house by Mr. Alexander Pope. It is a curious fact in the history of antebellum Washington, that a large number of the best houses were built wholly or in part of the lumber of other houses which were pulled down and in many instances brought in from the country. It seems to show some difficulty in obtaining lumber.

The records of the Superior Court show a good many curious things indicating a change of manners. One is the branding of criminals. On April 1, 1783, John Ward was found guilty of manslaughter. He was sentenced to be "brought on Monday before the associate Judges and burnt in the Brastet of the left thumb with the letter M." On Nov. 5th, 1784, Dempsey Woods was found guilty of manslaughter and was sentenced to "have your right arm or wrist tied down by the proper officer and receive the impression of the letter M on the bran of the right thumb by a hot iron." It is added that the above sentence was "put into execution immediately after in the presence of the court." In 1786, a man named Charles Harrington who was convicted of horse stealing was sentenced to be branded on the shoulder with the letter R, (rogue I suppose) to receive thirty-nine lashes, and to stand in the pillory between eleven and twelve o'clock.

The pillory and stocks were instruments of government without which our ancestors would have supposed it impossible to preserve good order. At the time when the Court House was inspected and accepted in 1785, directions were given that the northeast corner of the Court House lot be reserved for the stocks. This would be in the northeastern corner of Gen. Heard's present flower garden.

In chronicling the curiosities in the county records I must not forget to tell the young people something of the legal steps for getting married in the last century and the early years of the present. The ordinary has filed away in his office bundles tied up with tape, great numbers of yellow papers which are of two classes. In some there is an order from the father of a young lady to be married stating that he allows so and so to have a license to marry his daughter, naming her. The other class consists of bonds, usually to the amount of £500 or $2,500, furnished by the intending bridegroom as a condition of securing the license. I was a good deal puzzled by these bonds until I found one which stated that the money named was forfeited in case the ordinary should be prosecuted for issuing the license. The consent of parents in the case of a girl under age was absolutely necessary, and the bonds were required in order to insure that all was right. The ordinary seemed to have some discretion in regard to the amount of the bond, for I find one as large as £1,000 which would be nearly $5,000. I suppose he required a larger bond where he felt in doubt as to the consent. In most cases, the bond was executed not only by the bridegroom himself, but by some friend. Thus, when John Griffin married Sallie Williamson, Thomson Bird and he signed the bond for £500, and when Thomson Bird married Susan Williamson, John Griffin and he executed the bond. In the nineties of the last century, as they began to use dollars and cents in the place of pounds, shillings and pence the bond begun to change. It became $500, and so was of course much lowered in value.

There was one thing which puzzled me a good deal at first. It was why a man should give bond, when he could avoid it by carrying a permit from the lady's father. But I finally concluded that it was because asking the father for his written order was tantamount to a confession of lack of cash or credit to make the bond.

I have copied below one of these bonds.

Know all men by these presents that we William Richards and Jacob Mercer are held and firmly bound unto David Terrell register of probates for said county in the sum of five hundred pounds, to indemnify the said register for granting Marriage License unto said William Richards to marry with Nancy Mercer. Witness our hands this 16th day of May, 1799.

The following is an order.

Mr. Terrell will be good enough to grant marriage license to Mr. Anderson Durham and Rebeheah Jarrett, my daughter, I.C. Jarrett.
March 28, 1797.

It seems to me that an elopement must have been nearly impossible in those days, unless by an old fashioned Gretna Green sort of a journey to some place under less rigid rule.

The records of our Superior Court from 1784 to 1789 contain some curious illustrations of the *Articles of Confederation* under which the people of the United States lived prior to the establishment of the present Constitution in 1789. The Difficulty was as my reader remembers, that the General Government, having no power over individuals, could not raise money unless the states levied taxes. The Judge Walton presided in 1785, he called attention to neglect of the state to raise this money. "The act of the assembly for laying a tax throughout the state for the support of the government should be immediately attended to," and he goes on to argue the case at some length on the ground of "the support of our credit." He said, "Hitherto the U.S. in Congress assembled have in vain called upon us for our quota, and although the General and Superior devastation of our country yet° for a while Banishes the Idea of a Tax in the common way for that purpose, it has been, and is yet, in our power to maintain our credit by an impost on trade. It has been repeatedly asked of us, and that it has not been complied with is I presume principally owing to the Multitude of other business" &c. "I now earnestly recommend it to your observation." Then the Judge winds up with a peroration very much in the fashion of that time, when men thought they had not made a worthy speech unless they referred to the Greeks and Romans. "It is essential to proceed by certain forms, without which the record of established rights cannot be proved. This has been the practice since the original modes of the Greeks, continued by adoption of the Romans, and after the revival of letters through our English forefathers down to the American establishment.

The Grand Jury headed by their foreman, Gen. George Matthews (afterwards governor) followed the Judge's leading with great zeal. They said, "We present as a Grievance the inattention of the Honorable the Legislature to the requisition of the honorable the Congress for laying an impost on Goods and Merchandise imported in this state." They go to express fear that this will "disgrace us as a people and tend to destroy our credit at home and abroad." This was a somewhat notable grand jury, on which were found Sanders Walker, John Talbot, Thomas Grant, Jacob Early, John Nelson, James Findlay, Micaijah Megahee, Nicholas Long, Dionysious Oliver[1], Thos. Wooten, John Wingfield, Wm. Terill, Wm. Boren, Jas. Stewart, &c. About a year afterwards, another grand jury, whose foreman was Col. Benjamin Taliaferro, resumed the subject with no less emphatic deliverances. They presented, "As a great and dangerous grievance, the refusal of the state to grant power to Congress to levy an impost of 5 per cent on foreign articles of commerce imported into this state." They "take the liberty to recommend" &c. On this jury hardly less notable than the other were found Zachariah, John and James Lamar, John Freeman, Frank Merriwether, James Marks, Henry, John and Burwell Pope, Wm. Moss, Drury Cade.

In 1786 Micaijah Williamson applied for a license to keep tavern, as did also a man named Joseph Wilson. The Court took occasion to fix a schedule of charges for tavern keepers to make, and it may interest my readers to see it.

For warm dinner 1s 6d, for warm supper 1s, for warm breakfast 1s, for cold dinner 1s, for cold breakfast 8d, for cold supper 8d, lodging for night horse and finding him in fodder or hay 1s, good pasturage 24 hours 8d, good Jamaica spirits per gill 6d, good West India rum per gill 2d, good Madeira wine per bottle 4s 8d, all white wine per bottle 4s 8d, claret wine per bottle 3s 6d, Porter per bottle 1s 9d, Strang male beer per pt. 4d, good whiskey or brandy per gill 6d, good Clinava per gill 6d.

A shilling in Georgia currency at that time was nearly 22 cents, a penny about seven-fifths of a cent.

The old tavern kept by Micaijah Williamson on the site of Gen. Heard's residence had a tall sign with a picture of General Washington on it. It was the scene of a story which was repeated over Georgia against Gen. John Clarke when he became candidate for Governor many years afterwards. Gen. Clarke used to come in town and, like most men of that day get drunk. They did not all, however, cut up as he did, on such an occasion. He went into stores and smashed things, as tradition says; but

---

[1] Dionysius Oliver was the founder of Petersburg, a dead town on the Savannah River.

Judge Andrews used to say that he went back when sober and paid like a gentleman for the damages he had done. On one occasion it was said that he came into town intoxicated and galloping down Court street fired through the picture of Gen. Washington on the sign. This is the story his enemies told when he was a candidate. Judge Andrews said that his friends always denied its truth. After the death of Micaijah Williamson, Sr., in 1797, the tavern was kept by William Sansom, or as he is called in the record, "Major Sansom." It was about 1797 that a Market House was erected on the north side of our present Court House, a little south of the pump now standing. It was a small building erected by Wm. Prince, Sr., at his own expense, he having certain privileges in it for a term of several years. The people sent up a petition for it, and the directions given in the old MS. to which I have so often referred, say it was to be built half way between Major Sansom's house and Thomas Terrell's house. As I have before said there is, or was, some remnant of the foundation of Thomas Terrell's house near the present Court house steps. This market for awhile caused Court Street to be called 'Market St.' Wm. Prince sold meat in this market but I think he was not a regular butcher.

 It will surprise many readers probably, to know that the street which we call Main Street was at first called by the name of Broad St. The name appears to have been changed in 1805 when the town was incorporated. Whether the change from Broad Street was made on account of the extreme inappropriateness of the old name, I am unable to say.

 Judge Andrews told me (in substance) that the first jail of Wilkes county, as he described it, stood on the site of the present jail; that it was a brick house with quarters below stairs for the jailer's family, and that the rooms for prisoners were up stairs. The County records contain, in the proceedings of Inferior Courts, a description and contract for erecting just such a building. I doubt not that Judge Andrews remembered it personally, for he was born in 1799, and this building remained standing until 1817 or 1818. He came to Washington in 1821 to live. But he must often have been in the town before he came finally. His father settled in Wilkes, but was soon cut off into Oglethorpe. The place of my grandfather was just beyond the county line, and the 4d corn per quart 2d, for stablage for family did a great deal of their trading here.

 Judge Andrews was of course a perfectly trustworthy witness so far as his memory went. But he was under a mistake when he said that this old jail, which he remembered doubtless, was the first jail. There is in this case no evidence whatever superior to that of the official records of Wilkes county, and they show beyond the shadow of a doubt, that the county had three jails, although I never heard it from any of the old people to whom I have talked upon this subject.

The proceedings for building the jail which I have described begun in 1796. I read the full account a few days ago. They were completed and the jail accepted in 1798, from Benajah Smith who had it built. In the old book he is called "the undertaker." The judges of the Inferior court who called for bids were Richard Worsham (Mr. Samuel Barnett's grandfather.) Edward Butler, David Hillhouse, John Pope. There were three bids, that of Benajah Smith $2500, being the highest. They accepted the lowest, but it turned out that the bidder could not make a satisfactory bond, and then the other bidder backed out, leaving Benajah Smith in possession of the field. So he had the jail built, and it was ready for use in 1798. I find that there were up stairs two rooms, the criminal's room, "and the debtor's room," showing that they then imprisoned for debt in Georgia notwithstanding the colony had been established as an asylum for imprisoned debtors.

When we find that this jail was ready for use no earlier than 1798, there is already a strong presumption that the county must have had an earlier jail, since the early days of Wilkes county were not in the Golden Age. But there is more than presumption; there is positive evidence. The MSS. from which I have written so much about the old brick academy on Mercer Hill, is the official record of the Commissioners of the town of Washington acting as Academy Commissioners. After a meeting or two, they kept Academy and other business separate. But at the first meeting rec rded in the old MSS., 1785, we are told that Wm. Terrel undertaker of the county jail came to them and asked where he should put the jail. They reply by ordering that the gaol should be set on the south side of the lot 15 feet from the southwest corner. But this is not all the evidence to show that there was a jail earlier than the one described by Judge Andrews. In the records of the Superior Court, to be found in the Ordinary's office, I find that on April 7, 1796, William Triplett who is there called "high Sheriff of Wilkes county" appeared before court and said that the insecurity of the county jail was such that he could not be responsible for the keeping of prisoners, and he asked that this statement, or protest, should be placed by the clerk on the records of the court. This was accordingly done, and there it is to this day to prove that there was a county jail then, however insecure.

The present jail is the third. The description of the jail accepted in 1798 from Benajah Smith, shows that it was not our present jail which was then built; B. Smith's jail had two rooms up stairs and two down, and the latter two had several windows filled with glass.

I have not been able to find any account of the letting of our present jail, or of the contract and description; I was desirous to learn the cost and Mr. Dyson Clerk of the Court and I made a search through the records on Saturday last, but without success. But I found conclusive evidence of the date of the building and name of the undertaker. The records of the Superior Court show that on Tuesday Feb. 2, 1819, Justices Benjamin Porter, Matthew Talbot[2] and Wm. Evans being present the following entry was made. "The court having viewed the jail are of the opinion that the said jail is finished agreeably to contract with John Haliday Esq the undertaker, and therefore we do receive the same." From a few words previously recorded under date of April 1818, I judge that the old building must have been removed, and work begun in 1817.

I think I have shown clearly that Wilkes county has had three jails. I have argued this case at some length, because I am the first person who seems to have made the statement in our day, and a woman is not generally considered of much weight in such matters. But I do not think anyone will undertake to dispute my conclusion.

I think it may interest readers to know that in 1801, an order was issued by the Superior Court that $710 be paid to Major Ferdinand Phinizee (Phinizy) "for keeping in repair the Court House and Jail." Putting in repair is, I suppose, what they meant. The sum $710, is too large for the other purpose. This is evidently the ancestor of a rich and honorable citizen of Georgia lately deceased. It shows how numerous are the persons whose ancestors have some connection with Wilkes County.

(2) Matthew Talbot was President of the Senate, 1811, 1817, 1818, 1820-21 Ex., 1821, 1822. He was Governor of Georgia Oct. 24 to Nov. 5, 1819.

CHAPTER XIII

THE CULTIVATION OF COTTON

THE NINETIES OF the last century saw a great industrial revolution in the Southern States viz: the substitution of cotton for tobacco as the staple production of the agricultural class. Georgia and the Carolinas were the only cotton states settled; and in the up country, the north eastern batch of counties, with old Wilkes at the center formed the territory subject to the change. I have sought in the records, and in tradition, for some of indications of the change in progress.

The venerable mother of Mrs. Wm. Reese, Mrs. John Pettus, who died about thirty years ago at the age of ninety, was the last survivor of the great emigration from Virginia in 1784. She was a child of four years old when her father, Thomas Wingfield came to Georgia and took up lands at the northern end of Washington, building the older portion of the house burned a few years ago near what is now the big gully. Mrs. Pettus used to say that she remembered fields on the road between the big gully and town covered with tobacco in bloom.

In the subscription list taken up in 1796 for building the old brick Academy on Mercer Hill, Edward Butler subscribed 1000 lbs. of tobacco to be paid at the warehouse when his crop was made. This is the ancestor of our Mary Willis.

The records of the Academy and Town Commissioners for April 1789, show that they laid off an acre from the Common for the building of a tobacco warehouse. It stood on what is now Mrs. Stephen Palmer's back lot, between Main and Court Streets. It was built by Col. Jeter Stubblefield, who was to have the storage for fifteen years as compensation. The order for it says it should be large enough to hold 300 hhds. then these words are erased and a substitute made, "large enough to hold all the tobacco that may be brought to the warehouse for inspection." Long before 1793, the warehouse ceased to be of use, by the substitution of cotton for tobacco. In June 1794, the Commissioners passed an order that "the lot on which the warehouse stands, shall be sold to Mr. Francis Gordon, the only person having any claim having consented." But the warehouse lot was sold with the rest of the common, and I suppose the value of the house or lumber was the cause of the superior price that this lot brought, viz. £31, or $150. The change from tobacco to cotton was due to one man, Eli Whitney; and his invention of the cotton gin or engine. He was never in Wilkes County. He was when he made his invention, a Connecticut man staying as a guest on Gen. Nathanael Greene's place called Mulberry Grove near Savannah. The gin was patented in 1793. Mr. Whitney was shamefully treated about it. The principle of his invention is used in every gin made since, and it has not merely revolutionized our industry, but has caused him to be regarded as one of the great benefactors of the world. His patent was infringed, and it brought no less than sixty law suits. It was finally decided that his claim was entirely just, but this litigation took so much time that his patent expired in a few years after the decision was reached. The great injustice done him was in not extending his patent.

Whitney made a bad mistake in determining not to sell the right of manufacturing the gins. All exclusive rights are granted, not merely for the benefit of the owner, but because the public are also interested in any such rights of any value. It so happened that the train of events made this invention of wide and immediate value, first to all who could make cotton, and to the rest of the world. There was an immense body of people waiting, as it were to snap it up. Whitney determined to manufacture himself, and he did not have the money to do it fast enough. He formed a partnership with a man named Phineas Miller, who became Mrs. Green's second husband. Just as soon as the news of the invention got out, there sprung up a great immediate demand for such machines. As Whitney did not supply the demand fast enough, it brought forward a set of unscrupulous persons who began to evade the patent. They sold machines, and people went to work with them. Then when law-suits began, they interrupted people who did not mean to be dishonest, but were only anxious to begin work and keep at it as hard as they could. This made the owner of the patent unpopular, and juries were prejudiced against him.

In 1796, thirty machines manufactured by Whitney were in operation in Georgia. One at least of Whitney's gins was in Wilkes County. It was at work on Upton Creek in the possession of Mr. John Talbot. The place where the gin house stood is very near the site of Mr. F. T. Simpson's Mill on Upton creek, standing in 1890. A few weeks ago, I was at Mr. Simpson's house and he took me to see the spot.

Mr. Thomas Talbot, some time about 1848 or 9, told the following facts to my uncle Garnett Andrews. He said that pending the raising the money to manufacture the gins, visitors were not permitted to see them in operation. A man named Edward Lyon discovered the principle on which they acted, either by disguising himself in women's clothes, or else by sending his wife in to see it. Women were admitted it not being supposed that they would have sense enough to make any use of what they saw. Whitney and Miller afterwards had a lawsuit in which the claims of Lyon were fully tested and disallowed. When Mr. Talbot told this to my uncle, the cylinder of the Whitney gin was still in his possession, and he gave it to my uncle, who was greatly interested in it. I saw this cylinder myself. In 1848 or 9, my uncle was invited to make an address before the State Agricultural Association in Macon. He took with him this cylinder for exhibition. When he left Macon, he called for it. It was lost, or more likely, stolen: and he never recovered it. This was a great misfortune. If we had such a relic in our Library, it would be of the greatest interest to visitors.

I find no statistics of our county to show the rapidity with which the cotton culture spread and replaced that of tobacco, but the following general facts will indicate it. They show plainly that Whitney's invention was the cause of the whole change. In 1770, 3 bales of cotton were shipped from New York to Liverpool, 4 from Virginia, and 3 from North Carolina. In 1784, a vessel which carried 8 bales from the United States to Liverpool was seized in port on the ground that so large a quantity in a single cargo could not be the produce of the United States. In 1791, the cotton crop of the U. S. was 2,000,000 lbs. and 189,316 lbs. were exported. In 1792, the export was 138,328 pounds. In 1793, the year of the invention, 5,000,000 lbs. were the crop, the export 487,600. In 1794, when the cotton gin was first introduced generally, the crop was 8,000.000 pounds and the export 1,601,760 lbs. In 1800, the crop was 35,000,000 lbs., the export 17,789,803 lbs. In 1810, the crop was 85,000,000 lbs., the export of uplands 84,657,384 lbs.

These figures are taken from the source from which I got them, from *Hunt's Merchant's Magazine,* some of the tables being compiled by Prof. McCoy formerly of the University of Georgia. I think they show that the change from tobacco to cotton must have been made general in Wilkes near the beginning of the present century.

At first the work of separating cotton from seed was done in public gins kept by persons for pay. Mr. Charles Alexander's grandfather Felix Gilbert, with his brother and partner Wm. Gilbert, had a gin of this kind. Mr. James Roddy Sneed, within the past few days told me the Gilbert gin house was situated near the spot now occupied by the Seminary. Mr. Sneed says there was once a gin house where Mr. Wm. Fluker now lives (S. E. corner Water and Spring Sts.) Another, belonging to Mark A. Lane, stood on the present Academy lot at the corner of Jefferson and Liberty Sts., until some time in the twenties of this century.

As I have said, Whitney was never here.(1) Gen. Nathanael Greene seems to have owned lands in this county whether granted by Georgia or bought. The lands now owned by Mr. F.T. Simpson on Upton Creek, were bought by his father about 1817 from some Littlefields who were grandchildren of Gen. Greene. I myself knew some of Gen. Greene's descendants of that name living in Columbia, Tenn. These lands were not however granted to Gen. Greene. The deeds themselves show that they were originally surveyed for Wm. Barnett and his brother in law James Jack. I do not know how they came into the hands of Gen. Greene's heirs, who never lived in this county I am sure.

The cotton culture brings up the subject of the importation of negroes. Since I have been writing these chronicles of Wilkes County, the making of fire proof vaults in the Court House has caused an examination of old books in the offices of the Clerk and Ordinary of the county. In the Ordinary's office, a book has been found still older than the record of the court of 1779, supposed to be the oldest of the county records. This oldest book is a folio in leather, and contains the records kept by Barnard Heard who was appointed Register and Probate of Wilkes county as soon as the county was laid off in 1777. The office was substantially that of Ordinary. The entries were nearly all made during the Revolution and are chiefly records of wills, and inventories. The first will, that of a man named Richardson, was made in 1775 but was probated and recorded in 1777. He described himself as living in "the ceded lands of Georgia," the name by which the territory of Wilkes County was known at first. I looked over the inventories of property in this book, and I find that in a large number, there was negro property. The number of negroes owned really reached six.

The increase of cotton culture made negroes more valuable, and as Judge Andrews told me, the laws which were to stop the slave trade after 1808, made people very desirous to obtain a supply of negroes before that time. There was a negro trader called L. Prudhomme who was a refugee from San Domingo, who supplied many persons in the county. He lived somewhere in the southwestern corner of the court house square. Judge Andrews remembered that the father of Judge Vason bought some negroes from Prudhomme. I find Prudhomme's name among the subscribers

---

(1) "There is much tradition to prove Eli Whitney was in Wilkes county, and made gins there, and taught John Talbot's children. The old school house and gin shop are on Mr. Luke Burdett's farm, some six miles beyond Washington, on the Lincolnton road. Mr. Burdett told me that when he was a boy, his father bought the old Talbot farm and home, and that the old shop contained a number of Whitney gins, and that he and his brother dumped many of them in a gully in order to make room for other things, however, they kept one which I saw a number of years ago."
T. B. Rice, Greensboro, Ga.,
Historian of Greene County, Sept. 16, 1940.

to the brick Academy. From the court records, his business seems to have brought him a good deal of litigation.

I will add that Prudhomme made a fortune here and went to France to spend it.

The French revolution in 1789 was soon followed by a revolution in San Domingo. This caused Wilkes county to receive a number of refugees from that island. A family of them kept a store where Mr. Henry T. Slaton now lives on the Greensboro road. The place was long called *French Store* from this fact. Mr. Archibald Simpson married the daughter of the man who kept this *French Store,* and took her to Alabama. What is called the *French Mills road* to this day, owes its name to a mill kept by some of the San Domingo refugees.

Among the refugees, was a Mrs. Dugas. She had a son born in Washington, Louis A. Dugas, who became a distinguished physician in Augusta in this century. He was one of twins. Mrs. Dugas kept a school here for girls about where Mr. Charles Smith's house stands on the square now. Mr. Samuel Barnett's mother, and the late Mrs. Lewis Brown the aunt of Mrs. Andrews and of Mrs. Cornelia Pope, went to school to her. I have often heard the old folks speak of seeing Dr. Dugas and his twin brother suckled by a goat, a sight which evidently made a profound impression upon the little girls at school. In the old MSS. of the Academy Commissioners, it is recorded that in March 1806, Mrs. Dugas asked the Commissioners to patronize her school, and to appoint a day to examine her pupils. It is recorded that they made the appointment.

CHAPTER XIV

SETTLERS — WINGFIELDS

I WILL NOW SPEAK of some of the more noted families of settlers. The Wingfields are a marked instance of the immigration of a large body of kindred settlers which seems to have been common in the case of those who came from Virginia. The Wingfields came in 1784, the year when Georgia's land law was put in operation. The lands east of the Oconee were distributed by the "head right" system in which the settler selected his land and had it surveyed. The lands west of the Oconee were afterwards distributed by a land lottery.

The Wingfields of Wilkes were all descendants of John Wingfield and his wife Sarah Garland of Hanover County Virginia. The family came originally from Suffolk County in England, where there is a Wingfield Castle. They were gentry, and entitled to a coat of arms, of which Mrs. Reese has a copy, but it is part of the general good sense of the Wingfields that they never used it in this country. Such a thing has an antiquarian interest to all people, who are not too stupid to take an interest in their ancestors.

There are three branches of the descendants of John Wingfield and Sarah Garland. They descend from Thomas Wingfield; from Wm. Terrell who married Frances Wingfield, and from John Wingfield, who however, does not seem to have come to Georgia though his descendants did.

Thomas Wingfield who married Elizabeth Terrell settled in the northern part of Washington near what is now the big gully, having built the older portions of the house burned while in the possession of Dr. Tazewell Anderson. Thomas Wingfield's possessions included the farm of Mr. Foreman the property of Mr. Gil Cade and of Mr. Beal, and stretched round to the west and included the property of Mr. T. M. Green and Mr. Wm. Pope. He had several daughters nearly or quite grown. A Mr. Grimes, whose name is in the old county records, married one, and from them descend the Grimes family of Columbus. Another married Major Richard Worsham who had been an officer in the Revolution. He built a house long known as Worsham's Tavern which stood where Patat's house now stands on the square. After a while the house was kept by a man named Wm. Head, and was called Head's Tavern. Head added a dining room to the south and above it was a room known as Head's long room, in which stated Assembly balls were held in the winter. After being disused as a tavern, it was burned in the great fire of 1841.

Major Worsham was at one time a member of the legislature, and was a very intelligent man. When Wilkes county was making the uneventful history I have related, the French revolution of 1789 was going on, followed by Napoleon's Conquests. The news came to Washington with what would seem to us absurd slowness, but all the same, it was news when it came. Major Worsham's association with travelers made him get it comparatively soon, and it is said he was as much interested as are his grandsons Dr. Willis and Mr. Samuel Barnett in the history of our times. He would trace Napoleon's progress and draw maps on the ground before his house.

Major Worsham's daughters were the belles and beauties of their day, Sophia was the first wife of Mr. Osborne Stone, and through her the children of Mr. John Semmes descend from Thomas Wingfield. Miss Elizabeth Worsham married first Thomas Willis and then Samuel Barnett and so became the mother of Dr. Willis and the Samuel Barnett of our day.

In those days, men fought duels on small provocation. At a ball one night, Mr. Thomas Willis and a Mr. Henry had a dispute about a dance with Miss Worsham. She knew nothing of the result until it was all over for they did not discuss such disputes before ladies. But they fought a duel, and Mr. Henry, who was badly wounded, was carried to Judge Andrews' old house at Haywood then occupied by Dr. Gilbert Hay. In the ceiling of the old Andrews sitting room, are four hooks which were put up to hang a swinging bed for Mr. Henry.

Major Worsham had two younger daughters Emily and Martha, also considered great beauties, who in succession married Dr. John Pope, the uncle of Mr. Wm. Pope, who built Mr. Ed Hill's house. Thus the Popes who went to Florida and Texas were descendants of Thos. Wingfield. One of the latter was killed a few days since.

Major Worsham had a son, Joseph Worsham, who left a daughter that was the first wife of Mr. Frank Wingfield, another descendant of T.W., who settled near the big gully. The house in which Mr. Pharr lives on Main street was built by Mr. Frank Wingfield. He did not finish it, and for a while it was called "the old castle," from its dismal look. Mr. Scudder taught school in it at one time, and it was finished finally by Mr. I. T. Irvin.

Another daughter of Thomas Wingfield married Anthony Poullain, a Frenchman of noble birth, who came over I think with the French who helped us in the Revolution. He lived but a short time and left a son Dr. T. N. Poullain, of Greensboro, who died last year, aged ninety seven, the oldest living native of Washington when he died. The old house on the site of Mr. Marshall Sims' present house, was built by Dr. Poullain's father. The timber was used by Mr. Sims in building some outhouses, and Mr. Robert tells me he thinks some of the shingles are still used. They must be about a hundred years old. Dr. Poullain was a very polished old gentleman. His son Antoine Poullain, and his daughter Mrs. Moore, live in Augusta. In the early times there stood an old windmill for grinding grain on the Colley hill. It had the long picturesque arms of old fashioned wind mills, and was visible all over Washington.

Milldred Wingfield daughter of Thomas W., married John Sims - and her sons William and Rederic Sims are often named in the old records. They were afterwards merchants and cotton factors of character in Macon and Augusta, and in Albany and Apalachicola. Mrs. Sarah Garland Eve wife of Dr. Joseph A. Eve of Augusta, was her descendant. Dr. Eve and his wife were intimate friends of my father and mother and I do not believe the State of Georgia ever contained better people. An acquaintance with them made one think better of human nature. Mrs. John Pettus was the youngest daughter of Thomas Wingfield. She was a very lovely and refined old gentlewoman. She married her cousin of the John Wingfield branch and for a long time lived in the suburbs, on the eastern side of Spring street.

Thomas W. had a son Dr. Thomas Wingfield of Greensboro, who became the father of Mrs. Wm. C. Dawson, Mrs. McKinley, Mrs. Seymore. The Eatonton Wingfields descend from them.

He also had a son John who was an elder in the Presbyterian church present at that ordination under Mr. Alexander's poplar a hundred years ago. His son, Mr. James Wingfield was long postmaster of Washington, living where Mrs. Ellington now lives, and keeping the P. O. in the house of Mr. Smith on the other side of Court Street. Mr. Wingfield built the older part of Mr. A. Franklin's house on the eastern end of Main street, and facing west. He lived there but a short time, and left it a small one story house. Then Mr. Charles Bolton who afterwards went to Texas bought it, and made it a two-story house, and then Rev. James Dunwoody bought it and added a collonnade. So the little house grew up to be a big one. Mr. James Wingfield was the father of Leonora and Cornelia, of Frank Wingfield and Dr. Jim Wingfield, Mrs. Octavia W.'s husband. His sisters who married cousins, are well remembered here. Miss Rebecca W., who married Mr. Garland Wingfield of another branch, is remembered for her great kindness, and the good things she used to make, especially some wafers which she used to send to sick people, and which I always sigh for when I am sick. Three of these sisters married Mr. Stephen Pettus belonging to another branch of the Wingfield family and it is said that he courted a fourth, Miss Ann, who never married.

These ladies had a brother who became Dr. John Wingfield of
Madison. His daughter married Mr. James Nisbet of Macon; from
him descend Hazlehursts and DeGraffenrieds.
 This is the end of the Thomas Wingfield branch. The will of
T. W. is in the ordinary's office, with a list of his negroes
headed by his man Cupid.
 Wm. Terrel, who had our first jail built, is ancestor of the
Terrel branch. He seems to have come with several grown sons,
Joel, Thomas, Peter, David. Joel was father of Dr. Wm. Terrel
of Sparta for whom Terrel county is named. He was a rich intelligent liberal man, who made a liberal donation to the State
University. He left but one child, Lucy Terrel, one of the
most beautiful and lovely young women in the Georgia of my
youth. She married Edgar Dawson, also of the Wingfield stock
and lives with her children in Baltimore. Thomas Terrel had a
store on the square before 1817, near the Court House steps.
When Mrs. Vickers came in 1836, he was living on the east side
of the square, and was burned out in the fire of 1837. David
Terrel, who was the clerk of court for Wilkes county in the
last century was the ancestor of Mrs. Lucas of Athens and Mrs.
Alex Wallace of Atlanta. Miss Fanny Wallace, Librarian of the
young Men's Library in Atlanta, is his descendant. She and her
sisters are among the loveliest young women in the Atlanta of
1890. There are women in Atlanta who spend thousands in personal decoration but can never attain that look of refined
gentlewomen which shows itself in the most casual observation
of the Misses Wallace. The widow of our much esteemed Judge
Charles Wingfield was of the Terrel branch of Wingfields.
 And now I come to the John Wingfield branch. This John, son
of John W. and Sarah Garland, did not come but his descendants
did. The John and Garland Wingfield of the old juries were his
sons. This Garland W. was the uncle of the one remembered in
Washington as the husband of Mrs. Rebecca W. He married the
widow of Anthony Poullain, and is chiefly signalized to us by
having been turned out of the Methodist church for owning
negroes. This John Wingfield branch settled in the south western and southern parts of Wilkes county. The John Wingfield
of the old juries became neighbor there to the Simpsons and
the Butlers. One of his daughters married Wm. Simpson, the boy
who was brought from Virginia on horseback when a baby. This
makes the Simpsons, Lanes, Armstrongs, of this branch of Wingfields. Another daughter married Edward Butler. From her
descend Mrs. Samuel Barnett and Mrs. T. F. Willis.
 Of this branch were Stephen and John Pettus, through their
mother.
 The late Captain Archie Wingfield, with his daughters Mrs.
Terry and Mrs. Weems, and his sister Mrs. Dr. Ficklen the
elder, are of this branch. Captain John Wingfield, and his

brother the late Judge Charles Wingfield are of this branch.
Rev. Hope Hull married a sister of the John and Garland Wingfield of the old juries, and thus all the Hulls, including Mrs. Eliza Pope Hull's sons, belong to this branch of the Wingfield family. Mr. Garland Wingfield, who married Miss Rebecca W. was the son of the John Wingfield of the old juries. So was the husband of Mrs. Caroline Wingfield. The wife of Gen. David Merriwether was sister of John Wingfield of the old juries.

And having come to Gen. Merriwether I must correct an error. It was James Merriwether, not David, who was united with Duncan Campbell in a treaty with the Creeks. David Merriwether made another Creek treaty, his grandson says, together with Gen. Jackson. In White's *Historical Collections,* it is stated that the treaty was made by Gen. Merriwether and Daniel Forney.[1]

(1) Andrew Jackson, Joseph McMinn and *David* Meriwether, Commissioners for the U.S., signed the treaty with the Cherokee Indians on July 8, 1817. *William* Meriwether was a witness to the signatures.

Daniel M. Forney, of the State of North Carolina, and *David* Meriwether, of the State of Georgia, specially appointed for that purpose, on the part of the U.S., signed the Treaty with the Creeks at Indian Springs Jan. 8, 1821. Wm. McIntosh and twenty-three Chiefs, headmen and warriors signed for the Creek Nation. *William* Meriwether was a witness to the signatures.

Duncan G. Campbell and *James* Meriwether, Commissioners on the part of the U.S., signed the Treaty of Feb. 12, 1825 at Indian Springs with Wm. McIntosh and fifty-one Chiefs for the Creek Nation. *William* Meriwether was a witness to the signatures.

David Meriwether was in Congress, Dec. 6, 1802-March 3, 1807.
James Meriwether was in Congress, March 4, 1825-March 3, 1827.

CHAPTER XV

SETTLERS — THE GILBERTS

WM. AND FELIX Gilbert were brothers who came to Wilkes from the Shenandoah Valley in Virginia not long after 1784, as the name of Wm. Gilbert appeared in the court records before 1790. They are represented in the Washington of 1890 by Mr. Charles Alexander, who is the grandson of Felix Gilbert. There have been other families of Gilberts in the county, but not in any way related to these.

The family were Scotch by extraction. When they came to Georgia, traveling in their wagons, it is said they stopped for the night on property afterwards owned by them, but without a definite idea of remaining. But when they looked at the fine oaks, showing the value of the land it is reported that they agreed that it would be useless to go further, they never could find a better territory in which to settle. Mr. A. L. Alexander used to tell this. They became planters and merchants, and after the cotton gin was introduced, they bought cotton in and seed or ginned it for toll, in their gin house which was erected at the western end of Court street a few yards north from the site of the tobacco warehouse.

They made a fortune, and were the most important merchants here at the end and beginning of a century. In the course of time, Felix Gilbert married. His wife was the daughter of David P. Hillhouse an emigrant from Connecticut who was a brother of Senator James Hillhouse from that State. The name of David Hillhouse is found in the court records before 1790. Mr. Hillhouse was either accompanied or followed by Oliver Hillhouse Prince(1)---who was I presume his nephew, as I know that he was a kinsman. Mr. Prince became a noted lawyer in the early years of this century, having been admitted to the bar in 1806. His name will be long preserved in the legal annals of Georgia, by *Princes Digest* of the laws of the state. He was a great wit. I find, in the old MS. of the Town and Academy Commissioners, two Wm. Princes, father and son. I am disposed to think Wm. Prince Senior may have been the father of Oliver Prince, who is said by Appleton's *Encyclopedia of Biography* to have come to this state at an early age. Wm. Prince, Jr.,

(1) Oliver H. Prince was in the U.S. Senate Dec. 1828 to March 3, 1829.

taught school here in the old Academy on Mercer Hill.
   About the beginning of the century, a newspaper was established here called the *Monitor*. Alexander Milligan was the founder, but it soon came into possession of Mr. Hillhouse, or gave way to one founded by him called the *Gazette*. Mr. Chapman editor of the *Gazette* has in his possession two receipts for advertising done in the *Gazette* in 1802. Mr. Hillhouse died near the beginning of this century, and his wife Mrs. Sarah Hillhouse, then undertook to publish the paper, as a support for herself and children. She was a woman of sense and energy and excellent education. It is said that her penmanship attracted a good deal of attention from farmers who came into her office, as that was in those days by no means a general accomplishment among women. She had the printing done in her house, which stood near Mr. Hogue's front gate. Many persons will remember this one of the oldest houses about Washington. It may have been built by Mr. Hillhouse, as it had one mark of a New England house of early days, that is the gable end on the street. It seems to have been often the abode of printers, for when Judge Andrews came to Washington in 1821, Mr. Glen, then editing the paper, lived in it; and when I came here, it was inhabited by Mr. Kappel also a printer. Mr. Glen moved to Augusta.
   Mrs. Hillhouse became very successful with her printing establishment. When Louisville was the capital of Georgia, the reports of the Legislature used to be sent here and printed in Mrs. Hillhouse's printing office. She had two daughters, and a son afterwards known as David Hillhouse, who once edited a paper in Columbia, South Carolina. Her daughter Sarah was married to Felix Gilbert about 1805. Soon after Mr. Gilbert began to build the older portion of the brick house which Mr. Charles Alexander now owns. Before that time, he had lived in a house to the south of the present house in the old garden, where there is an old well still, to mark the earlier settlement. The new house was completed about 1808. With the exception of the old dormitory at Athens, Felix Gilbert's is the oldest brick house north of Augusta. It is the oldest private dwelling house of brick. The western wing was added by Mr. Alexander after 1820. It is not only the oldest house, it is to this day one of the best built. It is said there are bricks enough in it to build two modern houses. It is well proportioned with windows in deep embrasures, lofty walls, and the old plastering, has quaint old fashioned ornaments which are interesting decorations to this day. Mrs. Felix Gilbert died, just as the house was nearing completion. She left an only child named Sarah. In the old Alexander grave yard, the first grave was that of a little girl Sarah, the oldest child of Mr. Felix Gilbert. His youngest was not called Sarah until

after the death of her little sister. Mr. Felix Gilbert did not long survive his wife. He left his daughter to the guardianship of her grandmother. Mrs. Hillhouse finally built the house now occupied by Mr. Gabriel Toombs, or the older portion of it, and there Sarah Gilbert spent her childhood. I have heard Mrs. Lewis Brown tell of seeing her running around the walks of that front garden to get warm, which her thrifty and industrious grandmother thought was better than dawdling over the fire.

After his brother's death, Mr. William Gilbert completed the brick house and lived in it. The two brothers had amassed a large fortune, but Felix Gilbert was the best manager, and after his death his brother was unfortunate enough to lose a good deal. Mr. Wm. Gilbert never married, though he lived until some time in the thirties of this century. The property of the brothers was never divided. I shall speak of Wm. Gilbert again in connection with our town clock.

In speaking of persons and families who have lived here, it will be better to go on into subsequent years and complete the account. Mr. Adam Alexander, who was married in Mr. Gabriel Toombs' house to Miss Sarah Gilbert, was a native of Sunbury, a place now classed among the dead towns of Georgia. His father was a Scotchman and a physician. I presume he is the Dr. Adam Alexander mentioned in the annals of the Revolution. He married a German lady, the daughter of an officer in the Austrian army. I have seen the album of her father and I judge from it, that he was a man of education and station. Dr. Alexander had but two children, one Mr. A. L. Alexander, the other Mrs. Anthony Porter of Savannah. Mr. Alexander was a graduate of Yale college, New Haven, and he met his wife then, when she was on a visit to her uncle Senator Hillhouse. In giving an account of Mr. Alexander, whom I knew well for about thirty years, I wish to testify to his many merits and accomplishments. He was never in public life, and therefore was not so widely and well known to all classes of people, but I do not think any man who ever lived in this county would have given to an educated stranger a more favorable opinion of the community than Mr. Alexander. He was a polished and accomplished gentleman, a very handsome man, a wit, and also a Christian and man of unbending integrity. He was also, in an unusual sense of the word, a man of liberal education. Every thing he had learned at college was made of practical value. As long as he lived, he read the New Testament daily in the original Greek.

He was, through his whole life, a remarkably prosperous man. Mr. Alexander's first wife, Miss Sarah Gilbert, was one of the best specimens of the Southern lady of antebellum days. She was a woman of culture, fond of the best reading, a woman of meek and gentle spirit, and her industry would have shown the falsity of the statement which has come from the North, that Southern women were lazy, a statement repeated so often and so coolly in the teeth of evidence, that I sometimes fear that the very descendants of the women thus slandered will begin to believe it.

As I have spoken of Mr. Alexander and his family I must not omit to mention his second wife who was Miss Marian Dunwoody. She was one of the best of the old time Southern housekeepers, one of the kindest and most benevolent of women and a devoted wife, a lady in every sense.

About fifty years after the establishment of the *Gazette*, it was edited by Mrs. Hillhouse's great grandson, Mr. J. H. Alexander, now a well known and prosperous business man in Augusta.

CHAPTER XVI

SETTLERS — HAYS, PRINCES, ABBOTTS, BEASLEYS, GOODES

THE GILBERTS illustrate again the fact that the settlers of Wilkes often came in large parties of kindred families. Gov. Gilmer shows that this was true of the Broad River settlers. From Gov. Gilmer's account of the Gilberts one would suppose that the parents of Wm. and Felix Gilbert came to Wilkes. Their family traditions do not support this. But there were sisters who came, whether married after, or before they came. One of these married Dr. Gilbert Hay, who gave name to the place Haywood, which so long was the home of Judge Andrews. This property belonged at first to Mr. Thomas Wingfield, but Judge Andrews used to say that the first settlement on it was made by John Colley, ancestor of the family of that name. This John Colley had two sons called France and Spain. Dr. Hay seems to have come into possession of Haywood some time in the nineties of the last century. He built the older or eastern portion of the old house and probably planted the fine avenue of sycamore, which however have nearly all died and been replaced by other trees. When I first remember the place, in about 1837 or 8, their spreading branches entirely concealed the house from the street. The western part of the house, the newer, was probably built early in this century. Dr. Hay and Dr. Abbott were the chief early physicians, and Dr. Hay's office or "shop," stood where the eastern cottage stands under the big oak though there was another, which I think he occupied later, and in which Judge Andrews held his law school afterwards. I have already told how in 1805, Dr. Hay acquired the land east of the avenue. The lot on which Mr. Green's house stands was added to Haywood much later. A Masonic Hall long stood between the site of Mr. Green's house and the street, and both Gen. Graves and Mr. J. R. Sneed unite in saying that in their recollection a school was at one time kept there. When it was removed, the lumber was used in building the house now belonging to Mr. Wm. Pope. That house was built by Mr. Berry, but was soon after bought by Dr. Felix Hay the son of Dr. Hay, who was the father of the first wives of Dr. J.J. Robertson and Mr. James Roddy Sneed. I used often to tell Judge Andrews that if I owned Haywood, I should covet Mr. Pope's bit of woods as much as Ahab did Nabeth's vineyard.

Judge Andrews said that Dr. Hay was a very high toned old

fellow, but somewhat boisterous in manner, a wealthy and influential citizen, a man of culture, and a physician of high standing. He was a great hunter. When Governor Clarke fought a duel with Crawford, Dr. Hay was his second. Judge Andrews said that when he himself came to Washington in 1821, Dr. Hay's was the first house passed on the North side of Main street as you came down the Lexington road. He said that Dr. Hay then owned all the country between the Lexington and Greensboro roads, (except the old Academy lot,) the present freeman's town, the cemetery lot and the lots around it to the old Norman place, also the present property of Mr. Wm. Pope and Mr. Charles Irvin. He had a wheat field surrounded by a high fence where Mr. Hines' house now stands. Dr. Hay was buried at Haywood, but the occupants of the old graveyard were removed by his descendants to our present cemetery. The children of Dr. Robertson were the last descendants of Dr. Hay who lived in Washington.

After Dr. Hay's death, Haywood was owned by Hopkins Brewer, a lawyer who was a partner of Alexander Pope Sr., for whom he named his son Brewer. Judge Andrews bought it about 1835.

Felix and Wm. Gilbert had two other sisters here. One married Mr. Andrew Shepherd, but died soon and then he married Miss Hillhouse, a sister of Mrs. Felix Gilbert. This lady used to visit Mrs. A. L. Alexander and was called "Aunt Shepherd." She was an erect active old lady, a pattern of old fashioned courtesy. Mrs. Abner Fluellen of Columbus, the Hansells, Bakers of Marietta, and the wife of the noted Dr. Woodrow, are her descendants.

Another sister married Mr. Henry Gibson. This family moved to Americus, (where the Reeses are her descendants,) except Mrs. Caroline Wingfield, her daughter. She lived here like a hermit at the south east corner of Spring and Liberty.

Mr. Oliver Prince, of whom I have spoken as the nephew of Mr. Hillhouse, built the house in which Dr. Simpson now lives. He left Washington about the time when Macon was laid out, and the account of him states that he was one of the commissioners who laid out that city. Judge Reese tells me, however, that he was living in Athens at the time of his death by shipwreck. In 1836, (I think) the vessel *Home* south bound, from New York, shipwrecked off the coast of North Carolina. Mr. Prince and his wife were on board and were lost. They left three children. The person who last saw him said that his parting words were a message to his daughter Virginia, who grew up to be the wife of Dr. James Green of Macon. The younger daughter Fanny, became Mrs. King of Roswell. I was in Macon when she was married and I remember a conundrum that was made. "Why is Miss Fanny Prince like queen Victoria's oldest son: Because she is a prince and will be a king." Miss Basiline Prince is the daughter of Mr. Prince's son Oliver, who married a sister of Chief Justice Jackson. The house which was bought by Mr. Alexander Pope Sr., who added the southern rooms, up and down stairs, was much improved by Mr. William Simpson.

Dr. Joel Abbott(1) came here from Connecticut in 1794 and gained a very wide practice. He was distinguished as a physician, and was appointed by Georgia as her medical representative in making the U. S. Dispensatory. He was also a representative of Georgia in Congress. He built the older portion of the house which gained celebrity as the home of Gen. Toombs, and is I think buried on the property. No monument marks his grave, but there is a monument to a daughter of his who married a Rembert, in the enclosure in which he is buried. Dr. Abbott had a daughter who married a Billups, and from her descended Col. Joel Abbott Billups of Madison, and his late daughter the wife of Mr. Thomas Gresham of Macon. The house of Dr. Abbott stood nearer to the street than the Toombs house, a portion having been moved back. I think the southern central part is the portion of the old Abbott house. For a while, after Dr. Abbott's death, Rev. Alexander Webster, who is buried in the vestibule of the Presbyterian church, lived in the house. Miss Ann Quigley then taught school in it. Afterwards William L. Harris, a cousin of Mr. S. H. Hardeman, bought the place and built the front rooms, making it a very handsome house for that time. Mr. Harris married Miss Semmes, the daughter of Col. Andrew G. Semmes. He finally moved to Mississippi and then the house was bought by Gen. Robert Toombs. Judge Andrews said he was a most valuable public spirited citizen. Mr. Harris became Chief Justice of Mississippi. Gen. Toombs made many successive additions to the house. He added the colonnade, and then the western wing and finally the eastern wing, and kitchen. This last was added after negroes became free. Finally, Mr. Dudley DuBose remodelled the interior, putting in the folding doors. He also built the greenhouse. A great deal of good company was entertained there by Gen. Toombs in ante bellum times. Nearly all the distinguished lawyers of that day in the state have drunk good wine and cracked good jokes in the old dining room (northwest room) down stairs. There is not a room in Georgia which would have more interesting, eloquent and witty talk to report, if it could echo what was said within its walls.

A part of the old house of Dr. Abbott was moved to what is now the property of Mr. Lowe on Alexander Avenue, and forms part of the house which then belonged to Mrs. Royland Beasly, the mother of Mrs. Cotting. This, Mrs. Cotting told me, is the northern part of the house. Mr. Beasley's family were among the oldest settlers of Wilkes. He had a brother, Ambrose

(1) Joel Abbott was a member of Congress, March 4, 1817-March 3, 1825.

Beasley, who was either killed or wounded, Mrs. Cotting thought the former, at the battle of Kettle Creek. Mr. Beasley's sister, Miss Patsy Beasly, is one of the women who rode on horseback to Virginia: After she came here with her brothers, her father died in Culpepper Virginia, and it was necessary for some one to go and settle up the estate. Miss Patsy Beasley took the journey and when she got to Virginia, found a husband, and did not return. Mr. Royland Beasley was clerk of the court here. His wife was a Miss Lennard, also of a family which came early. The Lennards had a house which stood on Main street just opposite where the Methodist church now stands. The property on which Mr. William Sims now lives belonged to them. Mrs. Cotting tells me that her mother was turned out of the Methodist church because in marrying her father, she did not "marry in the Lord." At the N.W. Corner of Spring and Main Sts. there was a store kept in a large framed building by Lennard and Beasley. It was burned in the fire of 1841. Capt. Archie Wingfield's first wife was a Miss Lennard, and the firm afterwards became Lennard and Wingfield. The daughters of John B. Weems are descendants of Capt. W. and his first wife. The mother of Messrs. T. M. and T. B. Green was the daughter of this Mr. Lennard. Mrs. Beasley who is still living with her daughter Mrs. Jackson (in Jones county I think) is, since the death of Dr. T. N. Poullain the oldest living native of Washington. She was a good woman, noted for her skill and kindness in nursing the sick.

Several families of Goodes came from Virginia to Georgia. One of them settled a place called Chantilly on the hill to the west of mineral or Sulpher Spring. Mr. Samuel Goode, was the owner and I think builder of Chantilly. This spring, which gave its name to Spring street was noted in the early history of the county, and people used to come here from Savannah in the Summer to drink the waters. It is mentioned in Morse's old Geography published in 1796. A number of later comers have said that there was once a hotel at the Spring called Chantilly, supposing they had heard so. The older citizens to whom I have talked, who remember Chantilly, do not say that it was a hotel. Mr. J. R. Sneed, to whom I have lately talked, says it was not a hotel within his recollection. He came here in 1819, about six months old. Miss Emma Barnett, whose family were related to the Goodes, does not remember hearing of a hotel. This Mr. Samuel Goode was the ancestor of Mr. Samuel W. Goode now a real estate agent in Atlanta. There is an old family burying ground in the wood near the mineral spring and one tombstone with an inscription showing that the sleeper underneath was Mrs. Eliza Goode, the wife of Samuel W. Goode, and that she died in 1817, aged 33. While I am writing this article, Mr. Anderson, postmaster of Washington, received a letter from a gentleman connected with the college in Middlebury Vermont, who seems to be getting up facts about alumni for a catalogue, and who inquired about Hamilton Goode a graduate 1822, who was from Washington, Georgia. This is probably the father or grandfather of Mr. Samuel W. Goode of Atlanta. He lived here some time after Judge Andrews came, in the house now occupied by Mrs. Wilkes Sanders. He must have gone away some time in the twenties, or early in the thirties, for Judge Andrews occupied that house in 1835 just before buying Haywood. Also, Judge Andrews followed Mr. Edward Burton in the occupancy. I think that Mrs. Eliza Goode was a Napier and aunt of Miss Maria Randolph. In the old records, there is a "Thomas Napper" evidently Napier, that being the old pronunciation. One of his daughters married old Bob Randolph, another the father of the late Dr. T. N. Hamilton of Athens, still another a Mr. Kelsey. The sons of this Napier, and the Kelseys moved to Macon, and were well known, rich citizens, Leroy Napier and Skelton Napier. Mrs. Kelsey was the mother of Mrs. Macarty and Mrs. Geo. W. Price of Macon formerly, now of Atlanta. Mrs. Price and her sisters, Misses Harriet and Emily Kelsey, were natives of Washington.

Hamilton Goode, the graduate of 1822, was evidently the son of Mrs. Eliza Goode buried in 1817, who must have been married in 1801 or 1802. Thus it is probable that her husband built the place Chantilly very early in this century. The house was standing when Mrs. Vickers came in 1836 but the Goodes had gone.

There were at least three families of Goodes who came to Georgia, but their immigration was wholly independent. To one of them, belonged my grandmother, the daughter of John Goode and Francis Hunter. Judge Andrews used to say that he and Hamilton Goode whom he called "Judge Goode" could trace no kinship. Since that time, Professor George Brown Goode, Curator of the Smithsonian Institute, has written a book giving an account of the old Virginia family of Goodes, and tracing them in this country. He traces them back to England and the reign of one of the Edwards, and shows that they were entitled to a coat of arms. His account shows that all the Georgia Goodes are of the stock. But it is necessary to go such a long way back towards Noah, to establish any relationship, that it is merely a matter of antiquarian interest.

Note: Since writing my last article, I have learned that Mr. Samuel W. Goode of Atlanta, is the nephew of Hamilton Goode, called here Judge Goode. His father was Samuel W. Goode, his grandfather of the same name was the owner of Chantilly. Also, Mrs. Eliza Goode, the wife of the owner of Chantilly, was a Miss Hamilton, and was the granddaughter, not the daughter, of Thomas Napier.

CHAPTER XVII

THE LONGS

AFTER THE DEATH of Mr. Thomas Wingfield, who came in 1784, and built a house near the big gully, the house was bought by Col. Nicholas Long who is I think one of the most interesting of the early settlers. He was from North Carolina. Gov. Gilmer says that he was too young to do service in the Revolution but old enough to sympathize with the cause of Liberty. Gov. G. says also that he married, and immediately afterwards settled in Wilkes county. Mr. Long was on the Grand Jury which in 1785 censured the Legislature of Georgia because they did not vote money to support the Federal government. As he must then have been twenty-one years old, but could hardly have been much older, if Gov. Gilmer's statement is true, he must have married and emigrated young. Col. Long is represented to have been a polished gentleman, whose manners had, I judge, a little of that ceremonious politeness which marked a gentleman of the old school and is sometimes too much forgotten in this day. But there was nothing artificial or insincere about him; all accounts make him a man of great kindness of heart. Gov. Gilmer says he was "the most accomplished man of the southern country," that "his tall well formed person, expressive features, polished courteous manners, kind temper, cultivated taste and good understanding, made him the most admired gentleman of his day." All traditions of the old people tell us that the Longs were at the head of society when here and it was a society that contained a number of refined gentlemen. Col. Long who seems to have been a man of fine business judgment, made a large fortune by dealing in land. He bought and sold, not merely in Georgia but in other states, Tennessee and North Carolina; and some of these lands were disposed of in that ultimately illusive manner, on a lease of 99 years which makes the tenant forget that he does not own it in fee simple. Some of these 99 year leases are about beginning to expire with the close and beginning of a century, and some descendants of Col. Long are creating an alarm in some cities by showing a consciousness of the kind of title to the land on which they were built. One of them, noted as a litigant in our Supreme Court, was in Washington during the past year looking into the records in the Ordinary's Office.

Judge Andrews said that Col. Long was an army contractor with Farish Carter of Milledgeville in the war of 1812. Gov. Gilmer says, that the U. S. government appointed him Colonel of the 43d Regiment of Infantry in the war of 1812, but that the regiment was not fully raised and never in the field or Col. Long in command. Gov. Gilmer, who was appointed a lieutenant in this regiment, speaks "of having been at the barracks at Washington." Where these barracks were, it is impossible to tell now. It is perhaps in place here to say that there is still one woman in this county who draws a pension for her husband's services in the war of 1812. This is Mrs. Patrick Barnett. Within a few years there were two or three others, but Mrs. Barnett is the only one left now.

Gov. Gilmer tells us that the land dealings of Col. Long brought him into some connection with the Yazoo companies. Gov. G. does not attribute to him any complicity with the corrupt practices of some of the agents of the companies, but he says that these created such a storm of unpopularity for any one who had been connected with the companies, that Col. Long was never elected to any office. Judge Andrews said that he was a very fine stately old gentleman: He owned a plantation called *Belmont* which gave its name to Belmont Creek. crossing the Mallorysville road a few miles north of Washington.

Col. Long added to the house which Mr. Thomas Wingfield had built. Gov. Gilmer says that "his house and grounds were in better style than those elsewhere in any part of the county." I used to be in the house often when Mrs. Mary Ellington lived in it, and made it more attractive by the exquisite neatness of her housekeeping, and it always appeared to me a fine old house. There was a side porch on the north side of the house, from which a walk ran into the garden through beds of old fashioned flowers and continuing under a fine grape arbor, led to a path through the wood down to a beautiful and bold spring, which doubtless determined the place of the original settlement. In fine weather the view from this porch was charming.

In the beginning of this century, the Moravian school at Bethlehem Pennsylvania was the fashionable school for young ladies, and Miss Margaret Long was sent to it. Many years after, in the middle of this century, two Washington girls were again sent to this school. They were Miss Eliza Pope, afterwards Mrs. John Harvie Hull and Miss Mary Willis, the lady who afterwards received and was worthy of the beautiful monument of the Mary Willis Library. When Miss Margaret Long came home from school she was a great belle, and what not infrequently happened to belles of that day, had a challenge to a duel sent about her, but as I understand the

fight was averted by friends. I must not forget to say that
Col. Long had the first carriage brought to Washington, and it
was entered from behind. Margaret Long married Mr. Thomas
Telfair a son of Governor Edward Telfair. He became United
States Senator.(1) The house now occupied by Mr. George Beal,
and formerly by Mr. Thomas Callaway, was built by Col. Long
for his daughter. They were probably married about 1806, and
in 1813 Thomas Telfair became a member of Congress, where he
continued to go until 1817. In his last term the members of
Congress voted themselves increases of pay, and Georgia prompt-
ly requested them all to stay at home after that. Mr. Thomas
Telfair who had been a useful and active member of Congress
wrote a very dignified letter to his constituents. He took his
wife to Savannah and somehow I have not been able to understand
how, his sisters, the Misses Telfair came to live in the house
which had been built for him and his wife. I suppose they may
have come here for the summer and concluded to remain.

Col. Long and his wife both died of consumption, she first,
and he afterwards, in 1819. They had two sons, one Richard
Long, a young gentleman who had every advantage of education.
He married Miss Nancy Hay the daughter of Dr. Gilbert Hay. He
moved to Florida where his wife died of a cancer. At one time
Richard Long practised law here, and was sent to the Legislature. John Long moved to Washington county. Miss Eliza Long
was the first wife of the father of Gen. Dudley DuBose and
Mrs. Hunter. Miss Sarah Long married Mr. James Rembert
and moved to Memphis. While here, Mr. Rembert was a member of
the Legislature. Miss Eugenia Long was the first wife of Mr.
Lock Weems, but she died and he married Miss Shepherd daughter
of Andrew Shepherd, and moved to Columbus.

A daughter of Mr. Thomas Telfair and Miss Margaret Long
married one of the Cobbs from Columbia county (where John Cobb
the ancestor of Howell and Thomas R. R. Cobb first settled) and
the only descendant of Thomas Telfair was then Miss Alberta
Cobb. She went to Savannah with her aunts, the Misses Telfair,
and would doubtless have inherited much of the very large fortune which these ladies left to religious, and benevolent
purposes, but she ran away and was married to Mr. Arnold. I
remember well when this runaway match occurred. It occasioned
a sensation, for she was regarded as a great heiress. She
was in all married three times, and left a son and daughter by
her last marriage. She was proud and obstinate, and the aunts
were obstinate, and they never became reconciled. When the
aunts died, her son Telfair Wetter contested the will by which
so much money was left to the Presbyterian churches of Savannah

(1) Thomas Telfair was not in the Senate but was in Congress March 4,
1813 to March 3, 1817. He died Feb. 18, 1818. Edward Telfair, his
father was twice Governor of Georgia, Jan. 9, 1786-1787 and again
Nov. 9, 1790-1793.

and Augusta and the Savannah Library, but finally the Supreme court upheld the will.

During the past year 1889, Mr. Telfair Wetter, the great grandson of Gov. Telfair and Col. Nicholas Long, came to Washington and examined our records to get some links in a chain of evidence he was forging to recover some of the lands which Col. Long had somewhere leased for 99 years. He was a man of fine appearance and manners as became the aristocratic stock which he sprung from. Whether he would make money I cannot tell, but he has shown remarkable energy in trying to recover it. In the Ordinary's office, there are hundreds of packages of records of marriage licenses, all tied up carefully, and through these Mr. Telfair Wetter searched day after day, and he became quite a familiar figure. When I go into Capt. Anthony's office he constantly tells me that I remind him of Mr. Wetter by my interest in the records. He found the marriage license of Thomas Telfair and Margaret Long among the records.

CHAPTER XVIII

BRINGING THE GOSPEL TO WILKES

THE FIRST evangelists of our county were Baptists. They were born in North Carolina but they seem to have been converted and baptized in Columbia, so being myself a native of Columbia, I shall claim that Columbia sent over and started the spread of the Gospel in Wilkes. Columbia had the first organized church north of Augusta, old Kiokee Baptist church, which I remember seeing from the porch of my father's house, and to which I was first taken to church. I remember seeing, on a subsequent visit to Appling, the grave of Daniel Marshall the early evangelist of Columbia. There was a great square monument over it, through which a tree had forced its way. I looked at it with a good deal of interest for my grandmother named her youngest child Daniel Marshall, for the old preacher. He was the Doctor D. M. Andrews who was widely known and much beloved in this county, and the name remained in the family, for my cousin is Daniel Marshall Andrews to this day. Rev. Daniel Marshall was a convert of George Whitfield. I am disposed to think, from this commemoration of my grandmother, that the old preacher used to come up and preach occasionally in benighted Wilkes. But just before the Revolution, Silas Mercer came up from Columbia to settle. When the war came on, he went back to his native Halifax, North Carolina, and there was no gospel preached in Wilkes until the war was over. In the old record of Barnard Heard as Register and Probate of the county, there are copies of wills made and proved, all through the Revolution. They all begin with that language of quaint formal piety, characteristic of old fashioned wills, but there was no gospel preached here. Silas Mercer came back as soon as things were quiet, but before he reached Wilkes the Rev. Sanders Walker came up from Columbia, who persisted in the project of evangelizing Wilkes. Sanders Walker is said to have been by nature a man of fiery temper, but the Gospel changed him so completely, that he was called the "meek Sanders Walker." The use of the Gospel is to change men's hearts, and that it actually does, so it is a fact which ought to prove itself, if it is a true Gospel.

Sanders Walker came here in 1783. He seemed to have been at once recognized for a valuable citizen, for they put him straightway on the Grand Jury list: and in 1785 he was drawn on that jury with Governor George Matthews for a foreman which gave the Legislature a lecture for not voting money for the expenses of the General Government. They did not talk very meek, but I suspect that brother Sanders Walker with all his meekness could talk very boldly when he thought duty demanded it. Sanders Walker settled about Fishing Creek, and in 1783 helped to organize Fishing Creek church, the oldest church in Wilkes county, and except old Kiokee, which was formed in 1772, the oldest in the up country. It is now one hundred and seven years old. It has been moved, when rebuilt, but not far from the original site. Not long after, in 1784, Greenwood church was organized. This is now in Lincoln county, but just over the line. There is one thing about the old Baptist Churches. Wherever you hear of them at first, there, or very near there, you find them a hundred years afterwards. Then they have their church books, and I think some of the most interesting old records of Wilkes county must be those of the old Baptist Churches. In looking up this subject, I find a good deal of difference between Baptists and Methodists. The latter have not these old records, and it is difficult to locate the early Methodist Churches. I do not mean that Methodism did not take deep root for I think they did. The labors of the early Methodist preachers form a pathetic story, especially what is told in the *Journal of Bishop Asbury.*

Baptist preachers did a very hard work and were paid almost nothing. A touching story is told of the wife of Rev. James Matthews. Mr. Matthews was pastor of the church at Clarke's Station and lived on a farm at Clarke's Creek, from about 1788. He used to preach at Rocky Spring Church, now in Lincoln, and at Newford, and when he was absent, on this work, his wife used to hear wolves at night howling in the woods around the log cabin in which she and her children lived. Mrs. Matthews it is said complained much of her husband's absences, and on one occasion he determined to take her with him. A glorious meeting was in progress and she saw the good that he was doing, and was so much impressed by it, that she never afterwards complained when he left her to go and preach. This good woman was the ancestor of Col. Matthews of Oglethorpe, a noble Confederate officer, well known as a lawyer.

The Baptist preachers were scarcely paid anything at all and they did not stop for that, but kept on preaching the Gospel, pay or no pay, but somehow nearly all that I can read of in the early annals managed to collect a little independence, and in fact some got rich, and it was not always from marrying rich widows. I account for it in this way. Land was abundant, and the best was on rivers and water courses, and the Baptist churches were placed in such positions because "there was much water there." The Baptist preachers were thrifty and industrious

men, and so in the end they gained a competence. In 1784, the
Georgia Baptist Association was organized at Kiokee Church with
only five churches, of which two, Greenwood and Fishing Creek,
were in Wilkes. Then in the next year 1785, Phillips Mills and
Whatleys Mills Churches were organized in Wilkes. Whatley's
Mills is now Bethesda, of which my grandfather and grandmother
were members. I will mention that this church which is now in
Greene county, has an old brick building with curious old
twisted chimneys, which is exactly of the age of our Wilkes
County Court House built in 1817. Phillips Church is in many
respects one of the most interesting old churches in the county. Its records are complete from the day that the first sixteen members met in the mill of the old Revolutionary soldier
Joel Phillips and organized a church, June 10, 1785, one hundred and five years ago come next June. I do not know whether
Joel Phillips, who kicked the Tory out of the church was or was
not a member then. Also, we can turn to the record of July 7,
1787 and find that on that day, a young fellow eighteen years
of age named Jesse Mercer, son of the pastor Silas Mercer made
his appearance before the church assembled in conference and
relating his experience of grace applied for admission and was
received. This is one of the most interesting old records in
the county, and I wish the brethren at Phillips would put it in
our Mary Willis Library for safe keeping, where it would be
treasured as if it were gold. Silas Mercer was the founder of
this church and served it eleven years as pastor. He was followed by Jesse Mercer, who was its pastor for thirty seven
years. Jesse Mercer was ordained in the old church, which however, they no longer occupy. I have a great many times been
present at the conference of Phillips church. I was there when
the present pastor Rev. J. R. Young preached his first sermon
twenty five years ago. There are five Baptist churches in our
present Wilkes county that are over a hundred years old. They
are Fishing creek, Phillips, Ebenezer, Sardis and Clark station. As the Mercers Silas and Jesse, father and son, served
Phillips church as pastor, so Sardis church had Rev. Enoch
Callaway as pastor for 31 years, and since then has had his
son, Rev. Brantley Callaway, the present pastor, who has served
it for 20 years. But this is excelled by the record of Kiokee
church in which Daniel Marshall was succeeded as pastor by his
son Abram Marshall, and he by his son Jabez P. Marshall.
 There was not a church in Washington of any denomination until the twenties of the present century. There was preaching
here occasionally in the chapel or church, part of the old
brick Academy, on Mercer Hill. Mrs. Vickers reports Captain
Lewis Brown, one of our old inhabitants, of whom I shall speak
further on, as saying that when Rev. Hope Hull used to preach
in the old brick Academy, he could be heard distinctly on what

is now the public square. The old court house was also used to
preach in, situated in what is now Gen. Heard's garden. In the
life of Rev. Jesse Mercer it is mentioned that he used to
preach about once a week in the old brick Academy. But in the
early history of the county the country churches were the active organizations, and the town people, when they were church
members, belonged to country churches. I am afraid the gospel
did not flourish much in Washington. There was a theatre here
long before there was a church. It stood just north of the
present Methodist church, and a cross street led to it from
Main street. My aunt, Mrs. Garnett Andrews, used to say she
had some dim recollections of a curtain and scenery in the old
theatre. The alley was planted with trees. In Morse's old
Geography published in 1796, the author gives some account of
the diversions of the people in the various places which he
describes. He says in the up country of Georgia they were fond
of cock fighting. The up country of Georgia in 1796 was Wilkes
county and the counties formed from it.

CHAPTER XIX

PLANTING THE GOSPEL, Continued.

I THINK THERE can be no doubt that religion in Wilkes County was largely indebted to Jesse Mercer. Some years ago when Judge Andrews told me of his recollections of Wilkes, I had the curiosity to ask him what he thought of Mr. Mercer as a preacher. He described him as a man of wonderful native vigor of mind, and especially on the subject of religious experience, a powerful preacher. I have always been very much interested in reading and hearing of Mercer. He was a very intimate friend of my grandfather administered on the estate of my grandfather Andrews, and was in fact the guardian of my mother. My mother was just the age of his daughter Miriam who died in childhood and was her playmate. I suppose that this gave him an affectionate feeling towards her. She called him "Uncle Jesse" and his first wife "Aunt Sabry," and taught me in my childhood to call him "Uncle Jesse". I have an old album belonging to my mother in which he wrote four or five pages giving an account of the conversion of his first wife Mrs. Sabrina Mercer.

I remember Mr. Mercer coming to my mother's house when I was a little child, and that a pitcher of apple toddy sat on the hearth prepared for him. I remember when the napkin was raised from it the glimpse of the apples bobbing up and down, and the savory smell that arose, as if it were yesterday.

When the temperance agitation began Mr. Mercer gave up all use of spirits, with the sound judgment and high character that marked him and doubtless gave him his influence. I do not suppose he had ever misused spirits, for he was a man of great moderation in all things. Nothing shows a greater change in public manners than the social disuse of spirits. My grandfather who was a Baptist, distilled peach brandy for use and sale, and I have heard my uncle say that when he brought preachers home from church, the first thing was to go to the sideboard and lay out a dram for all.

When my uncle and I talked of the old memories of the county and town he told the following: "In those days there was in the county an excellent and universally esteemed old Baptist preacher Rev. James Armstrong. In those days all our ancestors drank spirits, as the temperance agitation did not begin until long afterwards. Many an old Baptist brother made peach brandy and whiskey and so did brother Armstrong, who like an honest old man as he was, took great pains with his whisky and it was generally considered the best liquor to be had in the county and in fact it went by the name of "Jimmy Armstrong". On one occasion, there was a 4th of July celebration in the grove between Judge Andrews' and W. A. Pope's, and Capt. Beard, (a gentleman living at the Randolph place) who was a hilarious old codger amused the company very much by giving as a toast "May we all be animated by the spirits of the Rev. James Armstrong."

I have spoken of changes in habit and custom. Some of the early Baptists practised the ceremony of footwashing and the following story is told of one of the early settlers, George Willis, the grandfather of Mrs. Lucy Simpson and most of the Willis family living in this county in our day. It was the fashion for men to wear knee breeches, long stockings and low shoes in the early part of this century. One day Mr. George Willis carefully dressed up for the occasion was going to Sardis church. He passed by a place where he was making charcoal, and he saw that the fire had gained so that it was likely to burn up the wood altogether instead of making it into charcoal. This was like the case of an ox or ass fallen into the ditch and so Brother George Willis stepped up and extinguished the fire. In so doing, he got his stockings covered with charcoal dust, but they were dark and did not show it. He then rode on to church, where a foot washing was part of the programme. Mr. George Willis who was to take part in the ceremony removed his stocking, in the presence of the congregation, when to his dismay and discomfiture, he found that the charcoal had sifted through the threads of his stockings and that his leg and foot were not soiled only but fairly black as if they had not been subjected to ablution with soap and water for a long time. I leave the reader to imagine the mortification of Brother Willis, the astonishment of the brethren, and the giggling and snickering of the congregation, as some participator in the ceremony dryly remarked, "I think Brother Willis's feet need washing."

In speaking of Jesse Mercer, I must not omit to mention his hymn book, *Mercer's Cluster,* which I suppose was the first book published by a person living in Wilkes. I have a special reason for interest in it, for my grandmother, Mrs. Nancy Goode Andrews, wrote two of the hymns in it. Unfortunately, I can identify only one of which the first line is, "Sister is come and I'll relate." I believe Mrs. Maude Andrews Ohl, and perhaps Miss E. F. Andrews are the only ones of her descendants who have published verses, though there are several book makers and scribblers of various kinds among them. I am afraid my grandmother's verses come under Carlyle's description of "rhyme that had no inward necessity to be rhymed, but should have told us at once without any jingle what it meant."

Mercer's Cluster was a useful book and I am sure it would be preserved with great care if somebody would give a copy of it to the Library. I have been much interested to know when the first edition was published. The *Life of Mercer* merely tells us that prior to 1817, when the *Cluster* was published in Philadelphia and copyright obtained, three editions had been published in Augusta, amounting in all to 2500 copies. I judge that the first edition, which was not bound, must have been printed early in this century. The edition of 1817 contained 2500 copies, and three others followed, the last in 1835. If all were as large editions as that of 1817, twelve or fifteen thousand copies of the book must have been circulated. The *Life of Mercer* says it was used in Alabama and Mississippi.

The Baptist church in Washington was not erected until after there were both Methodist and Presbyterian churches in the town, but I think it will be better for me to complete what is to be said, about the work of the Baptists. Silas Mercer had I think lived near the Phillips Mills church and there Jesse Mercer lived until about 1807, when he seems to have moved into Greene County near Whatley's Mills church, now called Bethesda. It was there that he was so intimately associated with my grandfather's family. In 1817, he moved to Powelton. My grandmother, who had become a widow, had moved to Powelton, and for a time he boarded with her, as I have heard my mother say. In 1826 or 1827, he moved to Washington, and shortly after married his second wife, Mrs. Ann (or Nancy) Simons. He bought the site of the old brick Academy, and built a house there, which was moved and another built on its site by Mr. N. Wylie in 1848. Mrs. Simons was the widow of a Captain Simons, who, Judge Andrews said, had been a wagon master under Gen. Jackson at the battle of New Orleans. He was a Jew. Mr. Mercer himself, in the obituary which he wrote of his wife, said she was married to Mr. Simons in 1798. She was the daughter of Mr. John Mills living on Little River. As Mr. Mercer got the greater part of the property which founded Mercer University from this wife, it is interesting to know something of Capt. Simons who made it. He lived five or six miles east of Washington on the Augusta road. Not far from his house, there is a steep hill over which the old Augusta road used to run. When all the merchandise and crops were transported in wagons this hill was the great dread of all up country wagoners going to and from Augusta. The old house in which Mr. Simons lived is very near the road. I saw it two or three weeks ago and I also saw "Simon's Hill." The old man used to be much troubled by being called on to help pull wagons out of the mud.

He was I suppose a man of strong plain sense, for he made a fortune and was sent to the Legislature, but he was a very uneducated man. Judge Andrews said that he could not read, and on one occasion Mr. Simons picked up a paper upside down; and looking at the pictures of vessels, he remarked that there must have been a great storm somewhere at the North. I presume his rough irreligious ways must have been a great trouble to his wife, and that she was much happier with Mr. Mercer. But he left her all his money to dispose as she pleased, and so it went to Mercer University. In Capt. Simonds' large old house, there is a big room upstairs called to this day the ball room. He is buried on a hill not far from his house in a small enclosure surrounded by a substantial rock wall, but there is no monument. The grave was in a field, but trees have grown up around it so that it is no longer visible from the road. I saw the grave a few weeks ago and a desolate looking place it is, and so I think Mrs. Mercer's grave is separated from those of both husbands. She lies in the Baptist Church enclosure in Washington. When Mr. Mercer buried her there, he doubtless expected to be placed by her; and for my part, I think it is a pity he was not.

She was an excellent wife very careful of her husband's comfort and clothing. It is said that when Mr. Mercer went to the tailor for new clothes Mrs. Mercer always went with him and was very particular to order that the backs of his waistcoats should be made of the best yellow cloth. Yellow was her favorite color and always graced the ribbons of her best bonnet and cap.

While Mr. Mercer lived in Washington the *Christian Index* was at one time edited and published by him in this place. He seems to have taken charge of the paper at the request of others. It is of local interest to remember that the *Index* was published in the house which stood on the site of the brick store of Irvin, Callan & Co., S. W. corner of Main and Depot streets. Mr. Mercer bought the place and also bought a new press and type. The Rev. W. H. Stokes came here to live, as assistant editor. I am told that in 1835, five papers were published in this place. Two of these were the *Christian Index* and a Temperance paper which was published at the *Index* Office. The paper gave Mr. Mercer a good deal of work and also subjected him to pecuniary loss. In 1840 he gave the press and other materials to the Baptist Convention and the publication office was moved to Penfield.

The Baptist Church in Washington was organized in 1828, with ten members who were dismissed from Phillips Church. Thus old Phillips Church is the parent church of the one here. Mr. Mercer was its first pastor. He died in 1841. From the minutes of the Georgia Baptist Association I find that its subsequent pastors have been, Dr. N. M. Crawford, Rev. L. J. Robert, Rev. Vincent R. Thornton, Rev. H. A. Tupper, Rev. B. W. Whilden, Rev. J. M. Springer, Rev. J. J. Brantly, Rev. H. A. Whitman, Rev. S. G. Hillyer, Rev. W. M. Harris the present pastor who came in 1887. Dr. Tupper who was a native of Charleston served the church from 1853 to 1872 longer than any other pastor. He was much beloved by Christians of all names and will always be affectionately remembered in Washington.

As I have been much encouraged in writing this account of the Baptists, by the following circumstance; it is perhaps not amiss for me to state it. When Dr. Tupper was about to leave Washington, he preached a farewell sermon. All the churches were closed and the Baptist Church was crowded. It was an affecting sermon and occasion, and I thought it would interest the general public, so I wrote an account of it for the *Christian Index* and signed it, "Presbyterian". Dr. Tupper had been appointed Secretary of the Foreign Mission Board at Richmond, Va., and those who had appointed him wished to show the Baptist Churches the reputation he had where he was best known. They thought the article I had written for the *Index* well suited for their purpose, so they printed thousands of copies on slips of paper and sent them all over the Southern States.

In Mercer's *Life*, we find the statements: that in 1832 the members of the Washington church were 49; in 1835, 93; in 1840, 87. It is stated that in 1835, the church sent $600 to the Georgia Association for benevolent purposes. Of the 63 members in 1835, a portion were of course negroes who had little to give.

CHAPTER XX

HOW METHODISTS BROUGHT THE GOSPEL

THAT THE YEAR 1784 was marked in Wilkes by a rush of the best class of immigrants becomes more strongly confirmed as we examine the records of family history. This same year 1784 was also noted by an event which had much effect in the end on our history in Wilkes, though it occurred in Baltimore, then so far away through slow communications. This was the ordination of Francis Asbury as Methodist Bishop. Bishop Asbury was prominent in bringing the Gospel to Wilkes county. He made no less than seventeen journeys to Georgia, in nearly every one of which he came to some part of old Wilkes. Notwithstanding the personal connection of John and Charles Wesley and George Whitfield with Savannah, there was no plant of genuine Methodism put to growing, until it was set out among the Virginians and Carolinians who settled Wilkes county. I have fortunately been able to borrow from my valued friend Rev. J. S. Bryan a copy of *Asbury's Journal* printed in 1821. It is a book of exceeding interest, especially when read by the aid of local history and tradition.

In a few weeks after the ordination of Bishop Asbury, a conference was held in North Carolina at which a Methodist preacher was sent to Georgia. His name was Beverly Allen, and he had been a traveling preacher in Virginia since 1782. He seems to have had a brother in Wilkes (now Elbert) and his work was probably confined to the up country. His work here occupied the year 1785. This was the year in which Phillips and Ebenezer Baptist churches were founded, and in which the first Georgia Baptist association was held, the year in which the first court house and jail of Wilkes county were built.

Beverly Allen was a very fine looking man, an orator of much power, of zeal as preacher, and he must have made many friends as subsequent events showed. The historian of Georgia Methodism tells us, however that he did not accomplish much for religion. He reported seventy conversions. He was sent to South Carolina for 1786. This first Methodist preacher soon proved an apostate. I will anticipate by telling his whole story, which while ceasing to be Methodism, is still a very interesting part of the history of what was original Wilkes. In 1791, he was in Carolina, and in 1792 he was expelled from the conference for criminal conduct. He then came over to Elbert, which had been cut off from Wilkes in 1790, and entered into the business of merchandise with his brother Billy Allen. They had a store on the road between Fishdam Ford on Broad river and the Cherokee Ford on the Savannah. They became involved in debt, but went to Augusta to buy more goods, with their money, instead of using it to discharge their debts. A creditor outside of the state applied to the U. S. courts, and the U. S. Marshal, who was the father of our distinguished John Forsyth, went to arrest them while in Augusta. They shut themselves up in a room and when Mr. Forsyth forced his way in, he was shot on the threshold by Beverly Allen. The Allens escaped to Elbert where the sheriff of that county soon sought to arrest Beverly Allen on a charge of murder. Wm. Barnett was sheriff (one of the Virginia Barnetts, our Wilkes Wm. Barnett buried at Smyrna church, was a North Carolinian,) and he had to burn a house to arrest Beverly Allen, who was concealed in it. Sympathy in Elbert was with the Allens, for in those days news traveled slowly and the circumstances were imperfectly understood. Sheriff Barnett did not consider his prisoner safe, and he tried to bring him to the jail at Washington, but after starting found that he would be stopped on the road, so he returned to Elberton. That night, he greatly strengthened the guard round the jail, but a mob of 200 men broke it open and released the Allens. Beverly Allen fled to Kentucky, which was nearly a wilderness, and he was never tried for his crime. His brother, against whom there was no criminal charge, lived and died in Elbert. These last events took place in 1794, the year in which the common was sold.

In 1786, the conference in North Carolina sent two preachers to Georgia, both Virginians, John Major and Thomas Humphries. They were good and zealous men, and at the end of the year they reported to conference 430 members. Henry Park, the ancestor of the presiding elder of this district in 1890, was among the converts of 1786 one hundred and four years ago. He lived in what is now Elbert county. This conference, which met in North Carolina, then made Georgia a district. The Washington circuit was one of two circuits in Georgia and it embraced the territory north of Augusta. So of course they had a presiding elder for 1789. His name was Richard Ivy, and the two preachers were Thomas Humphreys and Moses Park. They reported 1100 additions. The greater number of these were from Wilkes county.

The people who settled Wilkes had pretty largely Presbyterian training but a good many things had contributed to demoralize them. They had gone through with a seven years war in which most of them were fighters, they were settling a new country in which there were of course none of the recognized restraints, and thus they were in just the condition to need stirring preaching. The Methodist preachers came before the Presbyterians, and though they had not so high a standard of education as the Presbyterians, their life was and still is such as to give them unrivalled knowledge of one subject of the highest importance to them, the knowledge of human nature. They certainly looked for success to attacks upon Calvinism, and I think they really owed some, perhaps a good deal, to the fact that the Presbyterian and Baptist preachers of that day sometimes preached Calvinism theoretically, rather than practically.

The year 1788 was that in which the Baptist churches of Sardis and Clark's station were organized and it is also marked by the first visit of Bishop Asbury to Georgia, and the first conference in the state. The part which Wilkes played in the planting of Methodism is shown by the fact that the first six Conferences in Georgia were all held within the boundaries of original Wilkes, and all except the very first, within our present Wilkes. Bishop Asbury was present and presided in all. The first was held in the fork of the Broad and Savannah Rivers, in what is now Elbert county, near the site of old Petersburg. Gen. David Meriwether was then living in the Forks and joined the church that year. The next two conferences, those of 1789 and 1790, were held at Grant's meeting house. One of these, the conference of 1790 was just a hundred years before the conference which will meet here the present year, and the house in which it was held was the first Methodist Church built in Ga., so it seems to me of a good deal of interest to know the actual site of that house. In our records in the ordinary's office, we find the names of Daniel Grant, Thomas Grant, on juries. They were father and son, and they came to Georgia in 1784. They lived on the Double Wells, or Powelton road, between the place where Captain John Wingfield lives now, and Moore's Mill on Little River. The home of the Grant's was on the western side of the road. The place was bought from one of the descendants of Daniel Grant by Mr. John Pettus; the father of Mrs. Lucy Reese and Mrs. Mary Cozart. He bought it, Mrs. Reese thinks, about 1820. She spent her childhood in the old house of Mr. Grant. Her father removed to Washington when his children were still young. She remembers the old store of the Grants, in which they laid the foundation of a large fortune for those days, but has no recollection of the old church. There was, she thinks, a Methodist church called "Piny Grove" church, between their home and town. As the family of Mr. Pettus were Presbyterians, they were not of course so much interested in the old associations of the place with early Methodists. Mrs. Reese tells me within the past year, she visited the old place. The store of the Grants once stood at the fork of the' road and turning to the right or west, the house was reached. This house, in which Bishop Asbury was entertained many times in his seventeen trips to Georgia, has long since been removed, but like most of the houses built by the old Virginia settlers, it had a cellar, and a depression in a field, in which lie some bricks and other rubbish, still marks its site. I think it probable that the meeting house was near the store. In the account of the first conference at Grants, in 1789, Bishop Asbury tells us, "Here we have a house for public worship and also one at Meriwethers." Two days before, he was at Scott's on Little River and he said in his Journal, "Here they have built us a large chapel." Thus in 1789, there were three Methodist churches or regular preaching places in Georgia. But I learn from the historian of Georgia Methodism, that Grants was the first built in the state. In that house one hundred years ago, March 10, 1790, a little handful of Methodist preachers met to hold conference; to confer about the conquest of Georgia for Christ. In 1890, Georgia has divided into two conferences and the one which will come here this year is so large that everybody is wishing for a larger house than the present Methodist church of Washington. Bishop Asbury tells us in his Journal, "We had a rainy day yet a full house, and a living love feast." He tells us that he preached from Ezekiel II.7. "Thou shalt speak my words unto them whether they will hear or whether they will forbear."

This Methodist Conference met in March 1790. On July 20 of this same year 1790, the first Presbyterian ordination in Georgia, that of Rev. John Springer took place in Washington under Mr. Charles Alexander's great poplar.

In the old manuscript record of the Academy Commissioners to which I have so often referred, I find, in August 1790, the following entry, "ordered that the Commissioners do write to Bishop Asbury and that Florence Sullivan and Jame Williams be appointed a committee for that purpose." The Commissioners present were the two gentlemen named, Jno. King, Henry Mounger and Francis Willis (the ancestor of Dr. Willis who has given us the Mary Willis Library.)

There is not in the MS. any further mention of Bishop Asbury of this letter or the answer to it. At the time it was written, Bishop Asbury was in Pennsylvania. I guess,---for guessing is all I can do without further facts to go upon,---that the letter referred to a school which Bishop Asbury and Hope Hull had been planning in the conference at Grants in 1790. The Commissioners who were then very anxious to have a school in Washington, probably wrote to urge the Bishop to establish his school here. If this proposal were ever made, the negotiations came to nothing.

Thus I have given an account of three conferences. The next

one, that of 1791, met at Scott's meeting house on Little River. This was a new chapel in the Gartrell neighborhood. It was on or near the Augusta road in the south-eastern part of the county, and seems to have been built by a settler called Joseph Scott. In our county records I have several times seen the name Joseph Scott Riden, probably a descendant of this old Methodist. Bishop Coke was at Scotts at conference, reaching there just in time to preach. Bishop Asbury tells us in 1791, "The peace with the Creek Indians, the settlement of new lands, good trade, buying slaves &c take up the attention of the people," and he found "these things very unfavorable to the work of religion."

I have thus spoken of four conferences, the first in 1788 in the Forks on the Broad and Savannah, two at Grants and one at Scotts in the Gartrell neighborhood on Little River. There are still two old conferences to tell of, in Wilkes. In one, that of 1792, Bishop Asbury passed through Washington where he collected the members of conference and went on to hold the conference itself at some place which he does not name. It could not be Washington, for he tells us he preached, and the very next year when conference was certainly held in Washington, that is in 1793, and Bishop Asbury preached here: he says in his Journal, under date of March 10, 1793. "I have now had an opportunity of speaking in Washington, most of the people attended to hear this man that rambles through the United States." This shows that the conference of 1792, at which he preached, was not held in Washington. It must have been near, here and was probably at Coke's Chapel which was three miles from Washington, and as well as I can judge, on the Fishing Creek road.

After the conference was over, he says he "rode to Fishing Creek and had an uncomfortable time on the Sabbath at Bibb's Cross Roads." There was a chapel at Bibb's Cross Roads, and I should like to find this place now. There are cross roads at Sandtown, at Danburg, at Delhi, and probably one of these may have been called Bibb's Cross Roads.

Our town of Washington was the scene of a Methodist conference for the first time in 1793, ninety seven years ago. In this year was passed the act for selling the common, but the actual sale was in 1794. The fact that five conferences had been held in the county - three of them within a few miles of the town, before one was held in the town, shows of how much greater relative importance was the country than the town in the early times. In his subsequent visits to Georgia, Bishop Asbury repeatedly came to Wilkes and went all round the town without coming into it.

On the occasion of this conference, Bishop Asbury preached. His text which he gives us, is the first text on record as preached from in Washington, so I think I will print it in full "Wherefore I take you to record this day that I am pure from the blood of all men for I have not shunned to declare unto you the whole counsel of God." This sermon was preached on Jan. 13, 1793. Do not understand me to say it was the first text, for it is reasonably certain sermons, one or more, were preached at the Presbyterian ordination in 1790 and probably earlier. It is the first text recorded.

The question comes up, where was this conference held? That is, in what building? I think we can give a reasonably certain answer to this. It must have been held in the first court house. For a long time the chapel attached to the brick academy was used for preaching as we know but the old MS. shows us that this building was not fairly begun until several years after this conference met. Zeal for education, our Washington people seem to have had from the very beginning, but in 1793, they were swamped by their debt to Samuel Blackburn.

But we know from a good many sources that the old Court House was used for preaching, so when the Conference of 1890 comes, we can with a reasonable degree of certainty point to the site of the Court House in General Heard's garden and tell them that the Conference of 1793 met on that spot. Bishop Asbury tells us in his Journal that the preachers "had great peace and union, the Carolina preachers came up to change with those in Georgia, all things happened well. Bless the Lord O! my Soul." He adds "Our sitting ended in exceeding great love." On Sunday he tells us, they had sacrament, love feast and ordination. He says, "I felt very serious and was very pointed on Acts XX, 26, 27." This is the text which I gave in full above.

Our old Court House was the scene of many a rough encounter of words, and sometimes more than words as the records in the Court House show. Once our old friend and soldier of the Revolution Col. Micaijah Williamson and his son walloped a man there who called the old soldier a rogue. It is pleasant to think of the Methodist preachers having "great peace and union" there. The old Court House knew a great many eminent men, but never was any body in it more worthy to be remembered than Francis Asbury.

This Washington Conference united the Georgia and South Carolina Conferences, and as a result, conference afterwards met very little in Georgia. There was not another conference in Washington until 1834 after the Georgia and Carolina Conferences had again separated. Miss Emma Barnett tells me she has a dim recollection of this conference, though she was a child. Mrs. Vickers who came in 1836 found the people here talking of it and especially of the heavy mud which pulled off your shoes when you tried to cross the street. Now we have stone crossings. After this, there was no conference in Washington until that of 1857, which I well remember myself. The preacher in charge was Rev. J. O. A. Clark, whose wife was an old playmate and friend of my childhood, and I dined at her house with the Bishops and with Dr. Alfred Mann and his wife. Thus the conference which will assemble at the close of this year is the fourth which has met in Washington. They came in 1793, 1834, 1857, and now in 1890.

CHAPTER XXI

THE EARLY METHODISTS ~
BISHOP ASBURY, HOPE HULL

BISHOP ASBURY must of course be the central figure in any account of early Methodism in Wilkes. He was an Englishman, a traveling Methodist preacher, who came to America as a missionary in 1771, the year before Wilkes county was ceded by the Indians to the white settlers. From this time until he died in 1816, he kept a journal from which we get our most important knowledge of early Methodism in this country. There were other Methodist preachers from England, but when the Revolution began, they could not sympathize with the colonists against the crown, so they returned to England. Bishop Asbury remained, because he was more deeply interested in religion than politics, a fact to which he owed much of his subsequent success in preaching the Gospel. He kept up his work under some disadvantages, until peace came. His journal gives a brief account of his own travels and work, and it has the additional value that it gives us an example of what all the pioneer Methodist preachers did and suffered. He was a very shrewd observer and we get from him several facts of much interest in our local history.

Bishop Asbury was forty three years old when he made his first visit to Georgia in 1788, when the first conference of this state met in the forks of the Broad and Savannah. He had traveled on horseback through Virginia and the Carolinas, and he crossed the Savannah, going and returning, at Petersburg. He had traveled about two hundred and fifty miles during five five days not long before crossing. Just before leaving Carolina, he lost his way in the woods and was benighted, causing him to travel fifty miles that day. What the condition of the country was, to which he came in 1788, appears from his statement as follows. "I am told that during the late rupture the Indians butchered at least a hundred people."

Sometimes when Bishop Asbury came to Georgia, he would cross the Savannah river at Augusta and ride up through Columbia county, stopping there with a Methodist convert, Thomas Haines. Then he would come to Scotts on Little River and from there to Grants. This was his route when he came to the two conferences at Grants in 1789 and 1790. Sometimes after coming up to Grants in this way, he would travel back to Carolina by passing Bibb's Cross' Roads, to the east of Washington, and crossing the Savannah at Petersburg. Sometimes he would cross the Savannah far South in Scriven county, and travel two hundred and fifty miles in Georgia before reaching Wilkes. These journeys were all taken on horseback at first; but after a few years, he had some sort of carriage,--which in one place he calls "the felicity." Readers at this day cannot realize what these journeys were when the roads were cut up by the wagons which transported all merchandise. Wagons used very often to mire down in the streets of Washington, and require help and hard work to prize them out. I have heard my aunt, Mrs. Garnett Andrews, who lived for many years in Mr. William Ellington's house N.W. corner of Main St. and Alexander Ave., say that it was a common thing to see wagons mired down at that corner. In 1799, traveling in "the felicity," the Bishop tells us, "the Augusta road was gouged with wagons in a dreadful manner, in consequence of which were five hours going twelve miles to Thomas Haines." He says, "there were wagons heavily loaded with rum." In his journey to the conference at Grants one hundred years ago, he says, "Frequently we have not more than six hours sleep, our horses are weary and the houses are so crowded that at night our rest is much disturbed." But he constantly tells us, "I enjoy peace." He very often mentions the open houses and the impossibility of retirement or privacy. Often he rode all day without anything to eat until seven o'clock in the evening. But for my part, I do not see why the good women did not put up a lunch for Bishop Asbury to carry with him.

Bishop Asbury continued to come to Wilkes when conferences ceased to be held here. In 1796, he came through Augusta just after the great Yazoo freshet, so called because it happened the Year the Yazoo bill passed. He says, "I saw, how the flood had ploughed up the streets. I walked over the ruins for nearly two miles, viewing the deep gulfs in the main streets." The same year, he had to swim his horse across Little River. When he came in 1801, he passed through old Petersburg which he tells us "has about eighty houses well constructed for stores and about one hundred buildings in all. They are generally one story in height well painted, with convenient shed attached." His trips had now become extended tours through Wilkes, Oglethorpe, Green, Franklin, Elbert, Warren and other counties: and he mentions among the Methodists, many people well known to our traditions. James Marks on Broad River is one of them. So is Ralph Banks, the ancestor of Mrs. Pledger. Also the Tates in Elbert, Henry Pope, Burwell Pope, the Hills. He speaks of "Mother Hill." This is probably the widow of Abraham Hill, the great grandfather of Dr. John Hill and Mr. Edward Hill of our day. The will of Abraham Hill is still in the ordinary's office at this day. When Bishop Asbury stopped at Scotts in 1801, he went home, he tells us with Mr. Gartrell. ("Gateral.") In 1803, he made another extended tour and again lodged with Mr. "Gatral." He says, "There are many hindrances to the work of God in this section of country, some evitable and some inevitable; among the first, are Sabbath markets, rum, races and rioting: among the latter may be enumerated necessary business (so called), sudden and severe changes more peculiar to southern climate, which affect people powerfully and against which they have not the protection of warm dwellings. The houses are universally open and unfinished, and the churches and chapels are in no better state." But he adds, "My mind is kept in perfect peace, notwithstanding my daily labers and my sufferings in exposure to night air and day damps and hard fare and hard lodging."

Bishop Asbury was a somewhat delicate man, and it is astonishing how long he lived under these years of constant trial. I think it is the more surprising when we read in his journal of some of the remedies which he used. In 1814, when he made his last visit to Georgia, he was suffering from a hemorrhage of the lungs, and he tells that he was bled in the arm as a remedy.

He continued his travels to the last and there is something affecting in the sudden way in which his journal ends in 1816 because the overworked preacher had at last gone to his eternal rest. He was seventy years old when he died.

CHAPTER XXII

EARLY METHODISTS –
HOPE HULL AND JOHN ANDREWS

WHEN THE FIRST Georgia Conference was held in the Forks, in what was then Wilkes, but is now Elbert, the Rev. Hope Hull came to Georgia for the first time. He had been a house carpenter in Baltimore, when he was converted, and at the time when he came to Georgia, had for some years been a traveling preacher of much power. He was sent by this first Georgia Conference on the Washington circuit for the next year. This year, 1789, when Hope Hull came to preach to the people of the Georgia up country, was noted in far away France by the beginning of the French Revolution, and in the United States by the adoption of the Federal Constitution.

To the Methodists of Wilkes, Hope Hull became very much what Jesse Mercer was to the Baptists, though he did not remain in the county so long. He was on the Washington circuit but one year, but in 1794 he returned and married Miss Anna Wingfield of the omnipresent Wingfield family, John Wingfield branch, and he then located in the county. His wife was a sister of the Frances Wingfield who married David Meriwether. David Meriwether about that time gave a body of land for the establishment of a Methodist School which Hope Hull taught. This was near Coke chapel, and it was called "Succoth Academy." This was the first distinctively Methodist school in Georgia, and I am very much interested in finding its exact location. Col. Thomas Meriwether, now living in Wilkes, is a grandson of Gen. David Meriwether, and he tells me that he had in his possession the original deed by which that land was conveyed for a school, but that he gave it to Atticus Haygood, who deposited it in the Library at Emory College. I have sent for a copy, and I hope it will enable us to fix the site of Succoth Academy, Coke's chapel.

Hope Hull was not a classical scholar, but he employed Rev. Mr. Brown, a Presbyterian minister, to teach Latin and Greek. The old MS. of the Academy Commissioners shows very plainly the high estimation in which Hope Hull was held in Wilkes. He was Vice President of the Board and on the death of Rev. John Springer, President. I have already spoken of his preaching at the old Academy on Mercer hill, and being heard on what is now our square. He had that great advantage for a public speaker, a clear resonant, melodious and powerful voice. He was also a singer of great power and sweetness. Mrs. Lucy Simpson has showed me a copy of a collection of *Hymns and Spiritual Songs* published by him at Washington in 1803. I am not sure but this book is an earlier publication than *Mercer's Cluster,* which I took to be the first book published by a citizen of Wilkes county. Besides *Mercer's Cluster* was printed and published at Washington. It was doubtless printed on Mrs. Hillhouse's press, and is probably the only printing from her press now in existence, unless there remain in the state archives at Atlanta some of the reports or journals, of the Legislature which she printed when that body met at Louisville.

The old MS. of the Academy Coms. tells us that Hope Hull left Wilkes for Athens in 1804, after the establishment of a college there.

Mrs. Eliza Pope Hull's husband, was a grandson of Hope Hull by his son Asbury, a much respected citizen of Athens. There are many traditions of the influence he had in Wilkes. His name "Hope" was not much liked by white mothers, but it is common among negroes. Mr. Alexander Pope, the father of Mrs. Cooper and Mrs. Hull, owned an old negro preacher, "uncle Hope," whom the family used to call in to hold family prayers for them when Mr. Pope himself was absent. Dr. John Pope, long an elder in the Presbyterian church here, used to say that he owed his first strong religious impressions to the preaching of Rev. Hope Hull.

There has been an impression in Wilkes that Hope Hull once had a school on Mercer Hill. This must be an error, due to his position as President of the Board of Academy Commissioners. The journal of Bishop Asbury enables us to trace his location until he was put on this Board in 1796, and then the MS., just mentioned gives us further information until he went to Athens in 1804.

The first Methodist preachers who traveled in Georgia came from beyond the State. They were mostly Virginians. But just one hundred years before our present year 1890, when conference was held for the second time at Grants old meeting house on the Double Wells road, a native Georgian applied for admission. He was the first person born within the State, to become a Methodist preacher. His name was John Andrew, and he became the father of a noted Methodist Bishop, James O. Andrew. He was from the old Presbyterian settlement at Midway in Liberty county, which has produced so many distinguished and valuable citizens in our State. He came up to Columbia county to teach school and was converted and began to preach. He was about thirty years old, and had been twice married, but had lost both wives. After joining conferences in 1790, he was sent to the Washington circuit the following year. He met in Wilkes, Miss Mary Cosby, whose father was a Virginian settled here. The "Fortunatus Cosby" of our old records was probably her father or brother. The family were among the best of our Virginia settlers. John Andrew married Mary Cosby, who thus became the mother of Bishop Andrew. John Andrew then located, and his son James was born very near Washington. The house in which he first saw the light was on the Mineral Spring road, just beyond the Sulphur Spring, on the eastern side of the road, and just opposite to the old place of Overton Wingfield where Mr. Lemuel Sims lately lived.

We have Bishop Andrew's own authority for saying he was born in that place. A few years before his death he was in Washington with his last wife, who was a cousin of Mrs. Lucy Reese and a descendant of the original settler Thomas Wingfield. Mrs. Reese took Bishop Andrew and his wife in her carriage and drove them all around our town of Washington and its vicinity. During this ride, they passed by the place where Bishop Andrew was born in 1794 and he pointed it out to Mrs. Reese as his birthplace. I have the statement from Mrs. Reese's own lips.

CHAPTER XXIII

THE EARLY METHODISTS
DANIEL GRANT'S WILL

I HAVE THUS SPOKEN of the meeting house built by Daniel Grant and the conferences held there, and now I will speak of the Grants. I think it will perhaps interest my readers more, if I name some of the descendants in this day, of this builder of the first Methodist church in Georgia. Some persons who read this have seen in Atlanta, on Peachtree street, a handsome house surrounded by a beautiful grove and gardens where lives the widow of Mr. John T. Grant, a wealthy gentleman who died a few years ago. Also many have read in the social column of the *Constitution*, of the gay parties at the house of Mr. W. D. Grant. These are the descendants of the Daniel and Thomas Grant who came here in 1784, and who are found on the old jury lists of our court records; who are to this day remembered as the early supporters of the Methodist cause in Georgia. The children of Mr. W. D. Grant are doubly connected with Wilkes, as their mother is a descendant of Thomas Wingfield who settled near the big gully. The family are still Methodists.

The Grants settled as I have said, on the Double Wells road, between Washington and what is now called Moore's Mill on Little river. Their land now belongs to the widow of Judge Charles Wingfield. Daniel Grant was probably a rather old man when he came to Georgia, for he died in 1793. His son Thomas Grant had probably reached his prime when they came in 1784, for he had been a revolutionary soldier. They came from North Carolina, but were originally Virginians. Daniel Grant had been an elder in the Presbyterian church in Virginia, and was still a Presbyterian when he came to Georgia. But the Methodist preachers soon came to Wilkes and he finally became a Methodist. In the *Life of Bishop Andrew*, there is a letter from Daniel Grant to Mary Cosby the mother of Bishop Andrew. It was written just one hundred and one years ago and is a letter of encouragement to "Sister Polly Cosby," he calls her, who had met with much opposition from her family in becoming a Methodist. It shows that the writer had not ceased to be a Presbyterian because he could not have Presbyterian services, but that he was Methodist at heart. He considered class meetings, "a great means to keep the life of religion in the soul."

From his will, which is still among the records in our Court House, it seems that Daniel Grant had only two sons, Thomas and John Owen. He had four daughters. Judge Andrews told me of two Grants whom he remembered in the county, who were I suppose, the sons of Thomas Grant. One of these, Wm. Grant, was a merchant here, and kept his store where the Masonic Hall now stands at the north east corner of the public square. He married a Miss Mills, who was the sister of Jesse Mercer's second wife. A few days ago, I saw among old marriage licenses in the Court House, that of Wm. Grant and Keturah Mills. There was another Wm. Grant in Wilkes Judge Andrews told me---and he by way of distinction, used to be called "Gentleman Billy Grant," not as my uncle said, that William the son of Thomas Grant was not a gentleman, but because the other "had more manner." Besides William Grant, Thomas Grant the Methodist seems to have had another son called Daniel Grant, who kept a store early in this century on the Greensboro road beyond old Salem church (now Phillips church.) This Daniel Grant, my uncle said moved to Athens, and was I presume the father of the late Mr. John T. Grant and his son William D. Grant of Atlanta. Mr. John Pettus, the father of Mrs. Lucy Reese, was a clerk of the Daniel Grant who had a store on the Greenesboro road. Finally, Thomas Grant moved away from Wilkes, and from him or his son Daniel, Mr. John Pettus bought the Grant place where the old meeting house stood. The house which was the home of Thomas Grant had, as Mrs. Reese tells me, four rooms down stairs and two up. There was a staircase which ran up in what they used to call the hall room down stairs. I imagine the old house would be a contrast to Mrs. John T. Grant's house in Atlanta now, but it was one of the best houses of its times in Wilkes. It was painted red.[1]

[1] In the office of the Ordinary of Greene county, there is a thin, flexible back book on which is inscribed - *Free Persons of Color, in Greene County*. This book contained the names and guardians for all *Free Persons of Color*, and their guardians or sponsors, had to make returns for each year. There are a number of Grant Negroes listed in this book. On p. 132, Miss Bowen refers to "Daniel Grant, who kept a store early in this century - 1800 - on the Greensboro road beyond old Salem Church (now Phillips church). This Daniel Grant, my uncle said moved to Athens, and was I presume the father of the late John T. Grant, and his son William D. Grant of Atlanta."

This Daniel Grant lived in that part of Wilkes that was added to Greene county in 1802. He operated a Tavern, and was on the old stage coach route. Stage horses were changed at Grantville and there was a Post office there. He is the man who liberated his slaves whose record is in Greene county. Grantville is shown on an old map of Greene county; its date is unknown, but is supposed to have been published around 1830, and revised by Dr. J. H. Kilpatrick and John S. Callaway sometime between 1860 and 1880.

Mr. Grant is said to have sold his property about the time the Georgia Railroad was being built - 1833-37, and became one of the contractors who built the Railroad to Athens, or from Union Point to Athens.

The old Grant home and Tavern was burned some ten years ago, but the chimneys are still standing. There are a number of Grant tombstones near the old home.

T. B. Rice, Historian of Greene County
September 16, 1940

Thomas Grant is said by the historian of Methodism to have been one of the most useful Methodist laymen of his day in Georgia. He used to keep at his house below town, clothing of all sizes for Methodist preachers who might ride up wet, and want some dry clothes. He had a room for the preachers, which he called "Prophets' Chamber." When he died, he left a legacy to the Georgia and South Carolina Conferences. That of the Georgia Conference was $1500 and some land. When he went to New York in 1803, the journey lasted three months and three days.

I must now tell of the will of the first Daniel Grant who came in 1784 and died in 1793. To make what I say understood, I must tell my readers that Bishop Asbury, and especially Bishop Coke, thought that slavery was a great wrong and sought to make the emancipation of negroes a condition of church membership. Bishop Coke was very obstinate in this matter, and thus destroyed his influence. Bishop Asbury, who as I said, was more interested in spreading the Gospel than in anything else, soon saw that the only chance he could have to preach the Gospel in the south at all was not to make the emancipation of a man's negroes the condition of communion. That it was a condition however, at the very first, is proved from the fact which comes down to us through family traditions that Garland Wingfield was turned out of the church for owning negroes. The reader must take note that this is not the Garland Wingfield whom many of us remember, but his uncle. This excommunication must have taken place very early indeed.

Bishop Asbury submitted, not to make it a question of communion, but he was of the same opinion, as his journal shows plainly. He tells us that he thought the Yazoo freshet an "African freshet" that is, I suppose, a judgment for making negroes property. In that early day, there had not been much outside interference with the local regulations of Southern States and much freedom of speech on the subject was taken without offence. Bishop Asbury appears to have talked and reasoned about it in private, and he speaks of it in his journal without bitterness. These allusions to slavery are doubtless the reason why a reprint of Asbury's journal has not been made and sold at the South.

In 1793, the year when conference first met in Washington, the Bishop was here. His journal shows that after preaching here Jan. 12, he went out to Grants next day and preached. He staid in the old Grant home, and doubtless talked a good deal with Daniel Grant. Six months after, that is on July 4, 1793, Daniel Grant signed his will, in which he made provision for the emancipation of his negroes. Daniel Grant's will is in the old record book of wills in our court house, and I hunted it up. He begins by saying that he is in his "usual health" of body and also of mind, reason and understanding! yet knowing that it is appointed unto all men once to die he makes his will. Thus he lets us know that he acts very deliberately not hastily, from the fear of death. First providing for debts, he says, "whereas I am possessed of a small number of slaves, and being fully convinced that perpetual slavery is most unjust and contrary to the natural rights of all mankind, and wishing to release to the best of my power the oppressed, until some future laws can be made in their favor. (and wherever that shall take place it is my will and desire that they avail themselves thereof) in the meantime I do dispose of them in the following manner. In regard to those negroes which I have heretofore given my daughters, I do not consider them as any part of my property, and shall say nothing therefore of their liberation &c though at the same time requesting their owners to relieve these oppressed creatures in some way or other. I do therefore lend unto my son Thomas Grant the following servants, or negroes until the males arrive at the age of 31 and the females to the age of 28, at which ages they shall be liberated so far as only to pay to my son Thomas Grant and his heirs, the males 10 shillings; and the females 7 shillings yearly as a token of subjection and to indemnify him for their taxes and to prevent abuse from others." Then he goes on to state the exact future date in which each male will be 32 years old; each female 28. He provided that none are to leave the state without the written permit of Thos. Grant; and if they do so, they can be captured and made to work 12 months for every such "elopement." He asks his executors to obtain an act of the general assembly to ratify that part of the will. He desires his son to have these slaves taught to read, and at the expiration of their time to clothe them well.

After bequests to his sons he orders his property remaining to be divided into five parts, a part to be given each of his four daughters, and one part to make a charitable fund for teaching poor negroes and whites to read the Scriptures and to furnish them with books. Whether by accident or design we know not, but it is curious that this will was signed July 4.

The executors of the will were Thomas Grant, John Crutchfield and David Meriwether. Gen. Meriwether was a member of the legislature, and got an act passed as requested, for carrying out Daniel Grant's will. There were always since I knew this town, some free negroes in it who owed their freedom to this will. Old Adam, who used to be janitor at the Seminary in antebellum times, was the son of one of Daniel Grant's freedmen. They all called themselves Grant. There is now in Washington a negro of this stock called Daniel Grant. There are others also.

Bishop Asbury says on one of his visits to Georgia, that

he was told by James Mark that he would probably emancipate his negroes at death. The Bishop thought that he would probably change his mind and it seems that he did:

CHAPTER XXIV

METHODISTS IN WILKES AFTER 1800

THE FIRST Methodist preaching, beginning with the time of John Major and Thomas Humphries, created a revival spirit which lasted some years and caused Methodism to take firm root. But about 1794, this zeal began to cool and a decline followed. The spirit of speculation, employed in projects for acquiring land, began to be rife in 1794, and indeed commenced earlier. It of course culminated with the act of the legislature in 1796 which our indignant ancestors called the "Yazoo Fraud." A strong party spirit was roused by the discussion of the Yazoo bill, and thus men's minds were taken from religion. There was an actual decline in the number of Methodist church members. Towards the close of the century, the revival spirit roused again. All the writers, Baptist and Methodist, speak of the great revivals of 1802 and 1803 and the following years. We read of it in the *Life of Mercer*, and Gov. Gilmer also tells us of the effect on the Broad river people of the great revival of 1809.

In 1802, Washington was visited by Lorenzo Dow, who came again in 1803 and 1805. He was an eccentric old Methodist preacher born in Connecticut, who had been converted by the preaching of Rev. Hope Hull when Hull traveled a circuit at the North before coming to Georgia. Lorenzo Dow was at first connected with the Connecticut conference, but finally began to travel independently, and largely on foot, and in this way he went over a large part of the then settled States. His published *Journal* shows that he was much influenced by dreams and mental impressions which he considered sent by God for his guidance. He was however, a good man and did some good work and where known gained respect and confidence. In 1802, he came to Savannah by sea, and then in obedience to the mental impressions which he obeyed, he started on foot to Washington to see Hope Hull. He walked up to Augusta and then through Columbia, stopping to preach wherever he had an opportunity. Good brother Haynes in Columbia, heard and entertained him. Then he came to Captain Thornton's on Upton Creek, and from there he got up and walked nine miles before sunrise to Hope Hull's house. Early as it was, Hope Hull was up and in his corn crib. Hope Hull's treatment of him shows the sturdy good sense of this early Methodist, to whom religion in Wilkes county is so much indebted. Mr. Hull advised him to give up this traveling in obedience to supposed impressions by which he might be deceived, and strongly urged him to take a circuit. In his journal, Dow reports Hope Hull as saying, "that he did not know when traveling that he ever felt it impressed on his mind to go to one place more than another, but said he, if I heard of a place opened, or a house vacant of a minister, or a wicked neighborhood, my reason said I should go." This is worth a good deal as an illustration of Hope Hull's character, whose refreshing common sense cannot be fully appreciated except by a person of Lorenzo Dow's narrative of his presentments and dreams and how he wandered about in obedience to them. But Hope Hull's sound advice to look to his reason and not to imaginary revelations for guidance, had little effect on Lorenzo Dow who tells us in his journal that after he heard it he got to thinking about "Alexander's Life" and a dream he had "about the pit and a spring of water."

Nevertheless, Hope Hull appreciated the genuine piety and disinterestedness of Lorenzo Dow, and got him a hearing in our Court House, where he preached at night Feb. 16, 1802. He preached there twice, and he tells us "a young clergyman from Connecticut as I had done, voluntarily made a flowery prayer in which he gave me a broadside." Lorenzo Dow went to Lexington, Petersburg, and many other places, and one of his converts was Major John Oliver, who was probably a kinsman of Mrs. Pharr.

Rev. Micajah Lane, grandfather of the Lane's living here now, who died two years ago at the great age of ninety two years, used to tell that when a boy he came to Washington on an errand. He said there were many people out and they told him that Lorenzo Dow was to preach. After a while he said, Lorenzo Dow came walking down the Lexington road. Without saying a word to anybody on the right or on the left, he marched directly to the Court house, preached a sermon, and then walked out of Washington in the same silence in which he had entered the place.

Early in this century, camp meetings began to be a great institution for promoting religion. Bishop Asbury speaks of them in his *Journal*. Camp meetings are now rare, but when I first knew Washington well, in the forties and fifties, it was one of the summer pleasures for young folks to go to Independence camp meeting. Young people went for the pleasure of the trip and the company. Parties would be formed and young men would take young ladies out in their buggies in the morning, to return in the evening. On Sundays, the rattle of the passing vehicles could be heard in the morning before we left our room, and in the evening the air was filled with the dust of the returning caravan, and vocal with the lively talk of the young folks getting home from their day's excursion. Wheat's camp ground in Lincoln county was near enough to draw some visitors, while others who had friends camping at the great camp ground of White oak in Columbia county, would go down to stay all night on the camp ground. Last summer (1889) people from this place went down to Fountain camp ground in Warren, which has been frequented through this century by Wilkes people. I suppose it takes its name from Thomas Fountain an early Methodist with whom Bishop Asbury stopped in his journeys, as recorded in his journal.

Of course some people who went to these camp meetings were attracted by the company and not the religious services, just as the Christmas festival of other Christians is celebrated without regard to its significance, and in fact in a way wholly inconsistent with the religious object. These lively companies of young persons very often behaved badly, laughed and talked and disturbed services and perhaps were very sharply reproved by uncle Jimmy Danelly, or some other preacher. Any religious body would have this trouble very nearly in proportion to the extent of people whom it affected. But those who came from mere pleasure seeking were very often benefitted.

Tradition says that the first church built in Washington was the old Methodist church which in 1881 we saw moved and turned into Mr. Floyd's opera house. It must therefore have been built before 1825, when the present Presbyterian church was begun. The Methodists have no records whatever to tell of it, but Dr. Willis said it was built about 1821. With no more than this to guide me, I went to the records of deeds, or 'indentures,' in the office of Mr. Dyson clerk of the Court for Wilkes county, to look for the deed to the land on which the church stands. When I say that the deed is put in the index as "Alfriend to Grant," my readers can imagine what a job I had to find it, and I do not believe there is a Methodist in the county who would have taken the trouble that I did. I gave it up once, but I found a good deal in the old books to interest me, and in looking them over, I found a clue which after a good many searches led me to the actual deed. It is dated Dec. 16, 1819, but was recorded Dec. 19. I will give it, just as it was written, leaving out the mere legal verbiage. "Indenture between Edw. D. Alfriend and Nancy W. Alfriend his wife, of the county of Greene, of the one part, and Wm. Jones, John B. Lennard, William Grant, James Bradley, Arthur M. Charlton, Trustees of the M. E. church of the other part, witnesseth that for $1800 for that part of the lot hereafter described for use as a parsonage, and $200 for that appropriated to a church, to them in hand paid, they have sold, &c., unto said William Jones, &c., trustees, a lot, beginning on what was formerly Mrs. Griffin's, now the Female Academy line, running south along this line to the Female Academy lot, and bounded by said lot on the north east, and south to Liberty street, thence along said street, to the corner of William Rorie's lot, thence north in direct line with Rorie's lot to Main street, thence along said street to the beginning on formerly Mrs. Griffins, now the Female Academy lot, in trust for a parsonage house and church as above described, for the benefit of the presiding elder's family who may from time to time be appointed to travel on the Ogeechee District; &c, &c. Be it understood that all that part of the lot fronting Main street and running to the lower end of the female academy including all the houses on the same is for, and will belong to the parsonage for that purpose, and all the balance from the lower end of the female academy, running a straight line across the said lot from the lower end of the academy to Wm. Rorie's lot or line, will be and is for the church, on payment of the above $200."

The lot of Wm. Rorie is now part of the Academy lot. It is the part on Liberty Street nearest to the church lot.

The parsonage lot here spoken of is evidently that now occupied by Mr. Jesse and his sister Miss Clara Jesse. In one of the books in Mr. Dyson's office, there is another deed, made in 1830 by the trustees of the church conveying this parsonage lot to Mrs. Ann Anthony. She was the widow of Bolling Anthony. The deed states that she paid for it $730, which is a decline of more than one half on the $1800 which it cost them. I will mention that Mrs. Anthony lived there but a few years. The school boys at the academy gave her so much trouble running to her lot for water, and throwing balls over her fence and jumping over to get them, that it caused Mrs. Anthony to sell the place.

The church was completed, Dr. Willis says, about 1821. Rev. Geo. G. Smith the historian of Georgia Methodism, says that the town of Washington which had been on the Little River circuit, became a station in 1822. He thinks that the church was not built until 1824. I think that the deed in the clerk's office and the evidence of Dr. Willis show that the true date is 1821. Mr. Smith tells us that Thos. Darley was sent to Washington in 1822. He records a revival about 1828, and he says that Dr. Lovick Pierce, and Dr. Olin came to help the preacher in charge, John Howard. There was a great deal of skepticism here among the intelligent men who lived here in the early part of the century, but Mr. Smith says that a great sermon from Dr. Olin put it to flight. There were 14 members when the church was built, but this revival brought in 100. All the traditions in this place tell of a great revival here about that time, under the preaching of Rev. Alexander Webster the first pastor of the Presbyterian Church in Washington. The revival probably was in both churches. Mrs. Vickers, who came in 1836, tells me that people were still talking of it when she came, and also of the conference which met in 1834.

I shall write with some fullness that part of the history of the Washington church which follows the coming of Mrs. Vickers. I have regretted much that Methodists have preserved so little of their interesting history. I can write this much at least from authentic information and I will do so, hoping that I may inspire some one else to continue the record. Mrs. Vickers says that when she came, the principal members of the Washington church were Mr. William Jones and his wife, Miss Betsy Waddy, Mrs. Thomas Jones and her sons, Captain Pelot, Miss Mary Minton, Mrs. John Lennard and Mrs. Beasley, Mrs. Lewis Brown, Mrs. Willie, Mr. and Mrs. John Green, the families of Mr. Stephen Pettus and Mr. Garland Wingfield, the Berrys, Mrs. John Hay, Mr. Alex. Pope, Sr., and his wife, Mr. and Mrs. Micaijah Anthony. Mrs. Vickers[1] says that when she arrived, the windows of the church were glazed only in the upper half, the lower half being closed by a heavy wooden shutter. There were no stoves in the church until 1839. In 1839 there was another great revival, in which about 100 persons joined the church. Rev. Alfred Mann was the preacher, and Rev. Samuel Anthony the presiding elder. After Mann married Miss Julia Pierce a daughter of Rev. Lovick Pierce and sister of Bishop Pierce, and brought her here as a bride, when he came to fulfill his appointment. I myself well remember the marriage of Alfred Mann and Julia Pierce. I was a little child living in Augusta, and my father and mother were neighbors of the Manns, and I used to play with Alfred Mann's sister, afterwards Mrs. J. O. A. Clark. They were not married in Augusta of course, but I remember the roast turkey which his mother old Mrs. Mann, basted in the old way before the open fire when she was expecting her son's wife, and the iced pound cake she made and ornamented thickly with little prickles of icing. When conference met here in 1857, and I dined with Dr. and Mrs. Mann and Bishop Paine, I told the party of the cooking of that turkey. Alfred Mann and I lived to be the last survivors of the two families who had been neighbors, and the old recollections were a strong tie between us. I afterwards knew his wife Julia Pierce well. She was one of the most superior of a remarkable family, all of whom I knew well. I consider her one of the most superior women this state ever produced. She had sound judgment, and much of that womanly quality, tact and she was fond of the best reading. Dr. Mann's easy circumstances (until he was old alas?) and the fact that she had no children, and so went with her husband to all the conferences, state and

(1) All of the pamphlets of this *Story of Wilkes* skip from here to the third to the last paragraph in this chapter, except the Sims copy, so pages 140 to 145 were secured from the Sim's pamphlet.

general, gave her many opportunities and broad knowledge of the world, and with her keen sense of humor, made Julia Pierce Mann one of the most charming and entertaining persons I ever knew. I never knew a woman with so much humor, so keen a sense of the ludicrous, who so perfectly kept it under the control of good feeling and discretion. I have always considered it a great misfortune that she did not live to write down her father's recollections from his lips, and to add to them her own.

The year 1839 was noted for the great drought in the summer and fall. The Savannah river dried up until it could be crossed on foot, and there was yellow fever in Augusta, of which my father died. A religious meeting was begun here in the fall, and Mrs. Vickers remembers that at the beginning of it, there was a meeting one night to pray for rain. At that time, there lived here on the lot east of Gen. Heard's property on Court St., a saddler by the name of Bradford Merry, generally called Brad Merry. His wife was a good pious Methodist, but he was an unbeliever. When he heard of the prayer meeting for rain, he said "Well if it rains, I will believe in the prayers of the righteous, and it will make me believe in religion." They had a day of fasting, and they had a prayer meeting in the evening for rain. Mrs. Alfred Mann, whom I have heard tell the story, said there were no signs of rain, when they went to church, the skies were unclouded, and there had been a drought for months. While they were praying, the clouds came and soon there was a sound of rain, and there was a good deal of trouble in getting home through it. Then, it is said that Brad Merry became a Christian. Now I tell this story as history simply, without expressing opinions, but I must be careful and not lead the reader to suppose that this prayer meeting and its result caused the revival which followed. I have never heard any of those who told the story, say that this particular prayer meeting caused the revival. They attributed it to all the prayers. Among the persons then brought into the church, were Mr. and Mrs. Vickers, Mrs. Julia Toombs, Alex. Pope Jun., and his wife who had been Sarah Willie, Mr. and Mrs. Hester and others.

Rev. Samuel Anthony was the presiding elder of the district, and he was here for about three weeks. After the meeting the citizens wished him to live here so they bought the house now occupied by Mr. Kendrick, north west corner of Alexander Ave., and Water Street, and asked him to occupy it. He was here for three years, and after that it was for some years used as a parsonage for the preacher in charge of the church. The house had belonged to Mrs. Andrew Semmes then a widow living in the house now belonging to Mr. Jordan. Mrs. Cotting told me that the house bought for a parsonage was one which had been moved into Washington from the plantation of Mrs. Semmes' father in the country. It is therefore one of the oldest houses in the town, though not on its present site, and may give us some idea how the early settlers built. It cost the church $700.

When Mrs. Vickers came, a preacher named Johnson was in charge of the church. Wesley P. Arnold followed him, then came Alfred Mann. Next came a Mr. Wright, and then in 1841, Thomas Benning was here. There was another revival in 1841, that gathered in some of the best members that the church has known. Among these, were Isaiah T. Irvin, one of the best citizens who ever lived in town, county or state, and whose wife was already a member of the church, and Lewis Brown whose conversion was a very remarkable one. He had been a very dissipated man until middle life - or indeed a little past it. Mrs. Brown's niece married my uncle with whom I lived, and in the family, I have heard much talk of the drunken frolics on which "Uncle Brown" would go, and in which he was a terror to his devoted wife. After his conversion, he was perfectly and entirely reformed. He lived more than twenty years afterwards, and never had the smallest relapse. His wife had already been a Christian and he was a liberal and useful church member. Dr. George Palmer was converted in 1841 and proved a useful and honored member of the Methodist church. Dr. Fielding Ficklen the ancestor of the Wilkes Ficklens, who married a Wingfield, was also converted in the revival of 1841. Mrs. Vickers says either Rev. Sam Anthony or Rev. James E. Evans, who was his successor, was presiding elder then. She says James Evans, who was a Lincoln county man, used to tell her that he was converted when a very young fellow clerking in Washington and that people used to doubt the permanence of the work, but said he, "Blessed be God it has lasted yet."

Mr. Benning was afterwards expelled from conference for bad conduct and became a worthless man. I can remember hearing people speculate as to the genuineness of the revival on that account. I know nothing of the man or his agency in it, but the conversion of uncle Brown and of others proved itself. The parents of Miss Ann Kendrick were converted in 1841. Mr. Benning was succeeded in Washington by Rev. James Wiggins. When here, Mr. Wiggins was a man of the most austere and rigid old fashioned Methodist notions. He had afterwards a good deal of domestic trouble, and it made him cease to preach, and people used to say he was a backslider. I knew him well during this declension. It was merely a cloud of personal faith, no disbelief in God, and he was not guilty of immorality. He afterwards joined the Florida conference. While out of conference, I have often heard him play the violin on which he was a good performer. It looked odd, for old fashioned Methodists considered a violin to be the devil's own instrument and he had been so austere. But there was no wrong in it, and music was a great pleasure to him in great trouble. Mrs. Vickers says that

Washington was not a station when she came, but was made one 1842, the year that Mr. James Wiggins preached here. She is very positive in her recollections of this matter. G.G. Smith says the town was made a station in 1822. I do not myself know enough of Methodist ways to tell about it, but she thinks that it must have been put back into the circuit, if as Mr. Smith says, it was made a station in 1822, and then again made a station in 1842. I will continue from Mrs. Vickers lips, a list of the preachers since she came. After Mr. Wiggins, came W. J. Sassnett, E. H. Myers, who did not complete the year, being sent to the female college in Macon, while a man named Jackson came to fill his place, John P. Duncan, W. B. Bound, Josiah Lewis, Wm. Evans, Rev. Foote, Caleb Key, Daniel Kelsey, Samuel Anthony, J.O.A. Clark, Thomas Pierce, John Norris, George Grogan. This brought the church up to 1860, when the Civil War began. In a previous article, I stated that the conference came in 1858. I have been corrected, and am told that it was in 1857, by Mrs. Lucy Simpson, who was married to a Washington Methodist, Wiley DuBose, in that year, an event she is not likely to have misdated.

When Rev. J.O.A. Clark was coming in 1857, he influenced the church to sell the old parsonage and buy the present lot, south west corner of Water St. and Alexander Ave. Mrs. Vickers thinks it cost $2000. Mr. Clark was here two years, and during that time, his wife's mother Mrs. John H. Mann of Augusta, came to see her, and fell sick and died. She was one of the early Methodists of old St. Johns church, Augusta, a saintly woman. I had known her from my childhood. I had seen several persons die, and used to say that I should like to see some one die a triumphant death. I had that privilege in Mrs. Mann's case. I shall never forget it, nor the song by Mr. Robert Smith at her request. I do not mean that Mrs. Mann shouted or exulted loudly, but she was conscious to the last, and expressed her perfect confidence and readiness to go. I suppose I was the more impressed, because I had known that old lady's goodness from my very childhood. One of my Schoolmates was a girl who was left motherless when a baby, and there was no one to take her, and old Mrs. Mann sent for the child and reared it with her own. She was Mary Helen Walton, one of the first graduating class of Wesleyan Female College. She afterwards inherited a large property for those days.

During the war, Mr. Grogan was succeeded by Rev. Habersham Adams and he by W. M. Fulton, who proved to be a hypocrite. Mr. Fulton's story is a strange one. He was a native of Ireland, and I think professed conversion in Savannah, and then became a preacher. He married a widow, a most excellent Methodist lady with some property. He attracted great attention as a preacher when here and drew hearers from other churches.

Mr. A. L. Alexander, I think, detected that he preached a sermon of Melville, but had not spoken of it. Among the wounded Confederate soldiers, was a man from Missouri who was sent to the interior to recover. He saw Mr. Fulton in Augusta, and recognized him as an impostor who had married several women in succession and deserted them. I have not space to go into details, but it was when the fortunes of war had cut us off from communication with the outside world and the conflict was about to end, that Mr. Fulton found the toils were closing round him and he would be discovered.

From Augusta he returned to Washington and making some excuse left the town again. After going to Milledgeville, he walked through the lines into the Federal camp and represented himself as having been forced to leave on account of his union sentiments. The Federal officers received such an honorable martyr with an effusive welcome, and so helped him to go to the north and marry one or two northern women, for whom in the white heat of indignation that we then felt, we did not feel so sorry as we ought to have done. But he was found out, and after a while was identified as the culprit here. He had a peculiar bodily defect which rendered identification easy. One arm was longer than the other. When last heard from, he was under sentence of death.

I remember the remark of Mr. Alexander, who was noted for his wit when he heard of Fulton's representations to the Federal officers. "Yes," said he, "Fulton's union sentiments were exactly what we objected to." The poor woman who married him suffered terribly. The strange thing was that they had been married several years, and he had never done or said the smallest thing which had seemed inconsistent with the exalted religious character which she attributed to him. She said that he was a very quiet sleeper, and she had often thought of that verse. "The Lord giveth his beloved sleep."

After the trouble with Mr. Fulton, conference sent to Wilkes, Morgan Callaway, who is a native of the county, and therefore could command great confidence. Mr. Callaway too has married a Wilkes county woman Miss Georgia Ficklen, a noble woman who has made her mark in the Woman's Missionary Society of the Methodist church. Her goodness and energy does not surprise us, but that it should find a field among Methodists, since she was reared a Baptist of the Baptists. The list of preachers, continued up to 1890 is as follows: J.W. Yarborough, Dr. Eustace Speer, Alfred Mann, W. R. Branham, Peter Ryburn, Jesse Boring, W. P. Pledger, George Gardner, L. J. Davies, W.H. LaPrade, J. S. Bryan, Dr. Mixon. In 1881 Rev. George Gardner being preacher in charge, a new church was built costing $5300. It was dedicated by Bishop Pierce April 9, 1882. As I write this the Methodist are raising a subscription to enlarge and

145

beautify the building for the expected conference of 1890.
After writing my account of the Methodist church in Wilkes county, an additional fact about them was gained from the study of Presbyterian records. The old church building which is now Mr. Floyd's opera House, was certainly completed by May 1823, for Rev. Alexander Webster the Presbyterian minister whose tombstone is in the vestibule of the Presbyterian church, was ordained in that old Methodist church in the month of May 1823.

This statement is found in the old book of minutes of the Presbyterian church session. To this fact, I will add that the old Methodist church was built by a carpenter who then or afterwards was a Baptist preacher, Rev. Wyche Jackson. He was a great oddity. When he preached, he would select some one in the audience and address them by name. On one occasion, he preached in this old Methodist church, and in the course of his remarks told the audience that he had built the church and said he, "it was a good piece of work, was it not brother......." The brother thus addressed agreed that Mr. Jackson had done his work very well.

I will add to what I said about the Methodist church that Rev. G. G. Smith writes me that the first 70 converts made in 1785 were not due to Beverly Allen who did not fulfill his whole appointment. Mr. Smith tells me that he learned this after his book was printed. Some preacher from Carolina came and gathered in this 70 as he thinks.

CHAPTER XXV

THE PRESBYTERIANS IN WILKES

A VERY LARGE proportion of the early settlers of Wilkes county were the children or grand children of men who came from the north of Ireland not long before the Revolutionary war, and settled in the rolling region of Virginia and the Carolinas, where they did some of the best fighting of the Revolution. They are known as Scotch-Irish. There was a great emigration of the same people into Pennsylvania, and after the war, some Pennsylvanians came further south. They can be traced among the early settlers of what is now Elbert county. There was also among the settlers a good number of Virginians of Cavalier English stock. The Wingfields, Goodes, Willis, Hays, and others are of English blood, and there were some people of English race from Connecticut, as the Princes, Hillhouses, Abbotts. There were some settlers who were French Huguenots, as DuBoses and Remberts, as also a few Catholic French from San Domingo. I do not think any descendants of the latter remain in the county. There came also, in the nineties of the last century, some Maryland Catholics of English descent, the Semmes family, of whom I shall speak of at greater length further on.

But the great body of the settlers were of Scotch Irish origin. They had been reared Presbyterians, and in the Carolinas, there were numerous Presbyterian churches before the Revolution. Our old friend Gen. Andrew Pickens, who came over to help us against the British and the Indians several times, was an elder in Long Cane Presbyterian church, which is still in existence. In the battle of Kings mountain where there was a handful of Wilkes county soldiers, a number of the colonels were elders in the Presbyterian churches which abound in that part of the Carolinas.

The Presbyterian church of the United States was organized before the revolution, and there was a Synod of the Carolinas. This Synod organized at the close of the Revolution, "a Presbytery of South Carolina," which first met in 1784. Its jurisdiction extended over Georgia, and from the records of this body carefully preserved, we get our first knowledge of Presbyterian churches in Wilkes. There are three Presbyterian churches in the state which antedate the Revolution in Burke county and in Augusta. The first Presbyterian church of Augusta is about a hundred and twenty years old. But the Presbyterian church in the up country had its beginning after the Revolution.

At the meeting of the Presbytery of South Carolina in 1785, John Newton, who was what Presbyterians call "a probationer" that is, a received but yet unordained candidate for the ministry, was ordered by the presbytery to do missionary work in Georgia. He preached at Bethsalem, in Oglethorpe county, which is not the Lexington church. This John Newton is the ancestor of a number of Newtons living to this day in this portion of Georgia. Rev. Henry Newton, and Elizur Newton, the latter of whom died a few years ago, was long an elder in the Athens church, are descendants of John Newton. The people about Lexington liked the early John Newton so well that they called him for their pastor in October 1787, and he was ordained in Carolina in 1788. We are told that elders Park and Gilham from Bethsalem church went over to Carolina to the ordination, and received him in the name of the Bethsalem people.

While these events were going on, there were Presbyterians organizing in a part of Greene county then Wilkes,where Bethany church was formed about the same time. Greene county was laid off in 1786. It was formed from Wilkes county,(1) but in 1802, a small portion of Wilkes was cut off and added to Greene, Rev. F. T. Simpson who was at one time the pastor of Bethany church, says that he has seen the original grant to some of the land in the immediate vicinity of Bethany, and

---

(1) The original Greene county was *never a part of Wilkes*, it was formed *wholely* out of Washington county; but in 1802, there *was* a part of Wilkes cut off and added to Greene. See Watkins Digest of the Laws of Georgia, also Marbury & Crawford's Digest.

The Ogeechee River was the boundary between Washington and Wilkes counties when Washington was laid out in 1784. The Ogeechee rises at Union Point, and at this point was located the *Great Buffalo Lick* where the survey started in 1773. From that point the line ran from the Buffalo Lick to Cherokee Corner, etc., etc., and this became the line between Washington and Wilkes counties in 1784.

All the land north of the Ogeechee River, from Moore's Mill to Union Point, and the land north of the Atlanta branch of the Georgia Railroad from Union Point to Cherokee Corner, was a part of Wilkes county up to 1802. The south prong of Little River then became the boundary between Greene and Wilkes, as far down that stream as to where the Beaverdam of Wilkes, empties into Little River. In other words, the line between Greene and Warren ran about where Crawfordville now stands. Much of the land that Greene received from Wilkes in 1802, was given by Greene to help form Taliaferro county in 1825. Whatley's Mill, later named Bethesda Baptist church, *was in Wilkes when it was constituted in 1785* - one year before Greene was laid out from Washington county.

Bethany Presbyterian church was in Greene when established in 1786, and was never in Wilkes.

T. B. Rice, Historian of Greene County
September 16, 1940

that it is described as in Wilkes county. So Bethany church when organized, was in Wilkes county. There was a Rev. Daniel Thatcher, a missionary sent from North Carolina, who preached in the neighborhood and organized the church, and Mr. Simpson tells me it had then 50 members, so it began as a very strong church. At the time that Bethany was organized, Moses Waddell[2] was a young fellow about fifteen years of age teaching in the neighborhood. He was afterwards a minister, and became President of Franklin College now the University of Georgia. In 1787, the Creek Indians crossed the Oconee river and burned the newly built town of Greensboro. Bethany church celebrated its centennial in 1886. If the Bethany people are correct in placing their original organization at 1786, they have the same age as Phillips and Bethesda Baptist churches. It was the year when the Methodist Conference sent John Major and Thomas Humphries to Georgia. And also Bethany church is the oldest organized Presbyterian church in the up country.

In 1788, the year in which the first Methodist Conference was held by Bishop Asbury, in the Forks of Broad River, the Presbytery of South Carolina met at Long Cane church and petitions for ministerial supplies were sent to it from the following Presbyterian congregations in Georgia, viz: Bethany, Siloam (now Greenesboro) Goshen, also in Greene and near Greenesboro, Ebenezer (Mt. Zion.) Little Britain, (on Little River) New Hope, now in Madison county, Falling Creek and Bethlehem in Wilkes.

At this meeting of 1788, a license to preach the gospel was asked for by a teacher of Carolina who was destined to play a somewhat conspicuous part in Wilkes county, while he lived. His death in the prime of his usefulness, was a most severe blow to the Presbyterian church in upper Georgia. This was the Rev. John Springer, who was ordained a hundred years ago, come the 21st of next July, under Mr. Charles Alexander's great poplar. The first knowledge that we have of the Presbyterians of Washington and Smyrna is in 1790, when they sent up a call to the Presbytery, for Mr. Springer as their minister. They

(2) There is a tradition, supported by letters written by a grandson of Dr. Waddell, that seems to prove that his first school was in Greensboro, and began in the fall of 1786. According to tradition, Moses Waddell came to Greensboro when the town was being laid out. He was around 18 years of age, had a fair education, and applied as a teacher for the children of the first settlers. He was given the place, and taught during the fall of 1786 and the spring of 1787. After his school closed he is said to have returned to North Carolina for the purpose of bringing his parents to Georgia; and when he reached Greensboro, in an ox cart, with his parents and their possessions, he found that the town had been burned by the Indians, many of the people had been killed, the building in which he had taught had been burned, and he saw no prospect for a school in Greensboro, so he drove on to Bethany where he started his second school.
T. B. Rice, Historian of Greene County,
September 16, 1940.

must have been an organized church when they did so, and it is probable that Smyrna church was organized as early as 1788, and that the Presbyterians in Washington belonged then to the church at Smyrna.

Rev. John Springer was a native of Delaware, born 1745, so that he was forty five years old when he was ordained. He was converted at the age of twenty-two, but he did not go to Princeton College, N. J., until he was twenty seven years old. Thus he was fully able to appreciate the advantage of a good education, and all we learn of him goes to show that he was one of the best scholars of his time in the Southern States. There is still preserved in print a copy of a long letter from him, written in 1773 when he was at Princeton, to a Mr. Thornton, a gentleman in London, who seems to have been much interested in him. It gives an account of his conversion, and shows conclusively the depth of his religious convictions, and the strength of his piety. He was first called to Virginia as assistant tutor in Hampden Sidney College. This was during the Revolution. When Virginia became the seat of war, he went to North Carolina, where he began to teach. From that state he went to South Carolina where he became president of a college at Ninety-Six or Cambridge, and gained a very high reputation as a teacher. His delay in becoming a minister seems to have been due to a deep sense of his worthiness. Mr. Springer's application to the Presbytery for a license to preach was seconded by a letter from Gen. Andrew Pickens. Probably it was also through the recommendation of Gen. Pickens who must have been a well known and influential person in Wilkes county, that he was called to Georgia.

There was, of course, no church building at Smyrna in 1790, for Mr. Springer was ordained under the great poplar or tulip tree, which is still standing and visible above surrounding trees in all the eastern part of Washington. The trunk of the tree is now so large that a man on horseback stationed behind it, is entirely concealed from the view of persons on the other side.

This great poplar is one of the historical antiquities of Washington, but the cause of the interest which it excites is not generally understood and often incorrectly stated. It is sometimes said that the first Presbytery held in Georgia met beneath its branches. No such body as a Presbytery ever met there. Mr. Springer was ordained by the authority of the Presbytery of South Carolina, who sent a committee of perhaps three ministers to perform the ordination. These facts are sometimes expressed in Presbyterian language, by saying that Mr. Springer was ordained by the Presbytery of South Carolina. This merely means that a small committee of that body was sent, armed with their authority to perform the ordination. I have sometimes heard it said that this is the largest poplar in Georgia. We do not know that this is so, and indeed it is not probable, though ours is a very large poplar. The tree has a historical interest because under it was ordained Rev. John Springer, the first Presbyterian minister ordained west of the Savannah river, and of course the first Presbyterian minister ordained in Georgia. Who the ordaining ministers were, we do not know. Their names, however, are doubtless preserved in the records of the presbytery of South Carolina; if these were kept out of the way of Gen. Sherman's torch, which in Atlanta caused us the irreparable loss of Dr. John S. Wilson's MSS, materials for a history of the Presbyterian church in Georgia. One person present and assisting in the ordination of Mr. Springer, we know. This was John Wingfield, the brother of the late Mrs. John Pettus, the father of Mrs. Rebecca (or Garland) Wingfield, whom many of us remember, of Miss Ann Wingfield, &c., &c.

Mr. Springer was ordained July 21, 1790. The manuscript of the Academy Commissioners from whom I quoted so much, has an entry in September 1790 in which it is stated that the "trustees of the Presbyterian church" have made application to them for a lot on which to build a church. The Academy Commissioners, who had not yet sold the common, offered these trustees of "the Presbyterian church," the two lots of the common lying west of what is now the property of Mr. T. C. Hogue. They are the lots on which the new residence of Mr. T. M. Green has lately been built. They are numbered 107-108 in the plan of the town. For some reason or other, they did not see fit to accept this offer, as is evident. This is evidently the Presbyterian church which shortly afterward was built at Smyrna, and the petition and its result shows the substantial oneness of the Smyrna church with the Washington church.

Mr. Springer very soon began to teach, in addition to his ministerial duties. The early Presbyterian ministers did a great service to the cause of education. Mr. Springer had a school of very high character about three miles from Washington on the Mallorysville road. It stood where Mr. Huguley now lives about one mile south of the Armstrong place and on the same side of the road. It was called Walnut Hill and the road up the long hill on which it stood just north of Belmont creek is still bordered by occasional walnut trees. The distinguished reputation of Mr. Springer as a teacher is shown by several facts. Boys were sent to school to him from Augusta when the Augusta Academy was in a flourishing condition. Among these was John Forsyth afterwards Governor of Georgia, U.S. Senator, and Minister to Spain. Another eminent pupil of Mr. Springer was Rev. Jesse Mercer. It is one of the things most honorable to Mr. Mercer that after he grew to manhood and had married he went to studying to repair the defects in his early education which were occasioned by the state of the country at the close of the revolution. He selected Mr. Springer as his teacher and for two years lived near Mr. Springer on Walnut Hill in order to study under him. A strong friendship sprang up between the two men which lasted during Mr. Springer's life.

There was a great want of teachers in Georgia at that time and the thorough education which the Presbyterian church requires of her ministers made them very desirable teachers. Those who came to Georgia were apt to be urged into the work of education. Rev. Moses Waddell and Rev. Francis Cummins were distinguished teachers. Dr. Waddell taught John C. Calhoun, Gov. McDuffie, and Gov. Gilmer, before he became president of Franklin College. Dr. Cummins taught Andrew Jackson. I am disposed to think that the Presbyterian church suffered from this diversion of her ministry into another channel. There were certainly a number of places where a small nucleus of Presbyterians were disposed to form a church but not being able to get preaching, joined other churches. If our ministers could have preached nearly every day as did the Methodists, more work could have been done.

The Presbyterian ministers in Georgia up to 1795, were only Rev. John Newton at Bethsalem (Lexington) in Oglethorpe, and Rev. John Springer at Washington and Smyrna. But in that year 1793, a Rev. Robert Cunningham came to join them. He was a Pennsylvanian and he became pastor of the churches of Bethany and Ebenezer. (Mt. Zion.) He went to live among the Bethany people, who had built themselves a log church. As there were no saw mills, they made seats from slabs which were split from logs and hewed. This building lasted until about the beginning of the present century.

I have already spoken of Moses Waddell who taught school at Bethany, when Greene county suffered from an incursion of Indians who burned Greenesboro. He returned in 1788, and was converted under the preaching and influence of Rev. Daniel Thatcher, whom I have already mentioned as the organizer of Bethany church. He then determined to study for the ministry, and by Mr. Springer's advice went to Hampden Sidney College Virginia. He was so thoroughly prepared for college, that it was not necessary for him to remain longer than eight months before he graduated. Then he returned to Georgia and became pastor of New Hope Church, then in Elbert, now in Madison county. He was also pastor of a church called Carmal which I am unable to locate now. In 1793 or 1794, he opened a school in Columbia county, to which John C. Calhoun was sent as a boy thirteen years old. Waddell married Calhoun's sister Rebecca who however died a year after her marriage.

In addition to these ministers there was a Rev. Wm.

Montgomery who came to Georgia to take charge of New Hope church.

These five ministers were in the Georgia up country in 1796. This was the year that the Washington people made a serious beginning to build the brick Academy which they had so long been trying to erect. They set to work at it in earnest by electing John Springer the president of the Board of Academy Commissioners, and Hope Hull Vice-President. It shows the estimate put on this early Presbyterian in the county. Some knowledge I have gained of John Springer by reading his will, since I wrote about the Academy, convinces me that he was an excellent man of business and that the knowledge of this fact caused him to be put thus at the head of the educational interests of the county. John Springer's relations to Jesse Mercer and Hope Hull, with both of whom he was, it is evident, on terms of great intimacy show the character and high influence of the man. When we celebrate his centennial, Baptist and Methodists may well take an interest in our honor of a man whom Jesse Mercer and Hope Hull by their acts evidently endorsed as one of the most valuable citizens of Wilkes in his time. John Springer subscribed $50 to the fund for building the Academy. Of his ability to do this I shall speak hereafter.

Two events of great importance in the earlier history of the Presbyterian church in Georgia took place in Wilkes in the nineties of the last century. One was the ordination of Rev. John Springer already related which took place July 21, 1790, and will perhaps have a centennial celebration this year.

The other was the first meeting of Hopewell Presbytery on March 16, 1797. This body was laid off from the Presbytery of South Carolina in 1796, and I think it very certain that the settlement here of such a man as John Springer, together with a knowledge of the great degree of personal influence which he had attained, and probably also his personal advice as to the wisdom of such a step, caused the Presbytery to be set off. This is the beginning of the separate organized existence of the Presbyterian church in Georgia. The Church in Augusta soon after placed itself under the charge of Presbytery. Of course, this independence of the church in Georgia, was not complete until the formation of the Synod of Georgia. Thus we may say that the Presbyterian, like the Methodist church of Georgia had its birth in Wilkes county.

Hopewell Presbytery held its first meeting in what was called Liberty church, then standing nearly nine miles southwest of Washington.

On last Thursday I went with Rev. E. T. Simpson to see the

site of old Liberty church. The church organization of Liberty was moved, and is now represented by the Presbyterian church at Woodstock(3) in Oglethorpe county. Nobody now living ever heard preaching in Liberty church. Mrs. Ellington who is seventy-three years old tells me that when she was a child she rode by Liberty church with her mother, and the old house of hewn logs had then fallen in, and she remembers the sadness with which the sight seemed to impress her mother. The place where it stood is not very far north of the battle ground of Kettle Creek. It is on land, that now belongs to Mr. Henry T. Slaton, between the Greensboro and Scull Shoals roads. It was built by Archibald Simpson (the ancestor of Rev. F. T. Simpson, and Dr. Simpson, the Revolutionary soldier who married Kitty Nelson) James Daniel and -----Finley, aided by some others. James Daniel, was the grandfather of the late Mr. Robert C. Daniel of Woodstock, and of Mr. Samuel Daniel still living but now an old man. The Findleys were once an important family in the county. A son of this Findley became Rev. David Findley, a Presbyterian minister of some reputation who married Eliza Goode of Washington and went to Montgomery, Ala. Old Mrs. Lyle, who died a few years ago in that part of the county was the last descendant of the Findleys in the county. She survived to be the one Presbyterian in what had become a Baptist neighborhood but no persuasions could induce her to forsake her church.

When Hopewell Presbytery met in 1797, in this old and almost forgotten church, there were present the Rev. Messrs. Springer, Waddel Newton, Cunningham, Montgomery; the elders James Daniel of Liberty, Ezekiel Gilham from Bethsalem (now Lexington) and Lodowick Tuggle who was the first elder from Bethany. They elected John Springer moderator, and Moses Waddel clerk, or secretary. It was a small body, but no Presbytery that ever sat in Georgia was more ably officered. Mr. Springer preached from Luke IV. 18, and as it is the only text I can find which he used, I will give it in full: "the Spirit of the Lord is upon me, because he hath anointed me to preach the gospel to the poor, he hath sent me to heal the broken-hearted,

(3) Woodstock-Philomath - is located at, or near the point where Greene, Oglethorpe, Taliaferro, and Wilkes counties corner, and due to changes in county lines, has been in all of the above named counties. Whether it ever had a Postoffice by that name, I do not know; but Alexander Hamilton Stephens is said to have given the village that name when he taught school there. Philomath means - a place of learning. Woodstock, in Cherokee county, came into existence long after the above named village was established, and, in all probability, was given that name by someone who had moved into that section from north Georgia around 1825-1835.

T. B. Rice, Historian of Greene County,
September 16, 1940

to preach deliverance to the captives, and recovering of sight to the blind, to set at liberty them that are bruised, to preach the acceptable year of the Lord." It was a sort of Missionary sermon, evidently, and this was extremely appropriate, for the men to whom it was preached were missionaries, and upper Georgia was then missionary ground. We are told that Mr. Springer always preached without notes, which were often a disadvantage to Presbyterian ministers of the older time, especially those who came from the North. Mr. Springer however, was not a New England Man, for he came from Delaware, and so he shared that feeling, or instinct, which prompts us Southerners; and makes a man talk not read to his audience; desire to be talked, not read to. He is said to have been an attractive preacher, and I wish we could have had some sermon preserved. But since he did not write, he left no sermons. After his death, those who had esteemed and loved him wished to print something from him, but nothing could be found except the lecture and sermon which had been required when he was licensed, as "parts of trial."

These were published in 1805 by Hobby and Bunce in Augusta. He is said to have had a delivery of "uncommon ease and elegance." Doubtless, it was a sermon of great power, preached a hundred years ago on the spot where a few days ago I saw only a grassy bank with the evening sun shining on it, and no indication that a house had ever been there. But on the other side of the road, there is a buryingground which Mr. Henry Slaton has religiously resurrected. There are no inscribed tombstones, and piles of fallen wall show the places where the dead Presbyterians await the resurrection.

Here lie James Daniel and his wife, Archibald Simpson and Kitty Nelson, who rode on horseback from Virginia, and also Mary Sankie whom Archibald Simpson married when Kitty Nelson died. But they were dead and gone so long ago, and so many had been the changes, that Mr. Simpson could not identify the graves of his grandparents.

We drove away by an old road on which a hundred years ago, Rev. John Newton and Ezekiel Gillam (or Gillham probably) must have rode on horseback from Bethsalem or Lexington, to attend the Presbytery at Liberty church. The road was probably then through a nearly unbroken forest.

Dr. Wilson reports from the minutes of this Presbytery that there were then under care of Presbytery the following churches: Liberty, Bethany, Little Britain, Bethsalem, New Hope, Bethsaida, Siloam, Smyrna,[(4)]* Joppa, Carmel,

* Footnote (4) on page 155.

Sharon, Ebenezer, Providence, Concord, Beersheba and Unity churches. He says that at this meeting, the church of Hebron, then in Franklin now in Banks county, and also Thyatira church were taken under the care of Presbytery. Several of these churches are extinct and only Bethany, New Hope and Hebron retain the names that they had a hundred years ago.

Before the second meeting of Presbytery, one of this small number of preachers died, Rev. John Newton. And eighteen months after this 16th March 1797, namely on Sept. 3d, 1798, John Springer died. There was another loss to Presbyterianism in the August Proceeding this September. John Talbot, who was the most important member of Smyrna church and had given the ground on which it was built, died in August, and his death perhaps led to that of Mr. Springer. It was very warm weather and Mr. Springer spoke a long time at the grave, and was doubtless much heated; and when he reached home he went to bed with a fever from which he never recovered. He was violently ill, and generally delirious, but there were lucid moments in which he expressed his believing hope, and spoke earnestly to his surviving friends. We are told that he died greatly lamented. He was buried at Walnut Hill, and many years afterward, his wife was placed beside him. No monument was placed over his grave, though he left an ample provision for his family, but at that early day, it was nearly impossible to get tombstones. None was placed over John Talbot, though he was a rich man at his death, his will showing that he owned a hundred negroes

(4) The Academy and Siloam Meeting House were both built on Cemetery Hill in the town of Greensboro. The Academy was used until after the War Between the States; the Siloam Meeting House was used for public worship by Baptists, Methodists, Presbyterians as late as 1830.

The Methodists built a hewn log church in 1799 and discontinued their use of the Siloam Meeting House. Jesse Mercer and Adiel Sherwood constituted the Greensboro Baptist church, in the old Siloam Meeting House, in the town of Greensboro, on June 9, 1821, and both the Baptists and Presbyterians continued to worship there until 1830. In that year, these two churches secured a charter for 'The Union Meeting House' which was built at the corner of East and North Streets in the town of Greensboro. Each denomination had use of the building for two weeks during each month, and all expenses were equally divided between them (the writer has many of the bills showing where they were paid 50/50). The Baptists bought the Presbyterian's interest in 1850.

In the year 1828, Smyrna Baptist church was organized. It was located six miles east of Greensboro. A thickly settled community sprang up around this church, two or three stores were built, a Methodist church was built, and very soon, a village came into existence (the community clung to the name of Smyrna). The village grew until a Postoffice was a necessity; there was already a Georgia Postoffice called Smyrna, so a new name had to be created. The Baptist church had an unusual baptismal pool, in which there was a constant stream of clear water that suggested the 'Pool of Siloam', and this is supposed to be the origin of the name. Miss Eliza Bowen, in all probability, knew something of the old Siloam Meeting House and got it confused with the village of Siloam, which came into existence about the time she wrote her history.

T. B. Rice, Historian of Greene County,
September 16, 1940.

and a large body of land. I am indebted to Mr. Simpson for a visit to the graves of both these men. The Talbot cemetery is surrounded by a rock wall, and the place in which Mr. Talbot is interred is easily identified.

Mr. Simpson, who took me to Walnut Hill, had previously seen the grave of John Springer near a large oak still standing. This oak is a little in the way of the road which leads to the house of Mr. Huguely, who now owns Walnut Hill, and so it has led the drivers of wagons and other vehicles to turn and drive over the graveyard. Mr. Huguely tells us that he has endeavored to have the graves respected, but cannot control drivers and others who go up to his house. However this may be, the road now used, to go to Mr. Huguely's house, passes directly over the grave of Rev. John Springer who was in his time one of the most important and respected citizens of this county. Mr. Simpson and I could find neither head nor footstone, but after we left, Mr. Huguely who kindly continued to search, found one. It would be a fitting celebration of the centennial to put some enduring mark over Mr. Springer's grave.

My investigation of his history has impressed me very much with his character and ability. It may be thought that this is because I am myself a Presbyterian, but to answer this it is only necessary to refer to the friendship felt for him by such men as Jesse Mercer and Hope Hull, both of them men noted for sound judgment and high character. Neither Jesse Mercer nor Hope Hull nor John Springer were men of professional narrowness. All three were to a considerable extent men of affairs. Of Jesse Mercer in this character I shall have occasion to say more in a future number, in which I shall add to my article on the Baptists.

In collecting materials for these chronicles, I have drawn out two MS. documents which throw light on Mr. Springer's character, and the influence he had. These are the record book of the Academy Commissioners, and Mr. Springer's own will which I found in the Ordinary's office. The former shows plainly the public confidence in him as a business man; his will shows us a good reason for it, for to my surprise I found that he had accumulated a handsome property. He wills away about 3000 acres of land and forty negroes. His scholarship and ability, his piety and uprightness, his business capacity and administrative talent all make him one of the foremost men of his time in this state. He had been a very successful college president in Carolina before coming here, and the influence that he had evidently gained convinces me that if he had lived he would have been made president of Franklin College now the University of Georgia.

I have been somewhat impressed with the idea that in making him president of the Academy board, it was intended to invite him to be at the head of that school. If it had been in active operation with Mr. Springer at its head, it might have caused the college to be established here. Dr. Howe in his *History of the Presbyterian church in Carolina,* speaks of Mr. Springer and Hope Hull as teaching school together. They certainly did not do so in Washington. I am a little disposed to think they may have taught together at Walnut Hill, that this may have been the site of Succoth Academy and bought by John Springer. Certainly Succoth Academy was north of Washington. If I can ever get a copy of David Merriwether's deed, I shall probably know about this.

Long after Mr. Springer's death, his house at Walnut Hill was moved to Washington and placed on the site of Mrs. Dr. Lane's present home. This information comes through Mr. Simpson, from the late Mr. Frank Armstrong, who lived within a mile of Walnut Hill. The house was added to, improved, changed, but the Springer foundation was never taken away, so substantially, it is John Springer's house still.

The will of John Springer was made when he was in perfect health, in 1795. It shows that his children were Sally, Elizabeth, Nancy, William, Susannah, Mary Ann, and the two first were probably married when he died, but their married names are not given. He gives each one about 1000 acres of land and some negroes, and to his wife he gives the property at Walnut Hill with several negroes. He directs that from this, each child shall have bought for it, a good horse saddle and bridle. He also directs that each child shall have a feather bed and its furniture. This is a common legacy to daughters in the old book of wills. Mrs. Vickers remembers his son who was called "Billy Springer." He was a very large man. Also she remembers a daughter who married James Alexander, who kept a hotel here when she came.

Mrs. Ann Springer lived here for many years. She was a Miss Green, for her father, Wm. Green and her brother Solomon Green, are joint executors with her of Mr. Springer's will. She was a very peculiar woman. Her oddities were much talked of and long remembered. She lived at the northeast corner of the square. The building is now the Masonic Hall.

The will of John Talbot is found in the old record book of wills, just before that of John Springer. Mr. Talbot was the most important, intelligent, rich and liberal member of Smyrna church which was thus severely tried in 1798 to lose its able and accomplished pastor and its chief elder.

I have already written something of John Talbot, but I have learned some further facts since, which I will relate before proceeding to tell how the church at Smyrna was moved to Washington. A great deal of the interest of chronicles like these comes from biographical details. Mr. Talbot is spoken of as a "venerable man" when he died. His son Thomas Talbot died in 1853, aged 86, so that the latter was 31 years old when his father died, 17 years old when the old gentleman came to Georgia in 1784. It is a matter of curious interest only, that Mr. Talbot was a descendant of the Talbots who were Earls of Shrewsbury. General W. H. T. Walker our gallant Confederate who was killed at the siege of Atlanta by Sherman, was a descendant of our John Talbot. Freeman Walker of Augusta who married John Talbot's daughter Elizabeth was a lawyer distinguished for being the most polished gentleman at the Augusta bar, which was noted for its fine gentlemen. I have often heard Judge Andrews speak of his elegant manners.

John Talbot must have been one of the richest men of his day in this county. His will disposes of a large body of land and about a hundred negroes. Of his sons Matthew and Thomas Talbot, I have already spoken. His daughters, as named in his will, were Phoebe Cresswell, Mary Triplett and Elizabeth Walker. Before his death, he had erected good houses for them all and settled them. His daughter Phoebe married David Creswell, who was a surveyor, and so also was Matthew Talbot. Their names occur often in the book which records the head rights. The large house about a mile from Washington on the south side of the Augusta road was built for Mrs. Creswell. Mrs. Ann Sims and Mrs. John Phinizy of Augusta were her descendants.

In Mr. Talbot's will he leaves his wife about forty negroes and half this plantation, besides a good deal of other personal estate. As his daughters were already keeping house, I suppose that they did not need that usual legacy to the girls of that day, "a feather bed and its furniture," so we find that John Talbot left his wife "eight feather beds and their furniture," which, by contrast reminds us of William Shakespeare and that "second best bed" which he left his wife. Besides this, John Talbot left his wife, his three stills and their furniture, and also 100 gals. of whiskey. Times have changed since then. Mr. Talbot willed his library to his two sons Matthew and Thomas to be divided between them. This collection contained some valuable books, showing that Mr. Talbot was a man of great intelligence. The book *Morse's Geography*, published in 1796, from which I have quoted, was lent to me by Mr. Simpson, and was bought by him from a sale of some of John Talbot's books. A geography is a book which gets out of date very soon and one published in 1796 is now very antiquated and amusing; but it was the latest and best book on the subject at that time. The two volumes have been presented to the Mary Willis Library, and ought to be kept with great care, not merely because they are now curious relics but because they were part of the library of such an eminent citizen as John Talbot. Rev. F. T. Simpson owns one of the original subscription copies of that famous book *Edwards on the Will,* which also came from the library of John Talbot.

Albert Lamar well known in our time as a successful editor was a descendant of John Talbot. So also was Mrs. Octavia Walton LeVert. A son of his daughter Mary Triplett married Martha Randolph a sister of Miss Maria Randolph, and her daughter Dora Triplett (not the Dora Triplett now living but her aunt) was the most beautiful woman I ever saw. Her mother Mrs. Martha R. Triplett moved to Florida. The daughter there became acquainted with Mad Achilie Murat who was by marriage connected with the Bonapartes. She made a visit to France during the second empire and took Dora Triplett with her, who excited great admiration by her beauty, in the circles of the empire. Shortly after she returned, she died of yellow fever at Key West the first victim of a fatal summer. There are two pictures of her of which one is an imperfect copy. The other is a fine painting which is justly admired but it gives only an imperfect idea of Dora Triplett's remarkable beauty. She was a tall elegant blue eyed blonde, with hair of a pale cool brown. I think that the shade is called "Preston brown" from a celebrated beauty the Duchess of Preston.

I will now return to my chronicles of the Presbyterian church at Smyrna after the deaths of John Talbot and Rev. John Springer in 1798. Unfortunately, the records of Smyrna church have been lost, and perhaps destroyed, in moving the papers of Mr. Thomas Talbot. So we can learn little of the Presbyterian church in Wilkes until 1820. We know that Presbyterians met at Smyrna church in 1805 and that Rev. Francis Cummins then came into the body. Dr. Moses Waddell left Georgia in 1801, to teach at Vienna, and then at Willington. He returned to our state and Hopewell Presbytery in 1820, having been made President of the University of Georgia. Dr. Wilson tells that in 1820, the church at Washington, or Smyrna, had but fifteen members. But a better day was at hand. The church building at Smyrna had fallen into decay, and the church then moved to Washington. About that time or a little later they secured the services of Rev. Alexander H. Webster. He doubtless preached for them at first in the Methodist church.

It is sometimes said that the old Methodist church was at first a Union church for the benefit of all denominations. It is probable that money for aid in building it, was furnished by all, and this with a mere expectation or understanding that the Methodists who used it only one or at most two Sundays in the month, would allow others to use it. But the Methodists were the sole owners of the property.

The regular minutes of the Presbyterian Church are preserved from October 20, 1827, but there is prefixed to these a short account of Mr. Webster's connection with the church. It states that the church in Washington "had long languished, having no pastor spiritual guide or leader, and barely twenty members, who were scattered over the county." It goes on to say that Alexander H. Webster came to Washington in 1823 to take charge of the Academy as its rector; that he was a licentiate then, and was ordained in May 1823; "the ordination took place in the Methodist meeting house, there not being at that time any other house dedicated to the public worship of God in this place."

Mr. Simpson tells me that Mr. Webster had been as he has heard, a tutor in the college at Athens, and that he came from there to preach in Washington and was made Rector of the Academy and became pastor of the Church.

The deed for the lot on which the church was built was given by Dr. Joel Abbott, who was then living on the property which was afterwards owned by Gen. Toombs. This deed is still in the Ordinary's office, and I will give the substance in the exact words, omitting what is merely legal verbiage. "This indenture made 29th day of July, 1825, between Joel Abbott of the one part, and Thomas Terrel, Samuel Barnett, Andrew G. Semmes, Constantine Church, and James Wingfield, Trustees of the Presbyterian church in the town of Washington of the other part. Witnesseth that the said Joel Abbott, for and in consideration of the sum of two hundred dollars, being his donation to said church, &c., &c., hath granted sold, &c., all that lot of land adjoining Charles Quigley's in the town of Washington, beginning at the china tree on Main Street then south on Quigley's line to his southeast corner, thence west on said Quigley's back line to the head of Liberty street, thence south across the end of said street; thence east to a line which will run parallel with said Quigley's line at a distance of 20 feet east from it; thence north 202½ feet on said parallel of 20 feet east of Quigley's line; thence east 70 feet, thence north 150 feet, thence west 90 feet to the beginning, to have and to hold &c. &c., unto the said trustees and their successors, to the only proper use benefit and behoof of the said Trustees and their successors for the use of said church--and the said Abbott and his heirs will defend the same, &c. &c."

This is a curious deed and somewhat difficult of construction, except by the knowledge of the present actual boundaries of the property. I am disposed to think that the copyist omitted a few words before those italicised,* and that the omitted words would make the italicised "thence" refer to the point which is now the southwest angle of the church lot, and which is on the parallel described in the deed. If we give this meaning to the italicised "thence," the rest is clear,--- and I see no other supposed error of copyist which would make it clear. This could not affect the property, if there is any common sense in the law and the lawyers, say it is the

perfection of common sense. The deed confirms the statement
made to me long ago by Judge Andrews and printed by me at the
time, viz; that Dr. Abbott and Charles Quigley his neighbor
could not get along, and that Dr. Abbott said that he hoped by
putting a church and a street between himself and his obnoxious
neighbor, to be able to get along with him. The little street
ought to be called Abbott Street. The records of the Presbyterian church which contain lists of members, do not show that
Dr. Abbott was ever a member of the church. His descendants
are new Presbyterians and I suppose he and his family were of
the congregation.
   It will be seen that the property is inalienable from the
use of the Presbyterian church. It is the only Protestant
church in Washington of which this is true.
   The account prefixed to the Book of Minutes does not state
when the church was completed. I presume it was in 1826. The
book has written on the fly leaf the words "Presbyterian
church, Washington, Ga., 1826," and there is a list of, "Members added on examination." There are 24 of these at the
beginning without date. These are, I am sure, the original
members. After their names come others with dates, the first
being Samuel Goode, Nov. 26, 1826.
   The prefixed account states that Mr. Webster was instru-
mental in adding about sixty members. After this, it goes on
to say, that at the close of 1827, the membership reached one
hundred, and the church then took measures which released Mr.
Webster from his duties in the Academy and would have enabled
him, from January 1828, to devote his whole time to the preaching and pastoral work of the church. But he died Oct. 29,
1827. There was, as I have heard Judge Andrews and others say,
a great deal of sickness in Washington in the years 1827 and
1828. Mr. Webster, I have heard, died of the fever then preva-
lent. Mr. Webster was, by resolution of the members of the
church, buried in front of their building for worship. His
tomb was taken inside when the vestibule and spire were added.
Mrs. Vickers tells me that when she came to Washington in
1836, this addition was making.
   The death of Mr. Webster appears to have produced a profound
effect on Washington. Mrs. Vickers tells me that when she came
in 1836, people were constantly referring to the piety and
excellence of Mr. Webster and Miss Avis Minton. The latter was
a sister of Mrs. Pelot and Miss Mary Minton, who died in what
people called the "sickly years" of 1827 and 1828.
   Mr. A. L. Alexander, than whom there was no better judge,
and who remembered Mr. Webster well said that he was a young
man of marked talent and character. All traditions report a
great revival in the Presbyterian church in 1826 and 1827 under
the preaching of Mr. Webster. Rev. Micaijah Lane, a venerable

Baptist preacher who died a few years ago, told Rev. Mr. Simpson that he remembered it well, that he himself used to come in regularly from the country during the meeting to hear Mr. Webster and that a great many other country people came. The record of the church confirms this account of a revival, by showing that in 1826, 43 persons were admitted to the church by examination, and 21 in 1827. An examination of the register shows that among these, were some of the most substantial people in the place.

The following is a list of the original members of the church, who had belonged to it at Smyrna, as seems probable. The dates after each, show when they died according to the register of deaths, in the session book. John Wingfield, 1828, aged 87. This was the brother of Mrs. John Pettus, Rebecca Wingfield, wife of foregoing, Thomas Terrell, 1838. Sabina Terrell, 1857; Andrew G. Semmes, 1833; Mary Semmes, 1838; Thomas Talbot, 1853, aged 86; Hannah Banks, 1839; Elizabeth Hanson, 1841, aged 93; Margaret McRea (afterwards Mrs. Clark,) died 1838. Nancy McRea, died 1841, aged 64, (from the two foregoing the deed came by sale, for the Baptist church lot;) Catherine Hay, 1832, (this was the second wife of Dr. Gilbert Hay who had been Mrs. Graves, grandmother of Gen. James Graves) Mary Robertson, 1828; William Barnett 1828; Lillis Barnett, 1862; Eleanor Corbett, 1841, aged 71, Eliza Lobdell (removed about 1834.) Constantine Church 1826; Wm. L. Weems, 1826; Mrs. Ellen Robinson, 1838; (first wife of postmaster R;) Mrs. Mary Church removed 1833; Henrietta Plumb (drowned herself, date forgotten.) Wm. L. Weems 1826. He was a brother of Dr. Walter Weems; Susan Wingfield 1864, she was Mrs. James Wingfield daughter of an early settler, Francis Gordon; Avis Winton, 1827; Benjamin Paull 1843; Elisa Hodge afterwards Mrs. Archibald Wingfield 1832. Mrs. Eliza Webster, wife of Rev. Mr. Webster died 1832.

I find among baptisms, that of Alexander Semmes, infant son of Eliza Webster baptized May 4, 1829.

Mrs. Hanson was an aunt of the Weems brothers, who came from Virginia with them. They settled in the Hill neighborhood at first, and there Mrs. Hanson and Wm. L. Weems are buried. Thomas Terrell is the son of Wm. Terrell and he sold his lot to the town, to form part of the square. His wife was the aunt of Mrs. James Wingfield and lived to be a hundred years old.

Mrs. Ellington who went to school here in the twenties tells me she has some faint recollection of Mr. Webster. After his death, she went to school to his widow.

Constantine Church, one of the trustees mentioned in the deed I gave, built the older part of the house now occupied by Merriwether Hill. His residence lots numbered 62 and 77, of the town plan, are parts of the common and originally sold to

Dr. Thompson Bird. C. Church bought them from John Burch and his wife Ann C. Burch in 1819, for $300. Mr. Church built a small house but a few years after his death, the place was sold to Mr. Henry Terrel who added to the house and brought it nearly to its present condition.

The following is a list of the pastors of the Presbyterian church with the dates at which they came. It is carefully made out from the Minutes book. Alexander H. Webster, 1823; N. Hoyt, 1828; John Brown, 1830; John Boggs, 1831; Samuel J. Cassells, 1837; G. H. W. Petrie, 1839; D. McNeil Turner, 1852; I. S. Axson, 1854; John Jones, 1856; G. W. Boggs, 1857; .J. B. Dunwoody, 1859; A. D. Montgomery, 1863; E. M. Green, 1866; Wm. S. Bean, 1873; John Jones, 1879; J. D. A. Brown, 1883.

Rev. Mr. Hoyt made a strong impression on the church, though he remained but a year. He spent the rest of his life in Athens. He liked Washington and some time near the close of his life, he expressed a desire to preach a farewell sermon to the people here. All the churches were closed except the Presbyterian, and Dr. Hoyt preached to a very large audience, a sermon, of great power. This was in 1865. He remained in Washington several days, and went to see all the older people.

Rev. Mr. Petrie's pastorate marks the most prosperous period of the church. The membership was more than a hundred during his stay. He was much beloved and deeply regretted. Dr. Axson who was afterwards for a very long time the pastor of the Central Presbyterian church in Savannah, did not live here, but came once in two weeks to preach. He was a preacher of much power. Dr. Jones as will be seen has twice been pastor of the church, when he was a young man and again when an old man. Rev. John B. Dunwoody left the church to become chaplain in the Confederate army. Rev. A. D. Montgomery was pastor during the war, when old men had to fill the places of the younger ones who had gone into the army. Rev. E. M. Green was forced to leave by the bad health of his wife. The people here were very strongly attached to Mr. Green, but they never knew what a good preacher he was. He was a somewhat diffident man, and at first preached wholly with notes. After he left here he ceased his practice. I heard him often in Kentucky, where he has been a man of very great usefulness, and is widely esteemed. The church which he serves in Danburg Kentucky has increased very largely under his ministry, and has greatly beautified and improved its church building which is a fine old house. Mr. Green has been thrown much where there were both Northern and Southern Presbyterians, and without in the least compromising his strong Southern principles, has done a great deal to allay bitterness and encourage a Christian spirit.

Rev. W. S. Bean is probably the most accomplished scholar who has served this church since John Springer's day. Mr. Bean ought to have been put in the Theological Seminary as teacher of Hebrew, and probably would have been had he not been a strong Woodrow man.

When the church at Smyrna was moved to Washington, Thomas Terrell and Andrew G. Semmes were elders. In 1828, Samuel Goode, Felix G. Hay and Joseph W. Robinson were made elders. The records say Samuel Goode received a letter of dismission but no date is given to show when he left Washington. His name appears for the last time in the session meetings in 1829. Felix G. Hay, who was the father of Mrs. Anna Sneed and Mrs. Lizzie Robertson, died in 1829. The house in which Mrs. George Dyson now lives, northwest corner of Alexander Ave., and South Street, was built for his widow. She died in 1814. Joseph Robinson died in 1855 aged 70.

In 1829, Lock Weems, Archibald Wingfield and Benjamin Paull became elders. Locke Weems moved to Columbus in 1843. Benjamin Paull died 1843, and Archibald Wingfield died 1851, aged 71.

Joseph Mosley was made elder in 1832, moved away 1843. A. S. Lewis was made elder 1840, moved away 1843. Mr. Lewis was the husband of Miss Caroline Lobdell. She came of a family of Lobdells who once lived on the north side of Court St., near Jefferson. In 1844, Dr. J. J. Robertson was made elder. He died 1873. His first wife was the daughter of Felix Hay and his second Miss Elizabeth Bowen from Savannah. In 1856, S. C. Ellington and F. T. Simpson became elders. Mr. Ellington was a grandson of James Daniel, elder of old Liberty church, who was a member of Hopewell Presbytery at its first meeting. When he died 1882, aged 72, he had attended more meetings of Presbytery and Synod than any elder in Georgia. Mr. F. T. Simpson became a minister, and still lives. In 1863, Samuel Barnett became elder; in 1872 Charles Alexander; in 1882, Osborne Barnett and Chas. Smith. These live at the present time, S. Barnett and O. S. Barnett having by request, been dismissed from the office.

This church has had two legacies of $1000 each from Miss Maria Randolph and A. L. Alexander. At one time, they owned a parsonage, and a letter still existing in the possession of Miss Belle Weems, shows that one of the original members, Mrs. Elizabeth Hanson, gave $1000 towards buying it. The house, greatly altered, is now in possession of Mr. Chas. Smith and stands on Alexander Avenue, on lot 79 of the town plan. The money left by Mr. Alexander and Miss Randolph is invested, so that only interest can be used.

The book of the Washington Church Session shows that the Presbyterian church at South Liberty near Raytown, was organized 1828. Charles C. Mills, who was a brother of Mrs. Jesse Mercer, and also his wife, Mrs. Sarah S. Mills were in

1828 dismissed to join the church, at South Liberty. It was thus so called to distinguish it from North Liberty, where the first meeting of Hopewell Presbytery took place.

The church minutes do not show that Dr. John H. Pope or Thomas Talbot were, as I had supposed, elders in the Washington church, though their names are recorded among members. My summary of church officers is perhaps somewhat dull, but it seems important to preserve it in an easily accessible place.

I will now say something of the history of Liberty Church (North Liberty) where Hopewell Presbytery first met. John Springer was preaching to this church once a month when he died, and his death was a serious misfortune to them. After that, the church fell into disuses from the impossibility of securing regular preaching and then it began to decay, and then too, the original members died, and it seemed destined to extinction. But at some time between 1815 and 1822, the congregation rallied, re-organized and built another church on an elevated spot south of the battle ground of Kettle Creek, called Starrs' Hill. Here Dr. Francis Cummins who was settled at Bethany came to preach to them once a month. He ordained Cunningham Daniel as elder. This was the son of the old elder and original settler James Daniel.

They called the church at Starrs Hill, Salem, but the organization was merely a continuation of that at Liberty. About 1822, the approaching infirmity of age forced Dr. Cummins to give up the charge. For a while, Alexander Webster preached to them part of his time and again the loss of the Washington church was a loss to them, when Mr. Webster died. Then Mr. Cassels preached to them a few times. But about 1834, the road was moved which passed over Starrs' Hill, and this put the church in a place extremely inconvenient of access. So they moved again, and built another Salem on land given by Joseph Foster. They had diminished to seven members when this removal took place. These were Cunningham Daniel and his wife Jane Daniel and his sister Miss Jane Daniel, Charles Gresham and his wife Lucretia Gresham, Jas. Findley, Isabella Findley. For awhile John B. Cassels preached to them, a brother of Samuel Cassels, but finally he died, and was buried in front of the church, just as Alexander Webster was at Washington. Then Rev. F. R. Goulding for a short time preached to them. In 1839, they secured the services of Rev. John W. Reid, and the church began to prosper. But the school which Mr. Reid established at Woodstock became very prosperous and the church members moved there; and in 1848, it was thought advisable to build a church at Woodstock and transfer services there. The church building was then sold to the congregation of Phillips Baptist Church for $350, and the church is now called Phillips Church.

The Presbyterians then built a church at Woodstock. The

church had new elders, on going to the second Salem. Robert C. Daniel a son of Cunningham Daniel became an elder and after his death his son William Daniel and afterwards his son John Daniel became elders, the latter now holding office. Thus four generations of Daniels in direct succession viz., James Daniel, Cunningham Daniel, Robert C. Daniel and his sons William and John Daniel have served the old church which has been called Liberty, Salem, Woodstock. This family of Daniels have been elders in this church more than a hundred years without interval. Rev. Mr. Reid died in 1876. Since then Rev. Paul Morton has served them. But this church is in rather depressed condition.

I ought to add that when they moved from Starrs Hill they had to be readmitted to Presbytery, as they had fallen out from non-attendance.

* Unfortunately typewritten copy from which composition was done failed to indicate italicised words referred to on p. 160.

CHAPTER XXVI

THE ACADEMY -- OLD AND NEW

I DID NOT intend to continue my history of the Academy until I had written up some other topics belonging to the early part of this century, but the present movement to re-organize that school--in its administration at least have given more immediate interest to the history of it, and especially of its property. I have heard a good many speculations and doubts as to the terms on which the Academy lots are held, and as I have fully looked the matter up, I think it will be best to speak of it now. I could treat the subject as I have done that of the churches, viz; bring it up to the present time, without interfering with other matters.

My investigation into the history of the Male Academy has brought me to some conclusions which have surprised me. The school is one of the oldest in Georgia, the trustees deriving their corporate power - the power to own property, to buy, to sell, to contract with workmen and also with teachers - from the same act of the legislature which gave corporate existence to the Richmond Academy in Augusta. This act was passed in 1783. The Richmond Academy celebrated its centennial several years ago, and had a distinguished body of Alumni to show for the hundred years. I have lately seen in some of the public prints allusion to the Louisville Academy as one of the oldest in Georgia. The Act of the legislature establishing the Louisville school was passed in 1796, so that it is thirteen years younger than the Washington Academy.

I had at first supposed that our present male Academy had some later and special charter, and when I began to see evidences of its identity with the old school which was housed on Mercer Hill, I went to Judge Reese's office to examine, with his aid, the volumes of Reports, in order to look for a charter. Judge Reese very kindly helped me in the search, but the conclusion we reached was that there is no authority for the corporate powers of the Trustees, other than the Act of 1783.

Unless the Academy were a better school, I do not know that we have any cause to glory in its antiquity, but it is certainly a strong argument for making it better. The inefficient old school and shackling building are what we have to show for a hundred and seven years of struggle carried on by some of the best men who have lived in the town and county. No one can read even a meagre account of what they did, without seeing that from first to last, our citizens have regarded good schools as one of the first objects of public endeavor, and that they never gave up though they have repeatedly failed. The difference in their success and that of Richmond Academy has been due to the fact that the former, from the first, owned the Sand Bar Ferry (a valuable property when there were only toll bridges at Augusta) and also to another fact, that it has had a number of other legacies. It is in fact a very rich school and really, it is said older than the Act of 1783, deriving some income from property granted by the crown and antedating the Revolution. But its corporate existence under our state government follows the Revolution.

I doubt if any of the Trustees of 1890 ever read the Act of 1783 under which they hold the property, so I will give it in substance. It appoints Micaijah Williamson, Robert Harper, Daniel Coleman and Zachariah Lamar Commissioners to lay out the town of Washington, by dividing a hundred acres into lots. They were to sell them, receive monies into their hands &c, and to apply the same to building a free school for said county--to erect a building, and the overplus, after building a church, is to be a fund in the hands of said commissioners and their successors forever as trustees, for the sole purpose of carrying this law into execution, and said Commissioners are to be liable for any and every examination that the Commissioners of the Augusta Academy are by this act subject to, and in the same manner the Commissioners or a majority of them, their successors in office or a majority of them are empowered titles to make to such lots in the town of Washington, and the monies and funds in like manner to place out at interest, as to them shall likewise appear most advantageous, and proper masters to engage for ruling said school, and by laws to institute, and contracts to enter into, for the building of said church and school.

"That on the death neglect or refusal to act, or suspension of any all, or either, of the said commissioners, or trustees, herein named, others shall be appointed by his honor the governor to fill up the vacancy" &c.

The examinations mentioned above to which the Commissioners of the Augusta Academy are liable, are stated in the previous sections of this act. They consist in rendering under oath annually, "a just and true account of the fund of said seminary to the governor," &c.

The Commissioners appointed by this act have merely the powers and functions of school trustees, except that of laying off and selling lots, which is of course a merely temporary duty. They have none of the powers of municipal officers, though they are called "Commissioners of the Academy and Town of Washington" both in this act and in some of the deeds to property.

Subsequently, in 1805, the town of Washington was incorporated, and in 1823 the act of incorporation was amended greatly. Under this incorporation there were elected another kind of Commissioners of Washington, officers with carefully stated municipal powers and duties, and as this made some confusion about the names, the Academy officers began to be called *trustees,* a name applied to them in the act.

In the record of the Academy Commissioners, it appears that they were appointed by the Governor. Thus, as I related in my former account, Gov. George Mathews, the first new appointment, made his appearance before the board armed with the Governor's commission, and was received. I asked Judge Reese how the change in the mode of election was brought about and he said, that it is evident that the fund contemplated in the act ceased to exist, and so they ceased to make reports to the Governor. Finally, as there was a mere house, and lot, the Superior Court probably empowered the trustees to fill vacancies in the board by election. Judge Reese says that nearly all the trustees of the Presbyterian church as at first appointed, having died, the Superior Court empowered the board to fill vacancies. So in this way the act of 1788 finally gave rise to the trustees of 1890 in the Academy.

As late as Feb. 11, 1820, the Commissioners of the Academy sold some lots of land in the town, which had, I suppose, returned into their hands from default of payment on the part of those persons to whom they had originally been sold. These were lots 51, 52, 65, 68, 71, 72, lots which lie to the south of Dr. Simpson's residence property on Liberty Street, and now belong to him. In 1820, the Commissioners sold them to Augustus H. Gibson, at $150, that is $25 per acre. This is the last record of any sale by them of town lots.

By 1819 the community seems to have become dissatisfied with the situation of the Academy house on Mercer hill, especially for female pupils. It must have been very bad walking in winter, for there were no sidewalks, and the streets and roads were, as tradition tells us, dreadfully cut up by the wagons in which all crops were then carried to market. Also there were no india rubber shoes then, though rough wooden sandals called *clogs,* were fastened to the shoes with straps. There is evidence that there was, almost from the first, a disposition to have a separate school for girls, since Mrs. Dugas' school was patronized in the beginning of the century. But at sometime between 1817 and 1819, the old theatre began to be used for a girls' school. The exact time of the change from theatre to school we do not know. The oldest copy now in existence of a newspaper published in Washington, was issued July

4, 1817, and is in the possession of Mrs. Lucy Simpson. In it we find the following advertisement: "The Thespian Society having obtained the professional services of Mr. and Mrs. Durang, Miss Moore and Miss Lettine, of the Charleston theatre, will, on Friday next, commence anew the Theatrical Exhibitions-particulars in the bills of the day."

Thus it is evident that in 1817, the theatre was still used for that purpose. But on Feb. 1, 1820, the Commissioners bought the old theatre and its lot from Mrs. Sally Griffin, and in the deed still existing as recorded in the clerk's office of Wilkes county, the building is called the *Female Academy*. The Commissioners who bought it were Samuel W. Goode, Wm. G. Gilbert, Samuel Barnett, (father of the present Samuel Barnett, Sr.) John H. Pope, Andrew Shepherd, Duncan G. Campbell, John Burch. This theatre lot extended through from Liberty to Main street, but must have been very narrow, since its whole area was estimated at a quarter of an acre. There was a double row of china trees constituting an avenue on it, and the house was situated very near the present Methodist church. They paid Mrs. Griffin $550 for the property. She was the widow of John Griffin, who lived where Mr. Burwell Green now lives, and whose tombstone is on the place when I write. She was the daughter of Micaijah Williamson. Soon after this sale, she married Judge Tait and moved to Alabama.

When school was held in this house Dr. F. T. Willis was a pupil. His teacher was a Miss Hix. The doctor was not very fond of going to school, and when some one asked him why he was so averse to it, he replied: "Miss Hix is so ugly I do not like to look at her."

In 1824, the Commissioners of the Academy sold the property which they possessed on Mercer Hill, to Richard H. Long for $825. The deed was recorded April 10, 1827, three years after the sale was made, and shows that they had previously mortgaged the property to William G. Gilbert, probably as a security for borrowed money, and that Mr. Gilbert had cancelled the mortgage. The property sold to R. H. Long is described as "certain premises heretofore occupied as an Academy, with the land attached thereto, computed at 10 acres, lying around said Academy on the Greenesborough and Lexington roads, and bounded in other directions by the Stark tract of land lately purchased by said Long." I will step aside from my subject a moment, to say that in 1827 Mr. Long sold the Academy lot and the Stark tract, the whole estimated to contain 250 acres, for $2,500, to the widow, Mrs. Nancy Simonds; and the same year Rev. Jesse Mercer married Mrs. Simonds and moved to Washington. The deed of the Commissioners made to Long states, that they had sold the property "and invested the proceeds in other buildings for the use of the county, and better suited for Academy purposes."

This property was doubtless the Female Academy or theatre, of which I have related the purchase, and some of our present Academy property which they had purchased, probably with the money borrowed from Mr. Gilbert. The property of the old Female Academy was afterwards sold, as I shall relate.

The present Male Academy lot consists of three lots bought at different times. One, which is on Main Street, and contains the Academy building, was bought from Edward D. Alfriend in 1823 or 1824. Neither the deed nor the copy recorded in the office of the County Clerk Mr. Dyson, can now be found. The book of Deeds for 1822, 1823, 1824, is missing from the series in the Clerk's office. This is known to those who are acquainted with the records, but it is not known how it was lost. The loss could not possibly affect the title, because there exists a mortgage deed made to the Bank of the State of Georgia on the property, and in it this deed is described as made by Edward D. Alfriend. Alfriend, the former owner or his heirs, is the only person who could profit by the loss of his deed, and as we have express evidence of the strongest kind that he had made the deed any claim from him or his heirs is barred. As no claim could be substantiated, the possession would prove the right. We do not know whether Mr. Alfriend gave or sold the property, but there is a powerful presumption that he sold it, because he sold the Methodists the site for their house. The deed to the Methodists, shows that he was a citizen of Greene county, and therefore the more unlikely to make such a gift here. It is clear that the present Academy Trustees could make a deed conveying this lot which no one would undertake to dispute.

The other two lots are on Liberty Street, one south of the one just described, and bounded by the Methodist church lot on the east; the other (1)

(Page Missing)

only, but the bank has not been in existence since twenty years. It settled up its affairs and took no steps to claim the property thus tacitly recognizing the fact that they had been paid. It is evident that if the trustees were now to sell the property, there is no one who would dispute the title they conveyed, upon the ground of this deed of 1829 to the Bank.

But there is one lot then belonging to the Trustees and enumerated in the statement of mortgaged property, which was actually sold by the sheriff in 1832. This is the theater, or Female Academy lot, which the Commissioners bought from Mrs. Sally Griffin in 1820. I suppose this was unredeemed because

---

(1) This was the end of the other pamphlets. The rest of this book came from the Sims' pamphlet.

it was no longer of use to the Trustees, the new Academy having been erected: and also it was separated from the other property which they had acquired, by the Methodist church and parsonage (now the Jesse lot) and I suppose they thought a sale under foreclosure of this mortgage as convenient as any other. The lot was sold by the sheriff, and actually bid off by the Bank, and they at once sold it to the Methodist church, and to Mrs. Ann Anthony, who had in the meantime bought the parsonage lot. She bought about two thirds of the theatre lot. There are among the deeds recorded for 1832, deeds for this property, from John Burks sheriff, and he states that the property was sold under a foreclosure of mortgage, and bought by the Bank, and also that Samuel Barnett Cashier had directed him to make deeds to Mrs. Anthony and the church. Any one who looks at the Jesse lot now can see that the house in much nearer the western than the eastern fence and this due to this subsequent addition of a small strip of land on the east. The new Methodist church is, I am told, nearly on the site of the old one, only a trifle further north. It must originally have been built at the eastern end of the lot, probably to place it on top of the hill. Of the after addition to its lot, there can be no possible doubt. We know it by the statements in the county records. The lot was bought in 1820, from Mrs. Sally Griffin, for $550. The Bank bought it for $80 in 1832. The decline in value may have been due to the removal of the building. It is not unlikely that the lumber of the house was used in erecting the new Academy. Lumber was never destroyed in that day.

The gin house lot was bought by the Academy Commissioners from Mark A. Lane, Sept. 8, 1837. Mrs. Vickers tells me that the gin house was standing when she came, but was burned in the great fire of 1837. From the Minute Book of the Presbyterian Sessions, I find that this fire took place Thursday, August 24, 1837. The same record tells us that the fire caused communion in this church, which was to have taken place on the Sunday after, to be postponed. I presume that the destruction of the gin house diminished the price of the lot. As I have copied the other deeds, I will also copy this.

"This Indenture, made Sept. 8, 1837, between Mark A. Lane, &c., of the one part, and the Commissioners of the Washington Academy, &c., of the other part. Witnesseth that said Mark A. Lane, for $200 in hand paid, Hath sold, &c., to the Commissioners and their successors in office all that lot of land in the town of Washington containing one fourth of an acre more or less, and bounded as follows, &c., North by Thomas Terrell's blacksmith shop, East by the Academy lot, South by a Street running east and west between Mrs. Mary Semmes and the Methodist church, West by Jefferson Street, and known as Lane's gin house lot formerly owned by Stone and Lane." "Stone" is

Mr. Osborn Stone, from whom Lane bought the lot. Mrs. Mary Semmes was the widow of Mr. Andrew G. Semmes, and they lived opposite the Methodist church having bought that place of Col. Duncan G. Campbell. They were the protestant family of Semmes. Mr. Andrew Semmes died in 1833, as stated in the Presbyterian Record book.

I have thus given a history of all the Male Academy property, and its entire accuracy is beyond all question for the statements are all based on the authority of the county records. It took me several days to find these documents, but here they are substantially. I think they show plainly that the Trustees of the Academy could make good titles to the property, if there were any good reason for selling.

The mere account of the property is only one side of the history of the Academy, and would perhaps have been more entertaining if told in connection with the rest. I have written it separately and first, because the movement in regard to the Academy and the meeting on Saturday in its interest, makes it important to settle vague rumors in regard to conditions on which the trustees hold the property.

I have said nothing thus far of the Seminary, of which I shall write a full account later, but I think the history of the property will be more interesting if I give it in connection with the same branch of Academy history. It will be seen, in reading the deed, that the lot was bought from Mr. A. L. Alexander, and not a gift. In saying this, however, I must add that I am sure Mr. Alexander's contribution to the Seminary property was much greater than the value of this lot.

The composition of this deed is evidently wholly the work of Mr. Alexander who was educated for the bar, and admitted, and who kept up his connection with it by the payment of the annual tax. Those who knew him well will notice, on comparing it with the other deeds, that it is somewhat curiously characteristic of him. He had the land carefully surveyed by Caleb Sappington, and a plot drawn, and we find it contains 3 acres, 3 rods and 35 square poles. The deed was subscribed Oct. 5, 1838 before Lewis S. Brown justice of the Inferior court, and Mr. Gabriel Toombs was a witness. Mr. Toombs was then a young man in his prime, for it was more than a half century ago. Here is the deed.

"Know all men by these presents, that I, A. L. Alexander, in consideration of $550 in hand paid, have sold to the Trustees of the Presbyterian church in Washington and their successors in office, all that tract of land on which the female Seminary is now being built" (Here follows description of property) "with the following restrictions and limitations that is to say that the beforementioned lot of land shall be used for the purpose of a female Seminary only, and shall contain such buildings only, as may be necessary for the accommodation and well being of the same, and in no event shall said lot of land be used for other purposes than the one herein mentioned unless the consent of the said A. L. Alexander be thereunto first obtained in writing, it being expressly understood by the contracting parties, that on no other consideration would the titles to said lot of land and sale thereupon have been made. And on the conditions and Limitations aforesaid, the said A. L. Alexander, the said bargained premises, unto the Trustees aforesaid, does hereby warrant and defend, and to their successors in office against the claim of any other person or persons whatever. But it is furthermore provided, that if he shall at any time sell his premises adjoining said Female Seminary, then and in that case, all the benefit of the said limitation shall cease forever, and shall vest in the Trustees aforesaid. And it is furthermore agreed between the contracting parties, that if the Trustees aforesaid shall transcend and exceed the limitations and restrictions herein imposed upon them, and which it is expressly understood confines the use of said lot of land to the purposes of a Female Seminary only, and to be used for no other purpose whatever, then and in that event, the said A. L. Alexander shall not insist on the forfeiture of the land, but shall claim and receive a pecuniary penalty only, to be determined by a jury of the county."

CHAPTER XXVII

THE TRAGEDY OF POLLY BARCLAY

I CAN HARDLY make a book of the humblest kind about the chronicles of Wilkes county without putting in some account of a tragedy which created a great sensation in Wilkes in the early part of this century, and led to the execution in our county of the first white woman who was ever hung in Georgia. There is some disadvantage in repeating a story which I have printed not two years ago in the *Atlanta Constitution,* and which was copied all over the state. But I have lately found, after much trouble a brief report of the trial in the superior court records, and so I can add a little to my former account and improve its accuracy a little. The record, however, is meagre.

The first and most important revision is to say that the woman's real name was Polly, or Mary Barclay, not Bartlett as she has been called by tradition. There can be no doubt that the name in the indictment was correct and it was certainly Polly Barclay. The name occurs a dozen times in the minutes of the superior court for 1806 and it is always written Barclay. I think likely that even in that day it was called Bartley, for Judge Andrews, Mrs. Lewis Brown, &c., called it Bartlett, and they were living, when the woman suffered death. They were all children, but the case was evidently talked of with profound interest for years, and they must have heard the name as it was called by people who were grown at the time. So it must at least have been popularly known as Bartley. But there can be no doubt that the woman's murdered husband wrote his name Barclay.

In the account I wrote before, I gave the following years; of the murder as 1804, of the execution, as 1805. But I find from the court record that they were 1805 and 1806. There was a session of the Superior court beginning May 5, 1806. Judge Charles Tait was the presiding judge. On the second day of court, that is May 6, the grand jury brought in a true bill of indictment for murder against Wm. Nowland, Polly Barclay, Mark Mitchum. The foreman of the grand jury was John Clark, who afterwards became governor of Georgia. Among the names on it, I found those of Wm. F. Booker, John Turner, Benjamin Branham, John Johns, John Freeman, Benjamin Taliaferro, John Graves,

Andrew Sheperd, Garland Wingfield, Thomas Semmes, John Dyson and Richmond Terrell.

There had been a called session of the superior court in January 1806, but there is nothing about this murder case in its records, so that the evidence against these three persons must have come out after January. From tradition we learn that the murder took place in the fall or winter, after Mr. Barclay had sold his cotton in Augusta and returned, that his wife was not at first suspected, but that suspicion was aroused through something about the money, that then people talked, and various suspicious circumstances were told which when put together led to a belief in the guilt of his wife and her arrest. On May 7, the day after the true bill was found, there is a record of bonds made by Archibald Bryant for $500, and his security Wm. W. Smith for $250, for appearance of Bryant on May 8, and afterwards from day to day, to give testimony in favor of the state at the trial.

On May 8, the trials appear to have commenced with Wm. Nowland. The records in the clerk's report book give no particulars whatever of the trial except the names of the jurymen and their verdict as follows: "Joel Aycock, Allen Hartsfield, Wm. Goolsby, Thomas Williamson, George Peterman, John Taylor, Lewis Flemister, Francis Billingslea, Stephen Heard, Son Simeon White, James Billingslea, Tol Thornton. We the jury find the prisoner not guilty, Wm. Goolsby, Foreman." Just following this report, there are records of two bonds made the same day, to secure the attendance of witnesses in the case of the State vs Polly Barclay, et al. Roger Green is bound in $300 and his security John Lindsay in $150, for his appearance as witness for the state. Then Wm. Nowland is bound in $500 and his security Thomas Anderson in $500 for him to appear next day at nine o'clock as witness for the state. Just following these records on May 8, it is entered in the case of the state vs. Wm. Nowland, that "the defendant having made oath that he was not able to pay his fees, whereupon the said Wm. Nowland was discharged by proclamation."

The next day, May 9, 1806, came the trial of Polly Barclay. The clerk does not give us a word except the names of the jury and the verdict, as follows: "Joshua Chapin, Jos. Henderson, Jesse McLean, Bernard Kelly, Peter Stoval, Christopher Binns, Thomas Chevers Jr., John Rory, Wm. Kilgore, Thomas Hudspeth, John Carter, Charles Terrell. We the jury find the prisoner at the bar guilty but recommend her to mercy, Charles H. Terrell, Foreman."

Immediately after this record of the trial, follows a statement that the bonds were forfeited which had been made to secure the appearance of Roger Green as witness for the state. Roger Green the record tells us, was solemnly called three times and failing to appear, his security John Lindsay was three times called to produce the body of the said Roger as he had bound himself to do, but this failing also, the bond was declared forfeited.

It is thus evident that a strong effort was made to save Polly Barclay by running off a witness who was important.

The name of Mark Mitchum was included in the indictment on which Polly Barclay was tried. Immediately after the account of the conviction on May 9, the following is found on the record.

"The State   )
M. Mitchum et al) Indc. for Murder

nol pros. Entered by leave of court"

On the 10th of May, 1806, the record tells us as follows: "The prisoner being brought to the bar of the court, and being asked if she had anything to show why sentence should not be passed upon her and nothing having been offered, the court proceeded to pronounce the following sentence: That you Polly Barclay be taken from this bar to the place from whence you came, there to remain until Friday the 30th, day of this present month of May, and that on the aforesaid 30th, day of May you are to be taken by a proper officer to a gallows previously to be erected in or near the town of Washington, and then and there on the day aforesaid, between the hours of ten o'clock in the forenoon and two o'clock in the afternoon, you are to be hung by the neck until you are dead and may God have mercy on your soul."

I have given everything in the record of the session of the court in May 1806 which refers to this case. If we had no other evidence, we should not know who was murdered even, or any particulars of the crime. I have given all from the books without anything from other sources to explain it, because I wish to show the accuracy of every part of my statement and the authority for it. I could have made the story more entertaining if I had told it in another way. One thing, which I have not heard from any other source and which strikes me very much, is the short time taken in the trial and the brief interval between sentence and execution. A true bill was found May 6th, she was tried on the 9th, and it is evident that the trial occupied but a single day. Then she was executed just three weeks after she was found guilty. The swiftness of justice is considered a great public security, and an element in its certainty. In this respect, it contrasts with some cases of our day. I suppose one reason is a court of appeal complicates the matter.

We have no account of Judge Tait's charge to the trial jury, but his charge to the grand jury made on the first day of court is copied in the record, and though it contains no direct reference to Mrs. Barclay it is difficult to believe that in some things he said, both he and the jury did not think of the woman then accused by popular opinion at least, of so gross a crime. Judge Tait spoke of the important duty of punishing the guilty. Then after some other matters occupied his attention, he spoke of the criminal law of the state, of its great severity, and the importance of revising it and also the need of a penitentiary, and he urged the grand jury to recommend the matters to members of the legislature.

As the trial jury recommended the unhappy woman to mercy, the short shrift from so severe a sentence seemed very hard. The judge, however, had no alternative then as now to hanging. I suppose, if he had thought the execution of the law of doubtful justice, he could have put it off longer, and left time to get up a petition to Governor Milledge for pardon. Judge Tait very evidently thought the death sentence deserved. The jury too must have found the evidence very strong, since they could not have been long in their deliberations; for the whole trial, the examination of witnesses, the speeches of lawyers, the judges charge, and the session of the jury were over in one day.

Having thus given the facts in the case of Mrs. Polly Barclay, from the court record, I will state what we learn from tradition. I find from the popular comments on what I wrote about two years ago in the *Atlanta Constitution,* that the members of nearly every family long resident in this county remember to have heard Mrs. Barclay's story from some of their elders, but the occurrences happened so long ago that the recollection is indistinct. The story, as I tell it, comes from two sources. Rev. Micaijah Lane who died a few years ago at the age of ninety-two was a boy twelve years old when the tragedy occurred. He lived less than two miles from the place where the murder was committed. He heard the shot fired that killed Barclay, and he saw the execution of Mrs. Barclay. I did not hear Mr. Lane tell these facts, but I got them from his son Dr. James H. Lane, and from Rev. F. T. Simpson a listener and reporter of great care, much interested in preserving the county history. Mr. Lane's grandsons also heard the story from him, and I talked to them.

The mother of Gen. B. W. Heard was a young girl of perhaps fourteen or fifteen when Barclay was murdered, and Mrs. Heard lived not very far from the Barclays. Gen. Heard, who reports what his mother said about it, is a reporter much interested in the county history also.

All the traditions concur in saying that Mr. Barclay was not killed by his wife's hand. All the stories mention her lover and her brother, - ----- --- concur in saying that - - -- - - her brother. Gen. - -- - -- bers several Nowlands, - - - -

named Jenkins who - - -- brothers. Her mother - -- -owland had it seems been - -- married and once to Jenkins, there is reason to think they lived in Jenkins District of the county, and that the name of the district came from the family or some member of it. All the sources of the story concur in saying that the actual doer of the deed escaped. My belief when I wrote my former account, was that Nowland did the deed at the woman's instigation. But it seems impossible to reconcile this theory with Nowland's acquittal recorded in the minutes of the court. If the woman did not do the deed with her own hand, it would have been impossible to prove her guilt without also establishing that of the actual doer of it, and that it was not Nowland, seems to me to be settled by his acquittal. If he had escaped on the plea of a mental incompetence making him irresponsible, he would not have been held as a witness in the trial of Mrs. Barclay.

The traditions that I have heard did not give the name "Mark Mitchum," but I suppose that he was the lover whom they mentioned. From the record, it is evident that he did not stand trial, and I suppose that he ran away when he learned there was danger of a true bill being found by the grand jury. The *nolle prosequi* is very puzzling. If Nowland was innocent and the woman did not kill Barclay with her own hand, it is quite certain then some one else was the doer of the deed. There is no indictment except against the three, and so Mitchum must have been the murderer. But this, as I have said makes the *nolle prosequi* incomprehensible.

Tradition says that at --- -- - not long before the murd---- Barclay planned it at her h---- - -- a person whom she incite - ---- ---- the deed. There was prese - - time a half grown boy who -- - - her family. He was lying - -- the fire and supposed to be asleep but he heard and remembered the whole conversation. Not long afterwards Barclay was killed. There were two men who came up the road at night fall from the direction of Augusta and stopped at Mr. Barclay's cotton house which stood on the road a short distance from his house, made some noise, to make him suppose that some person was stealing his cotton. There were some visitors at the dwelling house who reported at the trial, that Mr. Barclay was not disposed to go out, but that his wife urged him to do so. Shortly after he went, a shot was heard, and those present reported that she said, "that shot killed my husband." When found, he was still living but the ball had cut off his tongue. He died in a few hours.

This was Saturday. The mother of Micaijah Lane had gone that day to the Baptist church conference at Fishing Creek, taking him along. Later in the evening Mr. Lane, then aged twelve, was out for the cows. He was late getting home and lingered in the yard playing in the moonlight. He then heard the sharp report of the gun which killed Mr. Barclay. Next day the murder was told and he remembered the report of the gun that he had heard.

Tradition says that the half grown boy was the most important witness on the trial, and that the lawyers tried hard to discredit his testimony, but did not succeed. He told the same story in spite of their efforts to make him contradict himself and was beli---d. ----- - first heard the story. Mrs. - --lay had, in the presence of that --- - -ered her brother $200 to kill - ---clay. If this were true, I suppose Nowland did not follow her wishes. He may have proved an alibi on the night of the murder.

All the lines of the tradition unite in reporting that the unhappy woman possessed uncommon beauty. It is said she was confident she would be reprieved, to the very last, and I suppose some application must have been made to Governor John Milledge, who was then our executive; for tradition says that when the sheriff came to lead her to execution, she clutched at a paper she saw in his side pocket, supposing it to be a reprieve. It has also come down to us, that she put on a fine silk dress to go to execution.

Mr. Barclay was buried, it is said, on the spot where he fell. It was marked by two unhewn stones which were placed upon it and they can be still pointed out on the old Elberton and Augusta road a few miles beyond Sandtown. The grave is on the edge of the road, and it is said that those who have worked the road have always piled up the dirt above the grave. On Mr. T. W. Callaway's valuable map of Wilkes county, the spot is marked as, "Murdered Bartlett's Grave." This name, however, should be Barclay.

Judge Andrews told me that Mrs. Barclay was hung on a large white oak tree which once stood on the north side of Main Street between Mr. William Pope's gate and that of Mr. Charles Irvin. I remember the trunk of this tree, and it was just opposite the point of land which runs down from the Orphanage property into Main Street. This statement of Judge Andrews was printed in the notes on Washington shortly after

Here the Book Ends.
See introduction for explanation.

INDEX

A bbeville, 79
Abbott, Joel, Dr., 40, 44, 71, 100, 102, 160
Academy, in Augusta, 47, 150
  Trustees, 171
  in Washington, 46, 66, 171
Act of Legislature-Established Louisville School, 1796, 47 167
Adams, Habersham, Rev., 143
  Jno. Quincey, Sec.of State, 8
Albany, 93
Alexander, A. L., 96, 98, 144, 173, 174
  A. L., Mrs., 101
  Adam, 98
  Chas., 43, 44, 64, 69, 72, 77, 88, 97, 164
  J. H., 99
  Jas., 32
  Samuel, Capt., 32
Alfriend, Edw. D., 138, 171
  Nancy W., 138
Allen, Mr.-Tutor, 63
  Beverly-Preacher in Va., 118, 145
  Billy, 119
Alligator Creek, 14
Allison House, 52
  Street, 45
Anderson, Capt. of Pickens Reg. 12
  Post Master, Washington, 73, 103
  Judge, 78
  Nancy, 48
  Tazewell, 91
  Thos., 48, 176
Anderson's Mill, 18
Andrew, Bishop, 54, 131
Andrews, Dan'l.-Marshall, Dr. 44, 109
  Garnett, Judge, 44, 78, 83, 84, 89, 92, 97, 113, 175, 180
  Garnett, Mrs., 112, 126
  H. F., Dr., 69
  Jno.-First Methodist Preacher, 34, 128, 129
  Martha, Mrs., 40, 54
  Nancy Goode, Mrs., 114
Ansley, Thos., 51, 55
Ansleys-Augusta, 55
Anthony, Ann, 139, 172
  E. M., Ordinary, Wilkes, 22, 40, 43, 49, 108
  Jas., 48, 51, 55
  Mary, 48

Anthony, Micajah, 51, 140
  Milton, Dr.-Founded Medical College of Ga., 55
  Samuel, Rev., 140, 141, 143
Apalachicola, 93
Appling, Daniel, 74
  Jno., 74
Armour, Jas.-Teacher, 71
Armstrong, Jas., Rev.-Baptist, 114
  Jno., 51
  Wm. S., Dr., 54
Arnold, Mr., 107
  Wesley P., 142
Articles of Confederation, 81
Asbury, Francis-Methodist Bishop 24, 110, 118, 121, 122, 125, 126, 127, 133, 148
Ash., Gen.-Brier Creek, 25
Augusta, 93
  Occupied by British, April, 1780, 11, 25
  Returned to American possession, 1781, 35, 125, 136
  Whigs in possession, 11
Axson, I. S.-Presbyterian Pastor, 163
Aycock, Joel, 176
  Richard, 23

B ailey, Wm., 23
Bakers - Marietta, 101
Bank of the State of Georgia, 171
Banks County, 155
Banks, Hannah, 162
  Ralph, 126
Baptists, 109
Barclay, Polly, 175-180
Barksdale, Jno., 51
Barnett, Dr., 54
  Emma, 103, 123
  Lillis, 162
  O. S., 164
  Osborne, 164
  Patrick, Mrs.-Pension, 106
  S., 164
  Samuel, 40, 56, 92
    Elder, 1863, 164
    Comm. Female Academy, 170
    Trustee, Presbyterian Church, 160
  Samuel, Mrs., 48
  Wm., 56, 89
  Sheriff, 119, 162
Beal, Geo., 107
Bean, Wm. S.-Presbyterian Pastor 163
Beasley, Mrs., 103, 140

Beasley, Ambrose, 102
  Patsy, 103
  Royland, 103
Beattie's Mill, Battle, 31
Bedell, Absolom, Judge-1779 -
  1780, 22, 26, 33
Bedingfield, Chas., 23
Beersheba, 155
Belmont Plantation, 106
Benning, Thos., 142
Benton, Thos. Hart, 28
Berrys, 100, 140
Bethany Church, 147, 154
Bethsaida Church, 154
Bethsalem Church, 147, 154
Bibb, Wm., Dr.-Senator, 55
Bibb's Cross Roads, 122
Bigby's Store, 74
Billingslea, Francis, 176
  Jas., 176
Billups, Joel Abbott, Col., 102
Binns, Christopher, 176
  E. G., 43, 76
  Walter, 44
Bird, Thompson, Dr., 59, 76,
  80, 163
  Williamson, 52
Blackburn, Gen., 61
  Samuel, Teacher, 60, 63, 75,
  77, 123
Blackstone's-War at, 31
Boggs, G. W.-Presbyterian Pastor, 163
  Jno.-Presbyterian Pastor, 163
Bolton, Chas., 93
Booker, Nancy, 49
  S., 49
  Wm. F., 175
Boren, Wm.-On Jury, 51, 82
Boring, Jesse, Rev., 144
Borroughs, Mrs.-Teacher, 69
Bound, W. B., Rev., 143
Bowen, Elizabeth, 164
Bowen, Oliver, Commodore, 34
Boyd, Colonel, 11
Boyd's Creek-Elbert County, 20
Bradley, Jas.-Trustee, Methodist Church, 138
Brandywine-Battles, 38
Branham, Benj.-Academy Comm.,
  65, 175
  Mary, 65
  Spencer, 73
  Thos., 51
  W. R., Rev., 144
Brantly, J. J., Rev.-Baptist
  Pastor, 117
Brewer, Hopkins, 101
Bridges, Mr.-Slain by Indians,
  20
Brier Creek-British defeat Gen.
  Ash, 25

Broad River-Court opened, 5
  Separates Oglethorpe and Wilkes
  from Elbert County, 12
  Conference held, 120, 122, 125
  Settlement, 37
Brown, Col., British Officer, 27
Brown & Grierson-Captured Augusta, 25
Brown, Jno., Rev.-Presbyterian
  Pastor, 74, 128, 163
  Lewis, Mrs., 90, 175
  Lewis S., 142, 173
Bryan, J. S., Rev., 144
Bryant, Archibald, 176
Burch, Jno., 170
Burdett, Humphrey, 52
Burks, Jno.-Sheriff, 172
Burnett, Daniel, 23
Burns, Andrew-Academy Comm., 63
Burton, Edw., 104
Butler, Edw.-Academy Comm.,
  J. I. C., 51, 84, 86
  Troup, Mrs., 42
Buyers and Prices, 73

Cade, Gil, 76
Caharobas-Chief of-at Augusta
  Treaties, 1763, 2
Cain, Jno., 51
Calhoun, Abner Wellborn, Dr., 54
  Jno. C., 151
Callaway, Mr.-Made map of Wilkes
  County, 12
  Brantley, Rev., 111
  Enoch, Rev., 111
  Job, 51
  Morgan, Rev., 55, 144
  T. W., 180
Campbell, Col.-British Officer,
  11, 22
  Duncan-Comm. to make Treaty
  with Indians, 38, 95
Carmel Church-Presbyterian, 154
Carnes, Thos. P., 74
Carnesville, 74
Carr's Fort-Battle of, 15
Carter, Farish-Army Contractor,
  106
  Jno., 176
  Thos., 23, 52
Cassels, Jno. B., 165
  Sam'l. J.-Presbyterian Pastor, 163, 165
Catchings, Benj.-J.I.C., 22, 26
Catholics, French, 146
Ceded Lands-by Indians 1773, 4
Chalybeate Spring, 62
Chandler, Major-Kings Mt.
  Battle, 30
  Jno., 51
Chantilly-Home, Goode Family,
  103

INDEX

Chapin, Joshua, 176
Chapman, Mr.-Country Residence, 44
  Editor, Gazette, 97
Charlton, Arthur M.-Trustee of M. E. Church, 138
Cherokees-Chief present at Treaties, Augusta, 1763, 1
  Cherokee Ford, 12
  Original inhabitants of Wilkes County, 1
Chevers, Thos., Jr., 176
Chickasaws-Chief present at Augusta Treaties, 1763, 2
Chisolm, Mr., Contractor of Court House, 60, 78
Choctaws-Chief present at Augusta Treaties, 1763, 2
Christian Index, 116
Christmas, Nathaniel, 51
Civil War-Close of, 52
Clark, Elijah, Col., Gen., 8, 14, 15, 16, 28, 62, 65, 68, 73, 74
  Hannah, Mrs., 33
  J.O.A.-M.E. Preacher, 124, 143
  J.O.A., Mrs., 140
  Jno., Gen.-Governor, 17, 19, 59, 175
    Commissioner, 65, 82
    Fought duel with Crawford, 101
Clark Station, 12
Clark Station Church, 111
Clark's and Sardis Station, 1788, 120
Clark's-N. C. settlers, 7
Clarke County, 16
Cobb, Alberta, 107
  Howell, 107
  Jno., 107
  Thos. R. R., 107
Cohron, Cornelius, 51
Coke, Bishop, 122
Coleman, Daniel-Commissioner to lay out town of Washington, 23, 40, 60, 168
  Jno.-Commissioner to lay out town of Washington, 26, 40
Colley, Frances, 8, 100
  Hill, 93
  Isabella, Mrs., 43, 77
  Jno., 52, 100
  Spain, 100
Collier, Jno., 52
Columbia, Tennessee, 89
Combs, Philip, 52
Commissioners of Washington, Academy, 172
Concord Church-Presbyterian, 155

Confederate Soldiers-Route taken returning from War, 52
Constantine Church, 160, 162
Cook, Jos., Capt., 58, 75
Corbett, Eleanor, 162
  Jas., 69, 76
Cornwallis, Gen., 11, 30, 32
Cosby, Mary, 130.
Cotting, Mrs., 102, 103, 141
Court of Oyer and Terminer, 22
  House-Preaching in Washington, 46
Cox, Wm., 55
Cozart, Jno., 42, 74, 77
Crane, Spencer, 51
Crawford, Geo. W.-Attorney, 6
  N. M., Dr.-Baptist Pastor, 117
Creeks-Chief present at Treaties, Augusta, 1763, 1, 2, 122
Creswell, David, 75, 158
  Phoebe, 158
  Samuel, On jury, 51, 73
Crocker, Wm.-Teacher, 69, 70
Crutchfield, Jno., 24, 134
Cultivation-Cotton, 86
Cummins, Alexander, 52
  Ebenezer H.-Tutor, 70
  Francis, Dr. Rev., 70, 159, 165
Cunningham, Jno. Major-R.S., 31
  Robt., Rev.-Presbyterian Pastor, 151, 153
Cuthbert, 51

D abney, Austin-R.S., 17
Danelly, Jimmy, 138
Daniel, Cunningham, 165
  Jas.-Elder, 153, 154, 164
  Jane, 165
  Jno.-Elder, 166
  Robt. C.-Elder, 153, 166
  Wm.-Elder, 166
Darden, Elizabeth, 51
Darley, Thos., 139
Davenport, W., 74
Davies, L. J., Rev., 144
Davis, Jefferson, President, Route through Wilkes County, 25, 52
Dawson, Edgar, 94
  Wm. C., Mrs., 93
Day, Robt., 23
DeGraffenried, 94
Delhi, Danburg and Sandtown Crossroads, 122
Dennis Mills, 31
Dodys-Settlers from N. C., 7
Dooly, Judge, 22
  Jno., Col., Capt., Commissioner to lay out town, 26, 40
  Attorney for State, 22, 24

INDEX

Dooly, Judge-Organized Troops against Col. Hamilton, 11
Double Wells or Powelton Road, 120, 129
Dow, Lorenzo, 136, 137
Downs, Wm. C.-Commissioner to lay out town, 26, 40
  J.I.C., 22, 26
DuBose, Dudley, Gen., 102, 107
  Toombs, 44
  Wiley, 143
Duncan, Jno. P., 143
Dunwoody, J.B., Rev., 93, 163
  Marion, 99
Durham, Anderson, 81
Durkee, Nathaniel, 77
Dyson-Clerk of Court, 85, 139, 171
  Geo., Mrs., 44, 76, 79, 164
  Jno., 176

E arly, Jacob, 51, 55, 82
  Peter-Gov. of Ga., 55
Ebenezer Church-Presbyterian, 111, 118, 155
Edmondson, Mr., 73
Edwards on the Will, 159
Elbert County, 5, 66
Ellington, Mrs., 74, 77, 106, 153, 162
  S. C., 164
  Wm., 74
English Families from Conn. Abbotts, Hillhouses and Princes, 146
Evans, Jas. E., Rev., 142
  Wm.-Justice-Rev., 85, 143
Eve, Jos. A., Dr., 54, 93
  Sarah Garland, Mrs., 93
Express Office, 74

F alling Creek Church, 148
Female Seminary, 173, 174
Ferguson, Col.-Sent by Cornwallis to Carolina, 30
Ferington, Jacob, 23
Ferry-of Thos. Carter, 51
Ficklen, Dr. Mrs., 94
  Boyce, 44
  Fielding, Dr., 142
  Georgia, Miss, 144
  Julia, Mrs., 44
Findley, David, Rev.-Presbyterian Pastor, 153
  Isabella, 165
  Jas., 51, 82, 165
First Court House, 78
Fish Dam Ford-On Broad River, 12, 119
Fishing Creek, 18, 179
Fishing Creek Church, 110
Fish, Ichabod Ebenezer, 71

Fiske, Ezra-Teacher, 49
Flemister, Lewis, 176
Floyd, Mr., 40,
Floyd's Opera House, 138, 145
Floyd's Store, 74
Fluellen, Abner, Mrs., 101
Fluker, Owen, 18
  Wm., 18, 44, 88
Foote, Rev., 143
Foreman, Mr., 74, 91
Forsyth, Jno., 119, 150
Fort Cornwallis, 32
  Heard-Stockade, 7
  James-Stockade, 5
Forston, Mr. and Mrs., 7
Foster, Jos., 165
Fountain Camp Ground-Warren Co., 138
France-Offered Col. Clark high command in Armies, 16
Franklin College, 17, 151
  County, 155
Freeman, Holman, Major-R.S., 23, 24
  Holman, Jr., 24
  Jno., 4, 24, 82, 175
French Huguenots-DuBoses and Remberts, 146
French Mills, 38
  Road-Domingo Refugees, 90
Fulsom's Fort-Indians collect at, 19
Fulton, W. M., Rev., 143

G addy, David-Contractor, 66, 70 72
Gaines, Daniel, 73
Galphin Claim, 6
  Geo., 5
Gardner, Geo., Rev., 144
Garland, Jno. W., 94
  Sarah, 91
Gazette-Newspaper, 66
Georgia and the Carolinas only Cotton States settled in 1790, 86
Georgia Baptist Association, 111
Georgians, by Gov. Gilmer, 34
Germantown-Battles of, 38
Gibson, Augustus H., 169
  Henry B., 51, 74, 79, 101
Gilbert, Felix H., 44, 69, 71, 77, 88, 96, 97
  Commissioner of Town, 40
  Sarah, 98
  Wm. G., 51, 88, 96, 98, 170
Gilham, Ezekiel-Elder from Bethsalem-now Lexington, 153
Gilmer, Geo., Gov. of Ga., 3, 100, 105
  County named for, 55
  Effect of religious revivals on Broad River people, 136

# INDEX 185

Gilmer, Geo., Gov. of Ga.,
 Gives opinion on Nancy Hart, 28
Glass, Jno., 23
Glen, Mr.-Editor, *Monitor*, 1800, 97
Glenn, Wm., 51
Goode, Eliza, 103, 153
 Geo. Brown-Professor-Curator of Smithsonian Institute, 104
 Hamilton, 104
 Jno., 104
 Samuel W.-Elder, 104, 161, 164, 170
  Owner of Chantilly Estate, 103
 Sarah, 38
Goolsby, Wm., 176
Gordon, Francis, 77, 86, 162
 Lord Geo.-Scotch settler, 3, 4
Gorham, Jno.-J.I.C., 23, 26
Goulding, F. R., Rev.-Pastor of Salem Church, 165
Grand Jury, 23
Grant, Billy (William), 132
 Daniel-Will of, 1784, 51, 55, 120, 132, 134
 Jno. Owen, 132
 Jno. T., Mrs., 55, 131, 132
 Thos., 51, 120, 131, 132
  Ex., Will of Daniel Grant, 134
 Wm. D.-Trustee, Methodist Church, 138
Grant's Meeting House, 120, 126
Graves, Dr., 66
 Jas., Gen.-Publisher of *Washington Chronicle*, 18, 66, 100
 Jno. Temple, Col.-R.S., 38, 39
Graves Mountain, 38, 66
Green, Burwell, 75
 E. M.-Presbyterian Pastor, 163
 Jas., Dr., 101
 Jno., Mr. and Mrs., 140
 T. B., 103
 T. M., 75, 103
 Theodoric, 41, 44
Green's House, 100
Greene County-Lands ceded by Indians, 1773, 5, 115
Greene, Nathanael, Gen., 38, 56, 87, 89
 Commander, Southern Division of U.S. Army, 31
 Nathanael, Mrs.-Widow of Gen., 87
Greenwood Church-Org. in 1784, 110
Gresham, Chas., 165
 Esther, Mrs., 39

Gresham, Lucretia, 165
 Thos., 102
Grierson and Brown, 25, 27, 31
Griffin, Judge, 59, 75, 76
 Mrs., 58
Griffin, Jno., 40, 59, 64, 75, 80
 Sally, Mrs., 170, 172
Griffing, Jno., 71
Grimes, Mr., 91
Grogan, Geo., Rev., 143

H aines, Thos., 126
Haliday, Jno.-Built Jail, 85
Hamilton, Lt. Col., 11
 T. N., Dr., 104
 Miss, 104
Hampden Sidney College, Va., 149
Handley, Jno., 75
Hansells, 101
Hansen, Elizabeth, 162,
Harper, Robt., 40, 168
 Wm.-Deputy Sheriff, 23
Harrington, Chas., 80
Harris, W. M., Rev.-Baptist Pastor, 117
 Sampson, 52, 74
 Wm. L., 102
Hart, Nancy, 27, 28
Hartsfield, Allen, 176
Harvie, Daniel, 57
 Lucie, 57
Hay, Catherine, 162
 Felix G.-Elder, 164
 G.-Commissioner of Washington, 40
 Gilbert, Dr., 44, 71, 75, 76, 100, 107
 Jno., Mrs., 140
 Nancy, 107
Haygood, Atticus, 128
Hazlehurst, Geo., 54
Head's Tavern, 91
Heard, Barnard, 7, 23, 24, 26, 36, 40, 89, 109
 Benjamin W., Gen., 1, 7, 58, 66, 67, 75, 77, 80, 141, 178
 Jesse, 7
 Jno., 7
 Robt., 25
 Stephen, 23, 24, 25, 32, 40, 60
 R.S., 17
 Heard County, 25
 Helped build Stockade Fort, 7
 Pres., Executive Council, 25, 176
 Wm., 52
Heard's Fort, 25, 26
Hebron Church-Presbyterian, 155
Hendly, Jno., 76

INDEX

Henderson, Jos., 176
Henley, Darby, 66
　Philip, 66
Henry, Mr., 92
Hester, Mr. and Mrs., 141
　Sarah, Mrs., 69
　Simeon, 65
Hill, Abraham, 126
　Edw. Y., Judge, 54, 74
　Henry, 3
　Jno., 51
　Jno., Dr., 126
　Joshua, Hon., 54
　Merriwether, 76
　Mother, 126
　Wellborn, 54
Hillhouse, David P.-J.I.C., 51, 55, 74, 84, 96, 97
　Jas.-Connecticut, 96
　Miss, 101
　Mrs., 129
　Sarah, Mrs., 72, 97
Hillyer, Junius, Judge, 24
　S. G., Rev.-Baptist Pastor, 4, 24, 117
Hines, (Hynes), Mr., 44, 45, 75
History of Georgia-by Chas. Jones, 34
Historical Collections of Georgia-by Rev. Geo. White, 22, 33, 34, 95
Hitson, Chiltson (or Eidson), 52
Hodge, David, 38
　Elisa, 162
Hogue, T. C., 73, 150
Haw River-Battle at, 31
Howard, Homer, 59
　Jno., 139
　Thacker, Mrs., 59
Howe, Geo. Dr.-*History of Presbyterian Church*, 157
Howell, Nathaniel, 51
Howley, Gov., 25
Hoyt, N., 163
Hudspeth, Thos., 176
Huguenots-French, 146
Huling, Jas., 77
Hull, Alexander Pope, 64
　Asbury, 57
　Clifford Alexander, 57
　Eliza Pope, Mrs., 57, 129
　Harvie, 64
　Hope, Rev.-Methodist Pastor and Pres. of Board, Trustees-69, 70, 95, 111, 129, 152
Humphries, Thos., Rev.-Methodist Pastor, 119
Hunt, Mr., 20
Hunter, Fred (or Dred), Dr., Mrs., 16, 65, 104
Hunton, Jno., 77
Hurt, Joel, 52

Hunt's Merchants Magazine - Cotton Culture, 88

I ndex- *Christian Index*-Temperance Paper, 116
Ireland, 143
Irvin, B. S., 44
　Chas., 101, 180
Isle of Wight, Virginia, 53
Ivy, Richard-Presiding Elder, 119

J ack, Jas., 51, 56, 89
　Jean, 56
　Jno., 56
Jackson, Absalom, 73, 74
　Andrew, Capt.-Gen., 115, 151
　Creek Treaty with, 95
　Harry, Capt., 54
　Wyche, Rev., 143, 145
Jail of 1784, 75
　Square, 77
Jarrett, I. C., 81
　Rebeheah, 81
Jefferson Street, 45, 172
Jefferson and Liberty Streets, 88
Jesse, Mr., 139
Johns, Enoch, 38, 66
　Jno., 175
Johnson, W. T., 76
　Wm., Rev., 41, 44, 142
Jones, Chas. C., Col.-*History of Georgia*, 1, 2, 16, 31, 32, 49
　Isaac, Rev., 70
　Jno.-Presbyterian Pastor, 1, 163
　Pelot, Capt., 140
　Thomas, Mrs., 140
　Toliver, Mrs., 23
　Wm.-Methodist Trustee, 138, 140
Jordan, Mr., 141
　Will, Dr., 12
Joppa Church-Presbyterian, 154
Joyner, Benj., 51
Justices of Inferior Court, Wilkes County, 1780, 22, 25

K appel, Mr.-A Printer, 97
Kelly, Bernard, 77, 176
Kelsey, Mr., 104
　Daniel, Rev., 143
　Emily, 104
　Harriet, 104
Kemmes, Mrs., 42, 74
Kendrick, Mr., 44, 76, 141
　Ann, Miss, 142
Kentucky, Danburg, 163
Kettle Creek-Band of Tories, 13, 14, 22, 103
Key, Caleb, Rev., 143
Kilgore, Wm., 176
King, Mrs.-of Roswell, 101
　Jno.-Comm. of Academy, 121

INDEX

King's Mountain-Battle of, 30
Kiokee Baptist Church-The first
  Church in Columbia County, 110,
  111
Krakatoa-Volcano, 27

L amar, Albert, 159
  Jas., 82
  Jno., 82
  Samuel, 26
  Zachariah, J.I.C., Trustee of
    Louisville Academy, 26, 40,
    60, 75, 82
Lane, Mrs., 41, 54, 76
  Mary, Mrs., 43
  Mark A., 88, 172
  Micajah, Rev.-Baptist Pastor,
    137, 161, 179
LaPrade, W. H., 144
Lee, Colonel, 32
  Robert E., 32
Lennard, Miss, 103
  Jno., Mrs., 140
  Jno. B.-Methodist Trustee,
    138
Lennard and Beasley, 103
Levert, Octavia Walton, 159
Lewis, A. S., 164
  Josiah, Rev., 143
Lexington Church, 147, 154
Liberty Church-Presbyterian, 154
  Street, 171
Life of *Father Mercer*, 1
Lindsay, Jno., 51, 69, 176, 177
Lipham, Capt., 51
Little Britain Church, Presby-
  terian, 148, 154
Little, Grace, 75
  Jas., Capt., R.S., 12, 17
Littlefields, 89
Little River, 2, 5, 12
  Parsonage, 75
Lobdell, Caroline, 164
  Eliza, 162
Long Cane, Battle of, 16, 31,
  33
  Church, 148
Long Creek, 7, 12
Long, Eliza, 107
  Eugenia, Miss, 107
  Jno., 107
  Margaret, 106, 107
  Nicholas, Col., 40, 44, 51, 71,
    82, 105
  Richard H., 107, 170
  Sarah, 107
Longs, The, 105
Louisiana Lottery, 71
Louisville Academy, 167
Lowe, Mr., 43, 76, 102
Lowry, David, 51
Lucas, Mrs., 94
Lumpkin, Geo.-On jury, 51, 54

Lumpkin,
  Jos. Henry - Chief Justice,
    35, 54
  Professor, 54
  Wilson, Governor, 54
Lyle, Mrs., 153
Lyndon, Dr., 43, 76
Lyon, Edw., 87

M acarty, Mrs., 104
Macon, 88, 93
Maddox, Mary Turner, Mrs., 24, 54
Madison County, 5, 17
Main Street, 45
Major, Jno., Rev., 119, 136, 148
Male Academy, 173
Mallory, Chas., Rev., 1, 9
Manack, Jno.-Indian Trader, 20
Mann, Alfred, Dr., Rev., 124,
  140, 142, 144
  Jno. H., Mrs., 140
  Milly, Mrs., 74
Manadue, Henry-Clerk, Court, 22,
  24
Mansemond, Virginia, 53
Map of Wilkes Co., Callaway, 12
Marbury, Horatio, 51, 71
  Leonard, 74
Marks, Jas., 51, 58, 82, 126
  Jno., 58
Marshall, Abram, 111
  Daniel, Rev., 109
  Jabez P., 111
Maryland Catholics, 146
  Riflemen, 50
Mary Willis Library, 73
Masonic Hall, 75
Matthews, Mrs., 110
  Anne, Miss, 61, 64
  Geo., Gen.-Governor, 37, 51,
    56, 57, 60, 61, 77, 82, 110
  Jas., Rev.-Pastor of Church at
    Clark's Station, 110
McCall, Col.-R.S., 28
  Hugh, Capt.-*History of Georgia*,
    1, 19
McClendon, Jacob, 23, 26
McCoy, Professor, 88
McDuffie, Governor, 151
McGhee, Jno., Esq., 38
McGillivray, Alexander, 19
McGirth, British, 11
McKinley, Mrs., 93
McLean, Jas., 23
  Jesse, 176
McRae, Margaret, 162
  Nancy, 162
  Robt., 65
McGahee, Micajah, 51, 55, 82
Mercer, Silas, 1, 3, 4
Mercer Hill Academy, 65, 84, 97
  111, 167
Mercer, Jacob, 81

INDEX

Mercer, Jesse, 1, 4, 112, 114, 115, 150, 156, 170
Mercer's Cluster, 114
Meriwether County, 38
  David, Gen.-R.S., 55, 64, 71, 95, 120, 134, 157
  Francis, 51, 55
  Frank, 82
  Jas., 95
  Thos., Judge-R.S., 37, 128
Meriwethers, 121
Merry, Bradford, 141
Methodist Parsonage-On Lot 61, 76
Milledge, Jno., I-Governor, 6, 180
  Jno., II, Col., 6
  Jno., III, Capt.-State Librarian, 6
  Polly, Miss, 6
Milledgeville, 144
Miller, Phineas, 87
Mills, Chas. C., 164
  Daniel, 51
  Jno., 115
  Sarah S., Mrs., 164
Minton, Mary, 140
Missionary Ridge, 15
Mitchum, Mark, 175, 177
Mixon, Dr., Rev., 144
Mobley, Jas., 23
Monitor, 97
Monmouth-Battle of, 38
Montgomery, A. D., Rev.-Presbyterian Pastor, 163
  Wm., Rev., 151, 153
Monument - Curious, 7
Moore's Mill- On Little River, 131
Moravian School-Bethlehem, Pa., 106
Morgan, Wm., 51
Morse, Jedidiah-*Morse's American Geography*, 48
Morton, Paul, Rev., 166
Moses, Park, Rev., 119
Mosley, Jos., 164
Moss, Wm., 51, 82
Mounger, Henry, 51, 121
Murat, Mad Achille, 159
Murrays-N. C. Settlers, 7
Musgrove's Mill-Battle fought-located in S.C., 16, 29
Myers, E. H., Rev., 143

N all, Jno., 51
Napier, Leroy, 104
  Leroy, Mrs., 54
  Skelton, 104
  Thos., 51, 54
Neeson, Mrs., 44, 76
Nelson, Jno., 7, 22, 74, 82
  Kitty, 8
New Hope Church-Presb., 155

New Purchase, 4, 7
Newton, Elizur, 147
  Henry, Rev., 147
  Jno., Rev., 147, 151, 153, 155
New York to Liverpool-Cotton, 88
Nisbet, Jas.-Lawyer, 54, 94
Norris, Jno., Rev., 143
Nowland, Wm., 176

O conee River-Creek Indians burned Greensboro, 91, 148
Ogeechee District, 139
Oglethorpe County - Cut off from Wilkes in 1793, 5, 66, 83, 147
Oglethorpe, General-Indian Treaty at Augusta, 2
Ohl, Maude Andrews, Mrs., 114
Olin, Dr.-Revivalist, 139
Oliver, Dionysius, 23, 82
  Jno., 137

P aine, Bishop, 140
Palmer, Mrs., 77
  Geo., Dr., 142
  Stephen, Mrs., 43, 86
Park and Gilham-Elders, 147
Park, Henry, 119
Paull, Benj.-Justice Sup. Court, 162
Penfield, 116
Pennsylvania-Emigration of, 146
Perkins, Gen., 4
Peterman, Geo., 176
Petrie, G.H.W., Rev., 163
Pettus, Jno., 132
  Jno., Mrs., 86, 93, 150, 162
  Stephen, 93, 94, 140
Pharr, Marcus, 51, 92
  Marcus, Jr., 44, 76
  Marcus, Jr., Mrs., 25
Phillips Church, 10, 111
Phillips, Joel, 33, 111
  Zachariah, 33
Phillips Mills, 33, 111
Phinizy, Ferdinand, 85
  John, Mrs., 158
Pickens, Andrew, Col., Gen. and Governor of S.C., 11, 16, 32, 65, 146, 149
  Francis, 16
  Joseph, 11
Pierce, Bishop, 140, 144
  Julia, 140
  Lovick, Rev., 139, 140
  Thos., Rev., 143
Piny Grove Church, 120
Pledger, W. P., Rev., 144
Plumb, Henrietta, 162
Pollard, Wm., 51. 55
Pope, Alexander, 79, 101, 129, 140
  Alexander, Jr., 141
  Alexander, Jr., Mrs., 141
  Burwell, 51, 82

INDEX

Pope, Eliza, Miss, 106
  Henry, 51, 82
  Jno. H., Dr., J.I.C., 51, 82, 84, 92, 129, 165
  Wm., 100, 101, 180
Popes, The, 92
Porter, Anthony, Mrs., 98
Posey, Colonel-R.S., 37
Poullain, Anthony, 52, 55, 92
  Antoine, 93
  T. N., Dr., 92
Powell, Ann, Mrs., 75
  Anthony, 73
Presbyterians in Wilkes County, 146
  Trustees, 169
Price, Geo. W., Mrs., 55, 104
Prince, Basiline, 101
  Oliver, 101
  Oliver Hillhouse, 96
  Wm., 40, 83
  Wm., Jr.-Rector of School, 70, 71
Providence Church-Presbyterian, 155
Prudhomme, L.-A negro Trader from San Domingo, 69, 89

Quigley, Ann, Miss, Teacher, 102
  Chas., 160
Quinn, Hugh, 73

Randolph, Bob, 104
  Maria, Miss, 104
  Maria, Mrs., 54
  Martha, 159
Ray, Jas. H., 69
Razapeth-(Prazepeth?), 65
Rector, Stephen Burroughs-Teacher, 64
Reese, Dr., 79
  Judge, 43, 45, 76, 167
  Wm., Mrs. (Lucy), 54, 65, 86, 91, 130
Reid, Jno. W., Rev.-Pastor of Salem Church, 165, 166
Rembert, Jas., 107
Rials, Joshua, 23
Richards, Wm., 81
Richardson, Walker-Will of, 51, 89
Richmond Academy-Augusta, 47, 167
Riden, Jos. Scott-Sheriff, 22, 122
Robert, L. J., Rev. 117
Robertson, Jas. J., Dr., 25, 29, 100, 101, 164
  Lizzie, Mrs., 164
  Mary, 162
Robinson, Ellen, Mrs., 162
  Jos. W., 164

Rocky Spring Church-now in Lincoln Co., 110
Rogers, Mr.-R.S., 31
Rorie, Wm., 139
Rory, Jno., 176
Rucker, Pressly, 52
Ruston, Jno., B., 64
Rutherford, Jno., 51, 54
  Milly, Miss, 54
  Wm.-Professor, U. of Ga., 54
Ryburn, Peter, Rev., 144

Safford, Reuben, 51, 55
Saint John's, Augusta, 143
Saint Paul's Churchyard, Augusta, 34, 57
Salem Church, 165
Sand Bar Ferry-Savannah, Augusta, 47
Sanders, Wilkes, Mrs., 104
Sandtown, Danbury, Delhi-Crossroads, 122
Sanson, Major, 83
  Jas., 52
  Wm., Tavern Keeper, 52, 83
Sappington, Caleb, 173
Sardis Church, 114
Sardis and Clerk's Station, 120
Sassnet, W. J., Rev., 143
Savannah - Ga. - River, 2, 12, 103, 136, 143, 164
Scott, Jos., 122, 125
Scott's Meeting House-Little River, 121, 122, 125
Scotch Settlement-Under Lord George Gordon, 3
Scudder, Mr.-Teacher, 92
Semmes Family, 146
  Alexander, 162
  Andrew G.-Trustee, Presbyterian Church, 160, 162, 173
  Andrew, Mrs., 141
  Jno., 92
  Mary, Mrs., 162, 173
  Thos., 176
Settlement-Town of Washington, 7
Settlers-Hays, Princes, Abbotts, Beasleys and Goodes, 100, 101, 102, 103, 104
Sevier, Jno.-1st Gov. of Tenn., 29, 30
Seymore, Mrs. 93
Sharon Church-Presbyterian, 155
Shelby, Isaac, 30
Shelverton, Walter, 44
Shenandoah Valley, Virginia, 96
Shepherd, Andrew, 101, 107, 170, 176
  Jno., 52
Sherman, General, 12
Siloam Church-Presbyterian, 154
Silver Bluff, S. C., 5

INDEX

Simonds, Nancy, Mrs., 170
Simons, Capt., 115
Simpkins, Eldred, 16
Simpson, Mr., 156, 157
  Dr., 79
  Archibald, 8, 90, 153
  F. T., Rev., 8, 54, 87, 89, 152, 158
    Pastor, South Bethany, 147, 164
    School Commissioner, 7
  F. T., Mrs., 38, 39
  Lucy, Mrs., 48, 129, 143, 170
  Robt., Dr., 41, 54, 76
  Wm., 8, 74, 94
Simpsons and Butlers, 94
Sims, Ann, Mrs., 158
  Frederic, 51
  Jno., 93
  Marshall, 93
  Rederic, 93
  Wm., 74, 93, 103
Slaton, Henry T., 14, 18, 90, 154
Smith, Benajah, 65, 69, 75, 84
  Chas.-Elder, 43, 75, 90, 164
  Geo. C., Rev.-Historian of Ga. Methodism, 139, 143, 145
  Harriett, 74
  Hoke, 54
  J. R., 44
  Manajah, 75
  Robt., 143
  Susanna, 73
  Wm. W., 176
Smyrna Church-Presbyterian, 154, 162
  Burying place of Jno. Talbot, 53
Sneed, Anna, Mrs., 164
  Jas. Roddy, 63, 79, 88, 103
Speer, Eustace, Dr., 144
Spring and Court Street, 45, 66
Springer, Ann, Mrs., 72
  J. M., Rev., 117
  Jno., Rev., Presbyterian Pastor, 68, 121, 152, 153, 163, 165
    Moderator and President of Academy Board, 64, 128
    Teacher, 150, 155
Stamper, Powel, 73, 76
Staples, Mr., 9
Starke, Ebenezer, 65
Starrs Hill Church, 165
Statistics of Georgia-by Rev. George White, 34
Staunton, Virginia, 61
Stewart, Jas., 82
Stith, Wm. (Chief Justice), 78

Stokes, W. H., Rev.-Asst. Editor *Christian Index*, 116
  Wm., 51
Stone, Osborne, 48, 92, 173
Stone and Lane, 172
Stoval, Peter, 176
Streets and Lots of Old Town, 45
Stroud, Thos., 23
Stubblefield, Jeter, 86
Succoth Academy-First distinctive Methodist School in Ga., 128, 157
Suffolk County, 91
Sullivan, Florence, 121
Sutton, Wm., 20

Tait, Chas., Judge, 170, 175, 177
Talbot, Jno., 51, 53, 82, 155, 156, 157, 158
  Matthew, Justice, Superior Court-Surveyor, 85, 158
  Thomas, 87, 158, 162
Talbot's House-Jno., 52
Taliaferro, Benj., Col.-Senator of Ga.-U.S. Senator-County named for, 51, 55, 57, 61, 82, 175
Taliaferro County, 2, 5
Tate, Chas., 51
Taylor, Jno., 176
Telfair, Edw.-Governor, 107
  Thos., 107
Teroudet, Daniel, 74, 76
Terrell, Chas., 176
  David-Clerk of Court, Wilkes Co., Reg. of Probates, 40, 45, 64, 81, 94
  Elizabeth (Mrs. Thos. Wingfield), 91
  Henry, 163
  Joel, 94
  Lucy, 94
  Peter, 94
  Richmond, 176
  Sabina, 162
  Thos.-Elder and Trustee in Presbyterian Church, 94, 160, 162, 164
  Wm., 51, 82, 84, 91, 94
Terry, Mrs., 94
Thatcher, Daniel, Rev.-Missionary sent from N.C.-Organizer of Bethany Church, 148, 151
Thomas Carter's Ferry, 52
Thornton, Capt.-on Upton Creek, 136
  Mr., 149
  Tol., 176
  Vincent R., Rev.-Pastor of Ga. Baptist Association, 117
Thweatt, Mr., 59
  Peterson, 59

INDEX 191

Thyatira Church-Presbyterian, 155
Toombs, Gabriel, 51, 67, 70, 98, 173
  Julia, Mrs., 70, 141
  Robt., Gen., 55, 102, 160
Tondee's Tavern-Savannah, 33
Tories-Cause trouble in N.C.-7
  hung for murder of Col. John Dooly-Treatment of Mrs. Hannah Clark, 20, 27, 33
Treaty of Peace-End of Revolutionary War, Nov. 1782, 32
Triplett, Dora, 159
  Francis, 24, 54
  Martha R., 159
  Mary, 158, 159
  Wm.-High Sheriff, 84
Trustees-Presbyterian Church, 173
Tuggle, Lodowick-First Elder from Bethany, 153
Tupper, H.A. Dr. Rev. Pastor Ga. Baptist Association, 117
Turner, D. McNeil-Pastor, Presbyterian Church, 163
  Jno., 175
Tyner, Noah, 20

U nited States to Liverpool-Cotton, 88
Unity Church-Presbyterian, 155
University of Georgia, 68
Upson, Judge, 17
Upton Creek, 56, 87

V ason, Judge, 89
Vickers, Mrs., 94, 104, 111, 139, 140, 142, 157, 172
Vienna-in forks of Savannah and Broad Rivers, 52
Virginia-Settlers who came from State, 86, 91
Virginians-Cavalier English Stock-Wingfields, Goodes, Willis, Hays, 146

W addell, Moses, Dr., Rev.-Rector of Academy-Pres., Franklin College, 4
  Teacher at Bethany, 69, 148, 151, 153, 159
Waddy, Betsy, 140
Walker, Elizabeth, 158
  Freeman, 158
  Sanders, Rev., 51, 82, 109
  W.H.T., 158
Wallace, Alex., Mrs., 94
  Fanny, Miss, 94
Walnut Hill, 157
Walton, Geo.-Judge-Chief Justice, 21, 23

Walton, Geo.-Signer Declaration of Independence, 35, 46, 51, 54, 81
  Mary Helen, 143
War Hill, 14
Ward, Artemus, 4
  Jno., 79
Warhurst, Timothy, 66
Warren County, 2, 5, 66
Washington Academy, 71, 172
  Chronicle, 18
  County-cut into lots-laid out, 40
  Town-Baptist Church Organized, 1828-Incorporated, 1805-Jesse Mercer-Common Sold, 69, 75, 115, 116, 133, 169
  Town, North Carolina, 49
Water Street, 45, 141, 143
Watauga Valley, 29
Wayne, Gen.-R.S., 37
Webb's Ferry, 12
Webster, Alexander H., Rev.-Pastor of Presbyterian Church, 145, 159, 162, 163
  Eliza, Mrs., 162
Weems, Mrs., 94
  Belle, Miss, 164
  Jno. B., 103
  Lock-Elder in 1829, 164
  Walter, Dr'., 162
  Wm. L., 162
Welborne, Curtace, 51, 54
  Thos., 51, 54
Wesley, Chas., Rev., 118
Wesleyan Female College-Female College in Macon, 143
Westmoreland County, Virginia, 7
Wetter, Telfair, 108
Whatley's Mills, 111
Wheat's Camp Ground-Lincoln Co., 138
Whilden, S.W., Rev.-Pastor of Ga. Baptist Association, 117
White, Geo., Rev.-Author of *Historical Collections*, 22, 28, 33, 95
  Simeon, 176
Whitfield, Geo., Rev.(Whitefield) 109, 118
Whitman, H.A., Rev.-Pastor of Ga. Baptist Association, 117
Whitney, Eli-Inventor of Cotton Gin, 87, 88
Wiggins, Jas., Rev., 143
Wilkes County-Callaway's Map-Change from tobacco to Cotton-Gov. Gilmer's Court held-Lands Ceded by Indians in 1773-Ordinary Court Minutes-Treaty of 1773 opened up County for settlement, 2, 4, 10, 22, 78, 87, 88

INDEX

Wilkes, Jno.-Member of English Parliament, 10
Wilkes Riflemen-During Revolution, 49
Wilkinson, Ann, 7
  Benj., 7
  Caroline, 7
Williams Creek-Bounded lands ceded by Indians in 1773, 2, 5
  Jas., 74
Williamson, Andrew, Gen.-Treachery of, 25
Williamson, Micajah, Col.-R. S.-fought at Kettle Creek, 17, 23, 31, 40, 58, 59, 62, 63, 65 68, 73, 74, 75, 77, 82, 123, 170
  Sally, 75, 80
  Sarah, 59
  Susan, 59, 80
  Thos., 176
  Wm.-first child born in Washington of white parents, 58
  Willie, Mrs., 140 141
  Francis, Col.-Member of f Commissioners, 62
  -Teacher, University of Ga., 69
  F. T., Dr., 40, 54, 62, 92, 139, 170
  Geo., 51, 114
  Jas. D., Col., 48
  Mary, Miss, 106
  Nathaniel-Teacher, University of Ga., 66
  Thos., 62, 92
Wilson, Dr., 154, 159
  Jas., Rev.-Teacher of languages, 71
  Jos., 52, 82
Wingfield, Dr., 65
  Anne, Miss, 65, 128
  Archie, Capt., 94, 103
  Archibald, 164
  Caroline, Mrs., 95
  Chas., Judge, 95, 131
  Cornelia, 93
  Frances, 38, 128
  Frank, 92, 93

Wingfield, Garland, 51, 54, 93, 95, 133, 140, 176
  Garland, Mrs., 65
  J. T., Mrs., 39
  Jas.-Washington P.M. Trustee Presbyterian Church, 93, 160
  Jno., 51, 54, 65, 82, 91, 150, 162
  Jno. T., Mrs., 38
  Leonora, 93
  Mildred, 93
  Octavia, Mrs., 77, 93
  Overton, 130
  Rebecca, 93, 162
  Susan (Mrs. James), 162
  Thos., Dr., 54, 69, 93, 105
Winton, Avis, 162
Woodrow, Dr., 101
Woods, Dempsey, 79
Woodstock Church-Oglethorpe County, 153
Wooten, Thos., 51
Worsham, Elizabeth, 92
  Emily, 92
  Jos., 92
  Martha, 92
  Richard, Maj.-R. S.-Commissioner of Academy, J. I. C., 40, 69, 71, 76, 84, 91
  Sophia, 92
Worsham's Tavern, 91
Wright, Rev., 142
Wright, Jas., Gov.-Appointed Gov. of Ga. by King George in 1773, 2, 5
  Jas., 38
  Jno., 38
  Polly, Miss, 39
  Sarah, 26
  Wm., Dr., 69
Wylie, Nicholas, 67, 115

Yarborough, J. W., Rev., 144
Yazoo Bill-23 million acres of Ga. land at 2¢ an acre-Act, Gov. Mathews signs, 57, 61
Yorktown, Siege of, 38
Young, Daniel, 74
  J. R., Rev., 111

www.ingramcontent.com/pod-product-compliance
Lightning Source LLC
Chambersburg PA
CBHW051811230426
43672CB00012B/2696